POLITICS, POSITION, AND POW

POLITICS, POSITION, AND POWER

The Dynamics of
Federal Organization

FIFTH EDITION

HAROLD SEIDMAN

New York   *Oxford*
OXFORD UNIVERSITY PRESS
1998

OXFORD UNIVERSITY PRESS

Oxford   New York

Athens Auckland Bangkok Bogota Bombay Buenos Aires
Calcutta Cape Town Dar es Salaam Delhi Florence Hong Kong
Istanbul Karachi Kuala Lumpur Madras Madrid Melbourne
Mexico City Nariobi Paris Singapore Taipei Tokyo Toronto Warsaw

and associated companies in
Berlin   Ibadan

Copyright © 1998 by Oxford University Press, Inc.

Published by Oxford University Press, Inc.

198 Madison Avenue, New York, New York   10016

Oxford is a registered trademark of Oxford University Press

LIBRARY OF CONGRESS CATALOGING-IN-PUBLICATION DATA   JK421
.S44
1998

Seidman, Harold.
    Politics, position, and power : the dynamics of federal
organization / Harold Seidman. – 5th ed.
        p.   cm.
    Includes bibliographical references and index.
    ISBN 0-19-509072-1 (pbk.)
    1. United States–Politics and government. I. Title.
JK421.S44 1997
351.73–dc21   97-26624
                                                     CIP

Printing (last digit): 9 8 7 6 5 4 3 2 1

Printed in the United States of America
on acid-free paper

FOR BENJAMIN GINSBERG

Who has made the Johns Hopkins Washington Center for the Study of American Government a living reality.

Contents

Acknowledgements, ix

I. The Politics of Government Organization

1. *Introduction,* 3
2. *Executive Branch Organization:*
   View from the Congress, 27
3. *Executive Branch Organization:*
   View from the White House, 51
4. *Nixon's New American Revolution,* 78
5. *Carter's "Bottom-Up" Reorganization,* 90
6. *Reagan: From the Positive to the Regulatory State,* 96
7. *Amputation Before Diagnosis,* 110
8. *The Executive Establishment:*
   Culture and Personality, 117
9. *Coordination: The Search*
   for the Philosopher's Stone, 142

II. The Politics of Institutional Type

10. *Administrative Agencies,* 161
11. *Advisory and Intergovernmental Bodies: Twilight Zone,* 197

III. Concluding Observations

12. *Concluding Observations,* 217

Notes, 222
Select Bibliography, 250
Index, 254

Acknowledgments

In writing the fifth edition of *Politics, Position, and Power,* I benefitted greatly from the accumulated wisdom of the National Academy of Public Administration Standing Panel on Executive Organization and Management. I know of no other group that is more dedicated to the cause of effective, democratic, and responsible government and knows better what it takes to achieve it. I am particularly indebted to Alan Dean and Tom Stanton for their support and insights. Benjamin Ginsberg encouraged me to write the fifth edition. Catherine Rossi was always there when I needed help in dealing with a balky copier or administrative problems. Benita Carr met the challenge of deciphering my handwriting and did the word processing.

H.S.

Washington, D.C.

POLITICS, POSITION, AND POWER

I

THE POLITICS
OF GOVERNMENT
ORGANIZATION

I

Introduction

Reorganization has become almost a religion in Washington. It has its Old Testament in the Hoover Commission reports, and New Testament in Vice President Gore's report of the National Performance Review. Various citizen organizations such as the Alliance for Redesigning Government have been created to preach the gospel of government reinvention and reform.

Reorganization is deemed synonymous with reform and reform with progress. Periodic reorganizations are prescribed if for no other purpose than to purify the bureaucratic blood and to prevent stagnation. Opposition to reorganization is evil and attributable, according to Hoover, to the "gang-up, log-rolling tactics of the bureaus and their organized pressure groups."[1]

The history of administrative reorganization in the twentieth century has been called "a history of rhetoric." Its orthodox credos are closely linked to religious and moral movements.[2]

For the true believer changes in structure and administrative systems can produce miracles. The emphasis is not on what the government does, but on how it does it. President Carter was going to reform the government by reorganizing it; President Reagan by privatizing it; and President Clinton by reinventing it. For modern

3

day Luddites in Congress, the abolition or reorganization of the Departments of Commerce, Education, Energy, and Housing and Urban Development is seen as a way to curb or destroy the evil federal government machinery and return power to the states and the people. Congressman William F. Clinger Jr. defended legislation to abolish the Commerce department as "pro-business, pro-downsizing, and pro-taxpayer."[3]

The myth persists that we can resolve deep-seated issues of substance by reorganizing. Rare indeed is the commission, presidential task force, or congressional committee with the self-restraint to forgo recommending organizational or procedural answers to the problems it cannot solve.

The organizational commandments laid down by the first Hoover Commission constitute the hard core of the fundamentalist dogma.[4] The devils to be exorcised are overlapping and duplication, and confused or broken lines of authority and responsibility. Entry into the "nirvana of economy and efficiency" can be obtained only by strict adherence to sound principles of executive branch organization. Of these the most essential are the grouping of executive branch agencies as nearly as possible by major purposes so that "by placing related functions cheek-by-jowl the overlaps can be eliminated, and of even greater importance coordinated policies can be developed"; and the establishment of a clear line of command and supervision from the president down through department heads to every employee, with no subordinate possessing authority independent of that of a superior.

The commission's report on "General Management of the Executive Branch" represents the most categorical formulation of the orthodox or classic organization doctrine derived largely from business administration and identified with the scientific management movement during the early decades of this century and the writings of Gulick, Urwick, Fayol, and Mooney. Government organization is seen primarily as a technological problem calling for "scientific" analysis and the application of fundamental organizational principles: a single rather than a collegiate executive; limited span of control; unity of command (a person cannot serve two masters); a clear distinction between line and staff; and authority commensurate with responsibility. For Luther Gulick, "work division is the foundation of organization; indeed, the reason for organization."[5] In his view, "the theory of organization, therefore, has to do with the structure of coordination imposed upon the work division units of an enterprise."[6] "Organization as a way of coordination requires the establishment of a system of authority whereby the central purpose or objective of an enterprise is translated into reality through the combined efforts of many specialists, each working in his own field at a particular time and place."[7] Organization structure should be designed to create homogeneous combinations of work units on the basis of major purpose, process, clientele or materiel, or place.

Orthodox theory is preoccupied with the anatomy of government organization and is concerned primarily with arrangements to ensure that (1) each function is assigned to its appropriate niche within the government structure; (2) component parts of the executive branch are properly related and articulated; and (3) authorities and responsibilities are clearly assigned.

The important caveats and qualifications emphasized by Gulick in his "Notes on the Theory of Organization," particularly coordination "by the dominance of an idea," the futility of seeking a single most effective system of departmentalism, the need to recognize that "organization is a living dynamic entity," the limitations of command, and the role of leadership, have been largely ignored by both his critics and his disciples.[8] Such reservations were not entertained by the Hoover Commission, whose report echoes, often in identical language, the organization "truths" first expounded by Herbert Hoover in the 1920s and early 1930s.[9]

Central to the understanding of orthodox theory are certain basic assumptions about the nature and purpose of organization and administration. The starting point is a rigid interpretation of the constitutional doctrine of separation of powers. Public administration is viewed as being concerned almost exclusively with the executive branch, "where the work of government is done,"[10] with only grudging recognition given to the roles of the legislative and judicial branches in the administrative process. Preoccupation with the executive branch is coupled with an ill-concealed distrust of politics and politicians as the natural enemies of efficiency. Politics and administration are regarded as two heterogeneous functions, "the combination of which cannot be undertaken within the structure of administration without producing inefficiency."[11] Execution of policy is a matter for professional, technically trained, nonpartisan career managers, not amateurs. "Efficiency" is held to be the single overriding goal of organization and administration. On this point, Gulick is unequivocal. In his words: "Efficiency is thus axiom number one in the value scale of administration. This brings administration into apparent conflict with the value scale of politics, whether we use that term in its scientific or popular sense."[12]

Since World War II, public administration theologians have become increasingly disenchanted with the orthodox dogmas. Skeptics and agnostics have dismissed the "principles of organization" as mere "proverbs" and exercises in "architectonics." Heretics have challenged the politics-administration dichotomy, notably Paul Appleby, who classified administration as "the eighth political process."[13] A few have even gone so far as to question whether efficiency and economy are "the ultimate good."[14] Behavioral scientists have attacked the assumptions about human behavior that they believe are implicit in the orthodox theology, namely, that authority flows from the top and employees are inert instruments performing the tasks assigned to them by their superiors. They condemn orthodox organization theory for almost completely ignoring the interplay of individual personality and interpersonal relations, informal groups, interorganization conflict, and the decision process in their conception of formal structure.[15] The literature of dissent is vast and growing.[16]

Overlapping and duplication are seen as a positive good rather than an evil by conservative organizations such as the Heritage Foundation. In its Mandate for Leadership II, Continuing the Conservative Revolution, the foundation asserts categorically that overlapping and duplication are "necessary" because they create "conflict and competition which in turn produces information which is useful for the political executive in controlling policy implementation."[17]

The Reagan administration condemned the orthodox theories as being too narrowly concerned with structure. Processes and procedures were considered to provide more effective means for establishing presidential control and reorganizing the executive branch.

Vice President Gore's report of the National Performance Review[18] would substitute a new theology for what it calls the "paradigm of private management," advocated by the Brownlow Committee and the Hoover Commissions, which resulted in "large, top-down, hierarchical, centralized bureaucracies." The report proposes to reinvent government by cutting red tape, putting customers first, encouraging employees to get results, and getting back to basics. The entrepreneurial government would "steer more, row less, delegate authority and responsibility, replace regulations with incentives, search for market, not administrative solutions," and measure success by customer satisfaction.

New theology's rejection of fundamental precepts of orthodox doctrine is condemned by some critics as close to heresy. The argument that government is broken and needs to be reinvented is interpreted as a thinly veiled rationalization of antigovernment bias and justification for drastic cuts in budgets and personnel. Where orthodox doctrine emphasizes presidential leadership and democratic accountability, the new theology emphasizes elimination of hierarchies and customer satisfaction. James Q. Wilson cites as the most striking feature of the Gore report, "the near absence of any reference to democratic accountability."[19] Provisions of the Constitution and laws that call for presidential accountability to the Congress and citizens, not to customers, are ignored. Ronald C. Moe and Robert S. Gilmour contend that "the president as chief executive can hardly be held accountable to the constitutional mandate to take care that the laws be faithfully executed if those laws are not his to enforce and the agents created by such laws are beyond his control."[20] The entrepreneurial management model is not and cannot be a substitute for political and legal accountability."[21]

Some argue that it is difficult "to find any organizational scheme that works better than another." The government's central management problems are "people problems." They predict that "government organizations, like those in the private sector are likely to be flat and loose in structure, organized around vision and values—intergovernmental and public—private distinctions will also be blurred by the invisible connectivity of electronic government. It matters little, of course, whether the voice or face at the other end of a terminal belongs to a public employee, as long as the service is of high quality."[22]

The debate between the old and new theologies reflects a fundamental disagreement concerning government's primary purpose. Is it government's primary purpose to govern and as mandated by the constitution, "to establish justice, insure domestic tranquillity, provide for the common defense, promote the general welfare, and secure the blessings of liberty to ourselves and our posterity"? Or has the dividing line between what is public and what is private become so blurred as to be indistinguishable with government's primary role as another market sensitive service provider to be judged by the degree of customer satisfaction and the bottom line? The outcome of the debate has profound implication for our constitutional form of government.

What the critics of the orthodox doctrines have not done is to provide a workable alternate set of doctrines for structuring the executive branch and designing federal programs. As the House Committee on Government Reform and Oversight found, "without determining government's proper role, efforts to redesign, reinvent, and reinvigorate any part of the government are likely to fail."[23] The committee stressed the need "to identify principles to drive and shape government, and apply those principles across the functions and institutions of the federal government."[24] The Standing Panel on Executive Organization and Management of the National Academy of Public Administration determined that it was feasible to identify principles "which have sufficient validity and scope of applicability to warrant serious consideration in any effort to reform the structure and functioning of the executive branch."[25]

The panel acknowledged its debt to Brownlow and Hoover. Building on the foundation provided by them, the panel endeavored to develop principles or guidelines adapted to significant changes in the federal government's role and way of doing business. The panel presented ten principles as guides to policy makers in restructuring the executive branch and enhancing government performance.

1. The principal objective of all government organizations and systems of management should be the faithful, effective, and equitable carrying-out of the provisions and intent of the Constitution and laws of the United States.

2. The Constitution vests the executive power in the president; and as chief executive the president must have the institutional capacity and support to exercise those executive powers effectively.

3. The departments and agencies of the executive branch should be organized as nearly as possible to reflect the major purposes which the government is seeking to pursue.

4. Executive departments and agencies should be organized in such a way as to enable the agency head effectively to establish basic policies with respect to mission, program goals, performance measures, resource allocation, legislation, and external relationships.

5. The head of each department and major independent agency should be held accountable for the quality of its management and be assisted by a principal official with the responsibility for providing advice and assistance on all aspects of the internal management of the agency.

6. Organizational design should be tailored to reflect the distinct requirements of different types of government programs so as to facilitate effective performance and to maintain accountability.

7. The quality of program administration in every executive agency depends heavily upon the management skills of the line administrators and other principal officials.

8. Legislation establishing executive departments or agencies or addressing aspects of general management should to the maximum feasible extent avoid the prescription of statutory detail and should empower the agency head to make the internal arrangements best suited to the effective execution of the laws.

9. The effective administration of programs is dependent on competent, motivated public service employees who are responsive to the policy direction of the political leadership but are selected, retained, and advanced on the basis of merit.

10. Employment of third parties (including state and local governments and for-profit and nonprofit contractors) to manage and operate government facilities and deliver public services does not eliminate the need for public management but merely changes its character.[26]

Dwight Waldo was correct when he concluded that

> . . . not only is the classical theory still today the formal working theory of large numbers of persons technically concerned with administrative-organizational matters, both in the public and private spheres, but I expect it will be around a long, long time. This is not necessarily because it is "true," though I should say it has much truth in it, both descriptively and prescriptively; that is to say, both as a description of organizations as we find them in our society and as a prescription for achieving the goals of these organizations "efficiently." But in any event a social theory widely held by the actors has a self-confirming tendency and the classical theory is now deeply ingrained in our culture.[27]

Publication of the *Papers on the Science of Administration* in 1937 may have marked the "high noon of orthodoxy in public administration theory in the United States,"[28] but someone apparently stopped the clock.

Orthodox doctrines were established by the Reorganization Act of 1949 (Chapter 9, Title 5 of the U.S. Code) as the lawful objectives of government reorganization. The president was directed from time to time to "examine the organization of all agencies" and to "determine what changes in such organization are necessary" to carry out the following purposes, which were declared by the Congress to be "the policy of the United States":

1. to promote the better execution of the laws, the more effective management of the executive branch of the government and of its agencies and functions, and the expeditious administration of the public business;
2. to reduce expenditures and promote economy to the fullest extent consistent with the efficient operation of the government;
3. to increase the efficiency of the operations of the government to the fullest extent practicable;
4. to group, coordinate, and consolidate agencies and functions of the government, as nearly as may be, according to major purposes;
5. to reduce the number of agencies by consolidating those having similar functions under a single head, and to abolish such agencies or functions thereof as may not be necessary for the efficient conduct of the government; and
6. to eliminate overlapping and duplication of effort.

Custom, culture, and role still require presidents, Office of Management and Budget (OMB) officials, and members of Congress to profess openly their faith in "economy and efficiency" as the prime goals of organizational and procedural reform, with the emphasis on economy.

Almost every president from Theodore Roosevelt to Bill Clinton, with the notable exception of Franklin D. Roosevelt, and every reorganization commission and every congressional sponsor of a reorganization plan has found it necessary to defend administrative reform as a means of reducing expenditures. President Clinton estimated that reinventing government would reduce the size of the civilian nonpostal work force by 12 percent and produce savings of $108 billion over five years. Sponsors of legislation to abolish the Department of Commerce claimed that it would save no less than $8 billion in seven years.[29]

"We have to get over the notion that the purpose of reorganization is economy," FDR told Louis Gulick in 1936. "I had that out with Al Smith in New York. . . . The reason for reorganization is good management.[30] The overwhelming weight of empirical evidence supports the Roosevelt view that reorganizations do not save money. Indeed, it is now recognized that the measurable and immeasurable costs may be substantial because reorganizations are disruptive and often require transfers and geographical relocation of personnel, physical facilities, and records.[31]

Principles, whether old or new, do not provide guidance or enhance understanding or the policy and political implications of organizational decisions. One must have knowledge of the tactical and strategic uses of organization structure, processes, and procedures as an instrument of politics, positions, and power.

Economy and efficiency or responsiveness to customers are not the prime objectives of public administration. Supreme Court Justice Louis D. Branders emphasized that "the doctrine of separation of powers was not adopted to promote efficiency but to preclude the exercise or arbitrary power."[32] The basic issues of federal organization and administration relate to power: who shall control it and to what ends? In a period of downsizing and budget deficits what we are witnessing is maneuvering for priority in obtaining scarce resources and, in some cases, assuring program survival.

EXECUTIVE BRANCH ORGANIZATION: THEORY VS. PRACTICE

Organizational and procedural arrangements are not neutral. We do not organize in a vacuum. Organization is one way of expressing national commitment, influencing program direction, and ordering priorities. Organizational arrangements tend to give some interests and perspectives more effective access to those with decision-making authority, whether they be in the Congress or in the executive branch. As Richard Neustadt has pointed out: "In political government, the means can matter quite as much as the ends; they often matter more."[33]

Institutional location and environment, administrative arrangements, type of organization, processes, and procedures can raise significant political questions concerning the distribution and balance of power between the executive branch, Congress and the Judiciary; the federal government and state and local governments; states and cities; the federal government and organized interest groups, particularly the principal beneficiaries of federal programs; and finally, among the components of the executive establishment itself, including the president's relationship to the departments and the bureaucracy.

If our democratic system is to be responsive to the needs of *all* our people, organization structure and administrative arrangements need to so balance the competing interests within given program areas that none is immune to public control and capable of excluding less powerful segments of our society from effective participation in the system and an equitable share of its benefits. Failure to maintain this balance has contributed to the present malaise.

The political implications of organization structure were recognized as early as 1789, when the states endeavored to control the extension of federal power by limiting the creation of executive departments. In 1849 the bill to establish the Department of Interior was opposed because "it meant the further extension of federal authority to the detriment of the states."[34] Reform and modernization of the army were blocked during the nineteenth century because it was feared that a nationalized army would diminish state power and control of the national guard.[35] President Reagan condemned the Department of Education as a symbol of intrusion into matters that should be left to state and local control.

Application of "economy and efficiency" as the criteria for government organization can produce serious distortions, if political and environmental factors are ignored, It led the first Hoover Commission to proceed from the indisputable finding that the Farmers Home Administration's functions duplicated and overlapped those of the Farm Credit Administration and the Agricultural Extension Service to the seemingly logical conclusion that the Farmers Home Administration ought to be liquidated and its functions divided between its two competitors. The conclusion was obviously faulty to anyone in the least familiar with the histories of the Farm Credit Administration and the Extension Service as creatures of the American Farm Bureau Federation and the most conservative elements in the agricultural community. The Farm Bureau was proud of its role in scuttling the Rural Resettlement Administration and Farm Security Administration, the immediate predecessors of the FHA.[36] If there were ever a case of letting the goats loose in the cabbage patch, this was it. The FHA was created to furnish special assistance to farmers who constitute marginal risks and possess little political clout. Commissioners Acheson, Pollock, and Rowe observed in their dissent that "the purpose of the Farmers Home Administration is to make 'good' tenant farmers out of 'poor' tenant farmers, and not to restrict credit to 'good' tenant farmers who can probably obtain credit from other sources."[37]

Powerful groups in the commercial banking, research, and educational communities favor overlapping and duplication for somewhat different reasons than the Heritage Foundation. Five federal agencies regulate depository institutions—three for commercial banks, one for savings and loans, and one for federal credit unions. The banking industry for the past fifty years has successfully blocked efforts to consolidate supervision and examination of commercial hanks in a single federal agency. One-time chairman of the federal reserve board, Marriner S. Eccles, described bankers' opposition to reorganization as "based on the old principle of divide and conquer."[38] As noted by the Senate Committee on Governmental Affairs: "the ability of commercial banks to select their bank regulators . . . permits and encourages a regulated bank to select the regulatory agency most inclined toward the type of activity engaged in by the bank."[39]

Overlapping and duplication among federal agencies making research grants does not alarm scientists and educators. On the contrary, diversity in support is held essential to maximize the opportunities for obtaining federal funds and to minimize the dangers of federal control. The Committee on Science and Public Policy of the National Academy of Sciences strongly endorsed a "plural system," which has many roots for its authority "and many alternative administrative means of solving a given problem."[40]

Assignment of administrative jurisdiction can be a key factor in determining program direction and ultimate success or failure. Each agency has its own culture and internal set of loyalties and values that are likely to guide its actions and influence its policies. A number of satellites grow up and around and outside the institution and develop a mutual dependence. Private bureaucracies in Washington now almost completely parallel the public bureaucracies in those program areas in which the federal government contracts for services, regulates private enterprise, or provides some form of financial assistance.

Shared loyalties and outlook knit together the institutional fabric. They are the foundation of those intangibles that make for institutional morale and pride. Without them, functions could not be decentralized and delegated with the confidence that policies will be administered consistently and uniformly. But because people believe what they are doing is important and the way they have been taught to do it right, they are slow to accept change. Institutional responses are highly predictable, particularly to new ideas that conflict with institutional values and may pose a potential threat to organizational power and survival.

There is an ever-present danger that innovative programs that challenge accepted norms, demand new skills and approaches, and create conflicts with agency constituencies will be assimilated into the "system" and their purpose muffled or distorted. One way to kill a program is to house it in a hostile or unsympathetic environment.

Orphan agencies or programs are by no means a rare phenomenon. Changing the name of the Bureau of Budget to the Office of

Management and Budget failed to provide a favorable environment for the management function. Since 1972, it has been recognized that the **M** had been so subordinated to the **B** that the capacity to provide government-wide management and leadership has been seriously impaired.[41] In 1994 a reorganization called "OMB 2000" in effect integrated the management and budget functions. The House Committee on Government Reform and Oversight expressed concerned about permitting policy and budget officials to dictate management decisions. The committee recommended establishment of a separate Office of Management outside of OMB.[42]

Inclusion of nonscience functions within an agency that considers science to be its primary mission often results in program neglect. When resources are limited, the National Oceanic and Atmospheric Administration, for example, is not disposed to give preference to nonscience programs such as nautical and aeronautical charting.[43] Inclusion of a nonlaw enforcement agency such as the Patent and Trademark Office in the Department of Justice would also be calculated to create an orphan.

Adherence to the principle of organization according to major purposes provides no automatic answers. Federal programs are likely to have multiple purposes. Disagreements as to priorities among diverse and sometimes conflicting objectives are a major source of current controversies. Is the major purpose of the food stamp program to dispose of surplus agricultural commodities or to feed the poor? Is mass transportation a transportation program or an urban development program? Are school lunches a nutrition function or an education function?

Should the federal water pollution control program have health protection as its principal objective, or should it be concerned more broadly with the development of water resources?

Major purposes cannot be ascertained by scientific or economic analysis. Determination of major purpose represents a value judgment, and a transitory one at that. Thus, President Nixon could argue in 1971 that the Department of Transportation "is now organized around methods and not around purposes," although transportation was assumed to be a major purpose when the department was established in 1966.[44] What is the secondary purpose for one, is a major purpose for another. To quote Miles's law: "Where one stands depends on where one sits."[45] Major purposes are not constants but variables shifting with the ebb and flow of our national needs and aspirations.

Debates about organizational type also may mask basic differences over strategy and objectives. Orthodox theory postulates that all federal agencies, with the possible exception of the independent regulatory commissions, be grouped under a limited number of single-headed executive departments and consequently ignores the other possible forms of organization. Except for the regulatory commissions and government corporations, the Hoover Commissions and President's Committee on Administrative Management took little interest in the typology of organization—a disinterest shared by most students of public administration.

The significance of institutional type has been underrated. In Part II we will endeavor to identify and analyze the rich variety of organizational types that have been developed within our constitutional system: executive departments, independent agencies, assorted commissions, boards, councils, authorities, wholly owned corporations, mixed-ownership corporations, "captive" corporations, institutes, government-sponsored enterprises, foundations, establishments, conferences, intergovernmental bodies, compact agencies, and a wide variety of interagency and advisory committees. The differences among these institutional types are more a matter of convention and tradition than of legal prescriptions. Yet some have acquired a "mystique" that can profoundly influence public attitudes and executive and congressional behavior for good or ill. Institutional type can be crucial in determining who controls—the president, the Congress, or the so-called special interests.

Institutional type, for example, was a major issue when Congress authorized the Marshall Plan. Republicans wanted the plan administered by a government corporation because by definition it would be more "businesslike."[46] A corporation would also make it more difficult for the State Department to meddle in the European recovery program. The compromise was to establish an independent agency outside the State Department and to authorize creation of a corporation, if and when needed.

Scientists devised a new government institution, named a "foundation," when existing institutions would not support their postwar grand design of "science governed by scientists and paid for by the public."[47] The ostensible aim was to duplicate within the executive branch a typical university structure. Effective control over the proposed National Science Foundation was to be vested in a twenty-four-member National Science Board to be appointed by the president after giving due consideration to nominations submitted to him by the National Academy of Sciences, the Association of Land Grant Colleges and Universities, the National Association of State Universities, the Association of American Colleges, or other scientific or educational institutions. The board would be required to meet only once a year. It would, in turn, select biennially from among its members a nine-member executive committee that would meet six times a year and exercise the board's powers. The foundation's full-time executive officer, a director, would be appointed by the executive committee unless the board chose to make the appointment itself.

A bill incorporating the scientists' proposal was enacted by the Congress but drew a strongly worded veto from President Truman.[48] Truman recognized that "the proposed National Science Foundation would be divorced from control by the people to an extent that implies a distinct lack of faith in the democratic process" and would deprive the president "of effective means for discharging his constitutional responsibility." He took particular exception to the provisions insulating the director from the president by two layers of part-time boards and warned that "if the principles of this bill were extended throughout the government, the result would be utter chaos." Truman's views only partially prevailed. The Congress deleted the most objectionable feature by making the foundation director a presidential appointee, but retained the basic structure desired by the science establishment.

Institutional advisory bodies often are as much of a potential threat to executive power as the National Science Foundation proposal, but they are far more difficult to combat. Creation of the National Security Council properly could be construed as a ploy by a Republican Congress to circumscribe a Democratic president's powers in areas in which he was constitutionally supreme. Not only did the Congress designate those officials who were to "advise" the president in the exercise of his constitutional powers, but it also included the curious provision that other secretaries and undersecretaries of executive departments could be appointed council members only with the advice and consent of the Senate. Advice is potentially one of the most powerful weapons in the administrative arsenal.

Up to now we have been discussing mainly the strategic implications of executive branch organization. But power relationships are not always involved in organization decisions. The president, the Congress, and even outside groups may use organizational means to obtain some immediate tactical advantage.

Herbert Hoover himself was not above using organization for tactical purposes. He claimed that he was "a much misunderstood man on this question of committees and commissions." According to Hoover:

> There is no more dangerous citizen than the person with a gift
> of gab, a crusading complex and a determination "to pass a
> law" as the antidote for all human ills. The most effective diver-
> sion of such an individual to constructive action and the great-
> est silencer on earth for foolishness is to associate him on a
> research committee with a few persons who have a passion for
> truth, especially if they pay their own expenses. I can now dis-
> close the secret that I created a dozen committees for that pre-
> cise purpose.[49]

Presidents have continued to employ committees and commissions to capture and contain the opposition. Committees and commissions can also offer an immediate, visible response in times of national catastrophe, such as the assassinations of President Ken-

nedy and Senator Kennedy or the *Challenger* disaster. Study commissions are employed as a kind of tranquilizer to quiet public and
congressional agitation about such matters as pesticides, crime,
and public scandals. Attention, it is hoped, will be diverted to
other issues by the time the commissions report. A poem appearing in Punch some years ago put it very well:

> If you're pestered by critics and hounded by faction
> To take some precipitate, positive action,
> The proper procedure, to take my advice, is
> Appoint a commission and stave off the crisis.[50]

Commissions may be employed to defuse sensitive political issues and to compel the opposition to share responsibility for unpopular actions. Presidents have resorted to bipartisan commissions to find the answers to such politically controversial questions
as funding of social security, tax policy, and base closings.

Interagency committees sometimes create an impression of
neatness and order within the executive establishments, even
when a president cannot or will not resolve the basic differences
and jurisdictional conflicts. If differences surface publicly and become embarrassing to the administration, the president's reflex reaction is to appoint another committee or to reorganize existing
committees. The pressure is almost overwhelming "to do something" that might do some good and certainly will do no harm. No
president can confess that he is stumped by a problem.

Pressure for immediate, tangible answers to highly complex
problems may result in reorganizations. President Eisenhower's
first response to the national trauma caused by the Soviet Union's
successful launching of *Sputnik* in 1957 was to appoint a special assistant to the president for science and technology and to transfer
the Science Advisory Committee from the Office of Defense Mobilization to the White House office. Creation of the Department of
Energy in 1977 was a response to the energy crisis caused by the
1973 oil embargo.

For many, organization is a symbol. Federal councils on aging,
mental retardation, physical fitness, consumers, and the arts, for

example, are more important as evidence of national concern than as molders of federal policies.

Some seek the creation of new federal agencies or reorganizations to enhance their status in the outside community. Their successful demand for an independent National Archives disassociated from the government's "housekeeper," the General Services Administration, in part stemmed from the archivists' desire to improve their standing as a scholarly profession. Establishment of the Department of Education is generally acknowledged to be a political payoff to the National Education Association.

The questions that now urgently confront us are as old as the republic itself. How can we maintain a government structure and administrative system that reconcile liberty with justice and institutional and personal freedom with the general welfare?

What we are observing today are the strains and tensions inevitably produced by revolutionary changes in the federal government's role and its relationships to other levels of government, institutions of higher learning and other nonprofit institutions, and the private sector. Dividing lines have become increasingly blurred. It is no longer easy to determine where federal responsibilities end and those of state and local governments and private institutions begin. These changes began with the "New Deal" in the 1930s, but the most dramatic developments have occurred since 1961 and have peaked in the 1990s when the federal government's legitimacy is being hallenged.

The Hoover Commission solution of "placing related functions cheek-by-jowl" so that "the overlaps can be eliminated, and of even greater importance coordinated policies can be developed" is not workable when you must combine the major purpose programs— health, education, manpower, housing—to alleviate the social and economic ills of a specific region, city, or neighborhood.

Senator Robert Kennedy posed the fundamental question when he asked: "Do the agencies of Government have the will and determination and ability to form and carry out programs which cut across departmental lines, which are tailored to no administrative convenience but the overriding need to get things done?"[51]

Straight lines of authority and accountability cannot be established in a nonhierarchical system. The federal government is compelled to rely increasingly for accomplishment of its goals on cooperation by nonfederal institutions that are not legally responsible to the president and subject to his direction. Federal powers are limited to those agreed on and enumerated in negotiated contracts. Success of the foreign aid, energy, space and defense research and development programs depends almost as much on performance by contractors as on performance by the government's own employees. The government, since 1948, has caused to be organized and wholly financed a host of university- and industry-sponsored research centers and so-called nonprofit corporations for the sole purpose of providing services to the government. Legally, these are private organizations, but many, such as the Institute for Defense Analyses, Aerospace Corporation, Lincoln Laboratory, and Oak Ridge National Laboratory, have more in common with traditional government agencies than with private institutions. In dealing with such institutions, regulations are the primary instruments of control.

In the years since World War II, the federal table has become crowded with dependents, each clamoring to be fed and demanding the biggest slice of pie. Whereas once the federal government was tolerated as a nuisance or at best a marginal customer, major industries, universities, and other institutions have now come to depend on federal funds for survival.

In contrast with the situation in World War II, and even that during the Korean War, a large share of defense production is performed by highly specialized defense contractors, many of whose products bear little resemblance to civilian items, and who have had little experience outside defense production. For many companies their most important customer is the U.S. government.

In 1996 the five leading government contractors were Lockheed Martin Corp., Mc Donnell Douglas Corp., Westinghouse Electric Corp., Boeing Co., and Tenneco, Inc., with annual sales to the government exceeding $38 billion.[52]

Unlike with the regulated industries, it is not enough for these federal dependents to maintain a strong defensive posture. Under our system of checks and balances, it is relatively easy to block action. It is far more difficult to persuade the executive branch and the Congress to do something, particularly when there are strong competing demands for limited resources. Offense demands a new team and a different strategy. Some industries, such as the railroads, have been penalized because they were too slow in getting their defensive team off the field.

Each of the dependents endeavors to manipulate the organization structure, processes, and assignment of program responsibilities so as to maximize its ability to obtain federal funds and to minimize federal interference in the allocation and use of funds. Scientists had these objectives in mind when they developed their original design for the National Science Foundation. Farm organizations were inspired by identical motives when they convinced President Eisenhower to support legislation that provided independent financing for the farm credit system and immunized it to effective federal control. Not all dependents were as successful as the farm credit organizations in gaining the four freedoms: freedom from financial control by the Congress, freedom from independent audit by the comptroller general, freedom from budget review by the president, and freedom to use federal funds. But for many, these freedoms remain the goals.

The struggle for power and position has contributed to fragmentation of the executive branch structure and the proliferation of categorical programs. With a narrowed constituency, agencies are more susceptible to domination by their clientele groups and congressional committees. Efforts to narrow the constituencies have been accompanied by demands for independent status or autonomy within the departmental structure.

Programs are packaged in such a way as to elicit congressional and clientele support. General programs have far less political appeal than specific programs. Support can be mobilized more readily for federal programs to combat heart disease, blindness, cancer, and mental illness than for such fields as microbiology or for general health programs. For this reason, in 1955 the National Microbiological Institute was renamed the National Institute of Allergy and Infectious Diseases. As was explained at the time, the institute had been handicapped in making its case to the Appropriations Committees because "no one ever died of microbiology."[53]

It would be a mistake to assume, however, that dependents always have the wisdom to know what is in their own best interests. The maritime unions became so obsessed with the idea that an independent maritime agency would solve all of their problems that they ignored the plain fact that any transportation agency outside the Department of Transportation would be in a very weak competitive position. In 1981 the maritime unions quietly supported legislation to transfer the Maritime Administration from the Department of Commerce to the Department of Transportation, thus conceding that a mistake had been made in opposing such a transfer in 1966.

Few would dispute that federal domination of science and education would be undesirable. Yet grave risks are run when public power is exercised by agricultural, scientific, and educational elites who are more concerned with advancing their own interests and the interests of the institutions they represent than the public interest. Serious distortions and inequities may occur in the allocation of funds among those eligible for assistance. Vested interests are created that are resistant to change and the reordering of priorities to meet new national needs.

As our one elected official, other than the vice president, with a national constituency, the president of the United States stands almost alone as a counterweight to these powerful centrifugal forces. Sometimes the executive branch takes on the appearance of an arena in which the chiefs of major and petty bureaucratic fiefdoms, supported by their auxiliaries in the Congress and their mercenaries in the outside community, are arrayed against the president in deadly combat.

Herbert Emmerich, a highly perceptive student of federal organization, has said: "The Presidency is the focal point of any study of reorganization. . . . The Presidency focuses the general interest as contrasted with the centrifugal forces in the Congress and the departments for the specialized interests of subject matter and of region."[54]

It is significant that the lasting contributions of the first Hoover Commission, the President's Committee on Administrative Management, and the earlier Taft Commission on Economy and Efficiency are to be found in their recommendations to strengthen the office of the presidency, not in the long-forgotten proposals for reshuffling agencies and providing more efficient and economical administration.[55] Institutional type and organization structure are important because they can help or hinder the president in performing his pivotal role within our constitutional system.

Structural and procedural reform also can be exploited by the president to alter the delicate balance within our constitutional system by eliminating or eroding the checks and balances resulting from the distribution of power within the executive branch as well as among the three branches of government. Watergate and its attendant "horrors" have raised fundamental and disturbing questions about the centralization of power in the White House, the fractionalization of presidential power among assistants to the president, and the division of responsibilities between the White House Office and the statutory agencies within the Executive Office of the President, the executive departments, and independent agencies. It is one thing to support and strengthen the president's capability to perform his pivotal role within the constitutional system. It is quite another to restructure the government so the president, in the words of assistant to the president Bryce N. Harlow, "is running the whole government from the White House."[56]

There is a growing awareness that we will not make progress by attempting to apply yesterday's solutions to yesterday's problems. The growth of third-party or proxy government raises a different set of issues from those considered by the Brownlow Committee and the first Hoover Commission. The contest for power and position now focuses as much on processes and procedures as on formal structure. The Senate Committee on Governmental Affairs has identified what it deems to be the most urgent problem facing reorganizers:

> The erosion of accountability in government which stems from the new patterns of administration is possibly the gravest threat to the health of our system. Fragmented authority and ill-defined responsibility fosters the sense that government is out of control. Those responsible for a given issue are difficult to identify and all too often are remote and unresponsive.[57]

2

Executive Branch Organization: View from the Congress

One could as well ignore the laws of aerodynamics in designing an aircraft as ignore the laws of congressional dynamics in designing executive branch structure and administrative processes. What may appear to be structural eccentricities and anomalies within the executive branch are often nothing but mirror images of jurisdictional conflicts within the Congress. Congressional organization and executive branch organization are interrelated and constitute two halves of a single system.

As noted by a National Academy of Public Administration panel: "The question of the proper nature and extent of congressional involvement in the details of administration is central to debates about the meaning of separation of powers as a criterion for carrying out the constitution. . . . Congress and the executive branch are separate but interdependent institutions collectively responsible to develop and implement federal programs as well as raise the revenue to pay for them."[1]

The Clinton-Gore reinvention strategy was fundamentally flawed because it assumed that proposed reforms could be accomplished by the executive branch without participation by the Congress.

Executive branch structure and administrative arrangements are not matters of mere academic interest to members of Congress.

Organization or reorganization of executive agencies may influence committee jurisdictions, increase or decrease the "accessibility" of executive branch officials to members of the Congress, and otherwise determine who shall exercise ultimate power in the decision-making processes.

To understand the organization of the executive branch, one must first understand the organization and culture of the Congress and the high degree of congressional involvement in administrative decisions.

It is highly misleading to speak of the Congress as if it were a collective entity. There are, instead, 535 individuals, 100 senators, and 435 representatives who in the final analysis are responsible and accountable only to the constituencies that elected them. A hierarchical structure is difficult to impose on an organization where everyone considers himself to be equal.

Under arcane senate rules any single senator may bring proceedings to a halt. Former majority leader Bob Dole complained that he had "43 independent contractors."[2] Newt Gingrich enjoyed some initial success in centralizing power in the House of Representatives and restoring the speakership to its dominant position under czars Thomas B. Reed and Joseph C. Cannon. He ignored seniority in selecting committee chairs, limited chairs to six-year terms, reduced committee staffs and increased the speaker's staff. Speaker Gingrich was hailed as prime minister and both the president and the legislative committees were deemed to be irrelevant. Czar Cannon's reign lasted for seven years (1903–10). Czar Gingrich's reign endured for less than three years.[3] Many members of the House of Representatives today would concur in the complaint by Cannon opponent Congressman William P. Hepburn: "No member ought to be compelled to go to another man, his equal and no more, a representative of a constituency no what superior to his own, and ask for the poor privilege of calling his measure to the attention of the House.[4]

The structure, procedure, and culture of the Congress tend to obscure the general interest, encourage particularism, and create an environment in which organized interest groups and special pleaders can be assured a sympathetic response. Consequently, dispersion, not integration, has been the dominant organizational thrust imposed on the executive branch. This has created a situation in which, in the words of former White House aide and HEW secretary Joseph A. Califano Jr.:

> Congress is eager to establish for each interest its own executive bureau or independent board. . . . The molecular politics of Washington, with power, and often authority and responsibility, fragmented among increasingly narrow, what's-in-it-for-me groups and their responsive counterparts in the executive and legislative branches, has the centrifugal force to tear the national interest to shreds.[5]

Congressional power is divided among what were once termed independent fiefdoms headed by all powerful barons: sixteen major standing committees in the Senate and seventeen major standing committees in the House of Representatives. In this respect the U.S. Congress is unique and differs from parliamentary bodies such as the British House of Commons where standing committees have marginal influence. Under Speaker Gingrich the barons are said to have been reduced to nobles subservient to the king.[6] While not as strong as they were under Democratic regimes, the power of committees and committee chairs should not be underestimated.

One of the most striking developments since enactment of the Legislative Reorganization Act of 1946, which cut in half the number of standing committees has been the proliferation in the number of subcommittees. The number of Senate subcommittees has doubled in the last fifty years with comparable growth in the House. There are sixty subcommittees in the Senate and eighty-five subcommittees in the House, a reduction of twenty-five from the previous high. Subcommittees tend to become independent power centers and may function with considerable autonomy.

Generalizations about congressional committees should be approached with caution. Each committee and subcommittee has its own culture, mode of operations, and set of relationships to executive agencies subject to its oversight, depending on its constituency, its own peculiar tradition, the nature of its legislative jurisdiction, its administrative and legislative processes, and the role and attitude of its chairman. Richard F. Fenno Jr.'s analysis reveals significant differences among House committees with respect to member goals, environmental constraints, strategic premises, decision-making processes, and conclusions.[7] Committees have only two things in common. First, power within a committee is earned by specialization. A new member is advised that "to make a great name for himself in the Congress a man must be a specialist."[8] Second, jurisdictional prerogatives are zealously guarded and raids by other fiefdoms are resisted with a jealous frenzy.

Growth of a congressional bureaucracy and institutionalization of committees and subcommittee has deepened the moats dividing the committees and has accentuated the innate disposition of the Congress to concentrate on administrative details rather than basic issues of public policy. Professional staffing for all committees became established only in 1946 with the passage of the Legislative Reorganization Act. Overall staffing has increased sixfold over the past half century. Approximately 19,000 persons are now employed on committee and members' personal staffs.[9]

According to Samuel C. Patterson, "committee staff members tend to adopt the goal orientations dominant among the members of the committee for whom they work." He has found that there is minimal communication among the professional staffs of the different congressional committees, even when they have overlapping jurisdictions, and that staff appear "to be very much isolated from one another."[10]

Staff develops alliances with the executive branch bureaucracy and the bureaucracies representing interest groups. Most are highly capable, but some develop narrow interests in particular programs, are highly parochial in outlooks, and provide a rallying point for those fighting reorganizations that upset committee jurisdictions. Roger H. Davidson and Walter J. Oleszek acknowledge that the House Select Committee on Committees seriously underestimated the ability of staff to mobilize outside allies to protect their domains.[11] Those who hope further expansion of the congressional bureaucracy will make it possible for the Congress to look at the big picture and regain legislative leadership are pursuing a will-o'-the-wisp. On the contrary, few would dissent from James L. Sundquist's observation that "as members become managers of professional staffs, the chambers disintegrate as 'deliberative bodies' in the traditional sense of legislators engaged in direct interchange of views leading to a group decision. . . . With each passing year, the House and Senate appear less as collective institutions and more as collections of institutions—individual member-staff groups organized as offices and subcommittees."[12]

Standing committees and subcommittees, like the major executive departments, tend to be composed of individuals who share much the same background, interests, and values. Members seek assignments that will best enable them to advance the interests of their constituents. Those from agricultural states or districts want to be on the agriculture committees, and preferably on the subcommittee concerned with the dominant crop produced in their area. Representatives from western states control almost a majority on the House Resources Committee, which has jurisdiction over reclamation projects, grazing, timber, and mineral rights—issues of primary interest to voters in those states.[13]

For fifty years senators and members of Congress have resisted any fundamental change in the committee structure. A succession of special committees established to examine and recommend reforms in congressional organization and operation were not able to accomplish anything more than minor improvements.[14] Speaker Gingrich renamed a number of House committees and abolished the Merchant Marine and Fisheries and Post Office and Civil Service Committees which do not have Senate counterparts and were perceived to represent predominantly democratic constituencies but did not otherwise upset existing jurisdictions.

Senator William V. Roth Jr. urged establishment of a Commission on Project Government Reform to reevaluate the organization and operations of both the executive and the legislative branches. Senator Roth reserved his harshest criticism for the Congress. He said:

> It is no wonder the people are angry. They see government as part of the problem, not the solution. This is especially true of Congress. Congressional procedures permit the avoidance of difficult problems and hard choices. Our committee structures a reflection of old priorities and bygone eras. Responsibilities are fractured and scattered so that nothing gets done. Accountability is diffused so that we can all point fingers at each other.[15]

The Budget and Impoundment Control Act of 1974 did provide an institutional structure for coordinating congressional actions on budget and fiscal policy. But except for budget and fiscal policy, there remains no place short of the floor of the Congress where important programs that cut across established agency and committee jurisdictions can be considered in their totality. Diffusion of responsibility provides opportunities to divide and conquer by playing off one committee against another.

Committee jurisdictions are overlapping and cannot be neatly delineated. Although one of the smaller executive departments, the Department of Housing and Urban Development is subject to oversight by no less than forty committees and subcommittees.[16] Turf problems among committees exercising jurisdiction over the Treasury and Justice departments are admitted to be one of the obstacles to eliminating the double clearance of travelers entering the country by the customs service and the immigration service.[17] Efforts to simplify administration of private pension regulation, currently divided among the Treasury and Labor departments and the Pension Benefit Guaranty Corporation, are complicated by the competing jurisdictional claims of the tax and labor committees.[18] A jurisdictional dispute between the Senate Labor and Human Resources Committee and Commerce, Science and Transportation Committee prevented enactment of annual authorizing legislation for the National Science Foundation.[19]

There is nothing more certain to doom a legislative proposal than a jurisdictional dispute among committees. Turf battles defeated legislation to reform the U.S. Intelligence Community.[20] House Government Reform and Oversight Chairman William F Clinger blamed turf warfare for failure to enact legislation abolishing the Department of Commerce strongly advocated by House Republicans. The bill had to clear eleven authorizing committees. When the bill emerged it provided for seven new agencies to replace one cabinet department. According to Congressman Clinger, the Department of Commerce owed its salvation to the House committee structure.[21]

Folklore has it that the camel is an animal conceived by an interagency committee. The camel is a perfectly fashioned animal compared with some spawned out of the maelstrom of conflicting committee jurisdictions. When jurisdictional problems could not be resolved, the Congress in 1966 created two agencies—the National Highway Safety Agency and the National Traffic Agency—to administer the highway safety program. The president was authorized to designate a single individual to head both agencies. All that was gained by creating two agencies, where only one was needed, was to give two Senate committees a voice in the confirmation of the agency head.

Organizational arrangements may be skewed to establish or maintain committee jurisdictions. H.R. 1756 (104th Congress, 1st Session) to abolish the Department of Commerce provided that the Patent and Trademark Office be transferred to the Department of Justice to preserve the House Judiciary Committee's jurisdiction. The Patent and Trademark Office's constitutional mandate is "to promote the progress of science" and no rational argument could be made for its transfer to a department whose primary mission is law enforcement other than to protect committee turf. It would be difficult to identify major purposes shared by the Patent Office and the Federal Bureau of Investigation, Immigration and Naturalization Service, and Bureau of Prisons, Justice's principal constituents.

The source of organizational conflicts and administrative deficiencies often have their roots in uncoordinated statutory mandates by the Congress. For example, between 1980 and 1992, the Department of Housing and Urban Development's statutory mandates increased from 54 to over 200 and substantially changed the department's mission. The National Academy of Public Administration panel concluded that simplification and drastic reduction in the number of statutory mandates were essential if the department were to be able to manage its programs effectively.[22]

Buried in the 1997 defense authorization bill were hundreds of directives by the Congress requiring studies of everything from costs of arms control to how federal agencies would assist local officials in countering the threat of biological and chemical weapons. The Department of Defense required 111 pages to list the reports requested in the 1996 appropriation and authorization acts.[23]

Organizational arrangements for the conduct of federal water resource programs violate each of the organizational commandments handed down by Herbert Hoover. Almost every objective observer has confirmed the Hoover Commission's findings that the existing sharing of water resource responsibilities among Interior, Agriculture, and the U.S. Army Corps of Engineers has resulted in poor planning, working at cross purposes, and wasteful competition. Entrenched interests within the bureaucracy and outside community constitute major obstacles to needed reorganization. But these obstacles would not be insuperable, if the schism in the executive branch did not have its counterpart in the Congress. As conceded by Robert A. Roe, chairman of the House Public Works and Transportation Subcommittee on Water Resources: "There ought to be, in the interests of the nation, just one committee that has total jurisdiction over water resources. But that's not going to happen. The political structure won't allow it."[24]

Congressional organization and executive branch organization with respect to water resources are so closely interlinked that they cannot be considered separately. Control over project authorizations and funding are the essence of congressional power. Jurisdictional rivalries within the executive branch pale by comparison with those among congressional committees. The Senate Energy and Natural Resources Committee and the House Resources Committee exercise jurisdiction over the Bureau of Reclamation and the Senate Environment and Public Works Committee; the House Public Works and Transportation Committee has jurisdiction over the Corps of Engineers; and the Agriculture Committee oversees the Soil Conservation Service.

The current organization of federal water resources functions results from a series of laws, each of which was directed toward a single objective, such as improvement of rivers and harbors, flood control, irrigation, and watershed protection. Given the original limited missions, the logic of assigning rivers and harbors and flood control functions to the Corps of Engineers, reclamation to Interior, and watershed protection to Agriculture could not be reasonably disputed. West Point was our first engineering school, and the Corps alone among federal agencies at the time possessed adequate engineering competence. The lands to be reclaimed were mostly arid western lands under Interior's jurisdiction. Agriculture pioneered a watershed improvement program that extended to the major watersheds of the Mississippi and its tributary, the Missouri.

In contrast with the early laws directed toward a single objective, the Federal Power Act of 1920 expressed a multipurpose concept of river basin planning and development. Clientele groups and congressional committees who had come to identify their interests with those of the Corps, Interior, and Agriculture did not object to the new concept—provided that it was carried out on their terms and by "their" agency. Instead of awarding custody to a single agency or dividing the baby into three parts, the decision was to produce triplets. Initially the three factions, the secretaries of agriculture, interior, and war, constituted the Federal Power Commission.

Since 1920 the Corps, Interior, and Agriculture have obtained parallel and, in some respects, identical authorities for multipurpose development of water resources, although Interior's jurisdiction is limited to the western states and Alaska and Agriculture's authority under the 1954 act is limited in terms of the size of the structure for watershed improvement.

Except when all parties are agreed on the dominant project objective, the decision as to which agency will undertake a particular multipurpose project requires a time-consuming, complex, and often bitter bargaining process. At some point the president must make a determination, but it is seldom final and can be upset by appeal to the Congress. Even the "peace treaties" negotiated by the Corps and Reclamation, under which one assumed responsibility for construction and the other responsibility for operation and maintenance of certain projects, have been negated by subsequent congressional actions.

The Kings River project in California is often cited as a classic illustration of the inherent weakness of federal resource management.[25] More significantly, this case history shows the linkages between organization and legislative policy. The Bureau of Reclamation and the Corps of Engineers were in agreement on the design of the project. The differences resulted from the conflicting water use philosophies developed by the two agencies in keeping with their individual legislative mandates. Reclamation emphasized water conservation and maximum water use, and the Corps emphasized local flood protection. This was not solely a bureaucratic contest for power. Economy and efficiency were not the issues. The significant disagreements centered on the policy issues raised by the choice among administrative agencies. These included differences over repayments and distribution of benefits, restrictions on acreage and speculation, operation of irrigation facilities, power development, and method of congressional authorization. Such issues cannot be resolved by reorganization, and regardless of who makes the initial decision, the president and the Congress will be the final arbiters.

Former congressman and TVA director Frank Smith concluded as follows:

> Ideally, the old concept of one single department of conservation and resource development, responsible for all Federal plan-

ning and action in the field, might still work if it could be achieved by waving a magic wand. It simply cannot be achieved, however, without a bloody, bone shattering fight, which would leave the landscape so scarred that the conservation cause would be lost in the critical years immediately ahead.[26]

The boldest congressional advocates of a Department of Natural Resources have been exceedingly timid in facing up to problems of congressional organization. Senator Edward Kennedy reassured the Congress that the sponsors of a bill to establish a Department of Natural Resources had no intention of upsetting the status quo and that, because of the special expertise acquired by the committees and their staffs, "legislative authority should remain where it is, relying upon effective administration of the programs to provide essential coordination."[27]

The natural allies for many agencies are the legislative committees Herbert Kaufman found, in his case studies of federal bureau chiefs, that "the more responsive a bureau and its chief are to the wishes of a committee, and the better their reputations, the more ardent the committee's defense of the bureau against attacks will be."[28] Complaints about unelected bureaucrats generally are directed by members of Congress against bureaus under the jurisdiction of committees other than their own.[29] As explained by one witness before the House Select Committee on Committees, "If you leave the same jurisdiction year after year, with the same bureaucrats appearing for twenty years, the same committee members for twenty years, and the same staff members, soon there isn't much to disagree about because everyone understands how they think their little piece of the world ought to be run."[30]

A close affinity often exists between a committee chairman and the senior career staff of the departments and agencies under his jurisdiction. The chairmen and ranking committee members probably know more about the details of an agency's program and are better acquainted with the senior career staff than most agency heads who serve for relatively brief periods. New secretaries quickly find that some officials whom they want to reassign are "untouchables." Others whom they may want to keep must be replaced because they have been declared *persona non grata* by the chair of the legislative committee or appropriations subcommittee. Even so revered a figure as Wilbur K. Carr, who served for forty-seven years in the State Department, much of the time as its principal executive officer, was packed off as minister to Czechoslovakia when a new appropriations subcommittee chairman refused to do business with him.[31] Probably more executive branch officials have been fired or reassigned as a result of pressure from the Congress than from the president.[32]

An executive agency's ability to withstand legislative committee pressures, assuming that it desires to do so, depends on many factors. Most vulnerable are the agencies that are required to do one or a combination of the following: renew their legislative charters at specific time intervals; obtain authorizing legislation before appropriations can be made; obtain congressional directives to undertake surveys and legislative authorization for individual projects; and keep committees "fully and currently informed" of pending action and supply copies of all correspondence. Singleheaded agencies are more resistant to pressure than are boards and commissions, and cabinet departments have greater immunity than do independent agencies.

The annual authorizing bill has been seized upon by the legislative committees as a means for obtaining leverage over executive agencies and counteracting Appropriations Committee influence over administration. Until 1948 most programs, with the exception of the civil works program of the Army Corps of Engineers, were either authorized on a permanent basis or for multiyear periods. In 1948 the foreign aid program was made subject to annual authorization, and since then the requirement has been extended to programs constituting almost one third of the federal budget.[33] Programs requiring both periodic authorizing legislation and annual appropriations include foreign aid, defense construction and procurement, space, maritime, intelligence, Department of Energy, Department of Justice, coast guard, National Science Foundation, Panama Canal Commission, Environmental Protection Agency (research and development), Bureau of Mint, U.S. Trade Representative, Federal Election Commission, and Travel and Tourism Administration.

As allies, the executive agencies and legislative committees make common cause against the "third house of the Congress": the Appropriations Committees. Lords of the executive establishment generally enjoy the cozy atmosphere of legislative committee hearings, where they are received with courtesy and the deference due their office. They shun, wherever possible, meetings with appropriations subcommittees, whose chairman on occasion may accord them about the same amount of deference as a hard-boiled district attorney shows to a prisoner in the dock. Before the House Appropriations Committee obtained new quarters, it was not uncommon for high officials to stand hat-in-hand for up to an hour in the corridors of the Capitol basement waiting to be summoned by their appropriations subcommittee.

Actions by the appropriations committees may override presidential directives or nullify laws enacted by the Congress itself.[34]

The appropriations "rider" is frequently employed for this purpose. Provisos attached to appropriations acts reversed administration regulations and policies on school busing and abortion. Riders have also controlled such administrative details as proposed reductions in the time period for marine corps basic training, the consolidation of training programs for navy helicopter pilots, and exemptions from environmental impact statements.[35]

Riders, at least theoretically, are subject to review by the Congress as a whole and sometimes can be eliminated on a "point of order" as legislation in an appropriation act. There is no effective way, however, for the Congress to review or amend the directives contained in Appropriations Committee reports that may tell an agency what to do, when to do it, where to do it, and how to do it. Reports do not have the force and effect of law, but agencies ignore such directives at their peril. A committee report was used to rescind one of the most important sections of the District of Columbia Reorganization Plan only a few months after the Congress had allowed the plan to go into effect. The plan conferred upon

the D.C. commissioner authority to reorganize the district government and to establish so many agencies and offices, with such
names or titles as he shall from time to time determine. The committee directed that the commissioner obtain its "prior approval"
before exercising his statutory authority, thus restoring an unsatis-
factory arrangement that the plan was intended to eliminate. Modernization of the D.C. government had been estopped for fifteen
years by the requirement that the Congress approve each transfer,
no matter how minor. Senator Mike Mansfield attempted to soften
the committee report by having Senator Robert C. Byrd (West
Virginia) agree on the Senate floor that he wanted merely to
be informed of "major changes in organization or financing
plans." Senator Byrd would have none of it and made the following
statement:

> . . . I want to emphasize that I for one do not want to bind the
> Appropriations Committee by a colloquy which leaves only so-
> called major changes subject to congressional approval when
> there can be wide variations of interpretations as to what consti-
> tutes major changes. I do not mean to be evasive, nor do I want
> to appear to be unyielding or difficult. I want the Appropria-
> tions Committee to be informed of all such transactions, as they
> have been in the past. And, as far as I am concerned, this is
> what the language means.[36]

Committee jurisdictions are the most important single factor influencing program assignments among executive agencies. Congressional dynamics can be equally significant in molding and
shaping the choice of administrative instruments, advisory arrangements, delegations, and field structure.

Institutional types are judged by their relative accessibility to
members of Congress, not by juridical concepts or abstract principles of organization. For members of Congress, the executive
branch is divided among the "president's men"—White House
staff, heads of executive office units, and cabinet secretaries—and
"agencies of the Congress"—independent boards and commissions and the Army Corps of Engineers. Administrators of inde-

pendent agencies, such as the General Services Administration and Small Business Administration, sit uncomfortably in a no-man's land between the "president's men" and "agencies of the Congress" and are considered fair game for both sides. These distinctions are based not on law, except possibly for the independent regulatory commissions, in which the Supreme Court has limited the president's power, but on "understandings" tacitly accepted by the president and the Congress.

Least accessible to the Congress are members of the White House staff. As a matter of long-standing practice, White House staff do not testify before congressional committees. To his later regret, President Kennedy departed from this custom in allowing James Landis in 1961 to present a series of reorganization plans related to the regulatory commissions. When four of the seven plans were disapproved, it was construed as a personal rebuff to the president. White House staff have testified, but in a personal capacity to explain charges that had been made against them.

Congress was particularly frustrated by its inability to obtain information and testimony from the president's special assistant for science and technology. Senator John McClellan complained that, "Unless legislative action is taken by the Congress to establish some medium through which reliable information and supporting technical data is made available to Congress by officials who are responsive to its needs, the committees of the Congress will continue to be denied information necessary to the legislative process in establishing policies in the fields of science and technology."[37] The reorganization creating the Office of Science and Technology in 1962 was, in part, the president's response to congressional demands for better access to his principal science adviser.

Presidents ask for trouble when they co-opt a congressional agent as a White House aide. The Congress regards such "two-hatted" arrangements as a violation of the rules of the game. Atomic Energy Commission chairman Lewis Strauss invoked his position as a special adviser to the president on atomic energy affairs in flatly refusing to answer questions asked by the joint committee.[38] Lingering resentment from this incident was one of the factors that led the Senate to reject Strauss's nomination as secretary of commerce.

President Nixon's designation of the secretary of the treasury and the director of the Office of Management and Budget as assistants to the president, and the secretaries of HEW, HUD, and agriculture as presidential counselors, was seen by some members of the Congress as a device for limiting congressional access to these officials. The director of the OMB, the heads of other executive office units, and the cabinet secretaries spend much of their time meeting with members of Congress and testifying before committees. But Congress recognizes that it is subject to certain restraints when dealing with these officials. These restraints were noted by Senator J. William Fulbright in opposing the 1950 reorganization plan to transfer the Reconstruction Finance Corporation (RFC) to the Department of Commerce:

> Under the accepted principles of our government, the Secretary of Commerce is a member of the Executive family. He looks primarily to the president for his policy and his influence. We all know he is removable at the discretion of the president. It is customary also, whenever a cabinet nomination comes up here, whether we like him or not, it is generally understood that we confirm him, in contrast to some of the other agencies, the Federal Reserve or one of the others which we look upon more as a congressional agency. I think the cabinet is in a little different position in relationship with the Congress than the heads of these independent agencies.[39]

Senator Fulbright acknowledged, "We rarely, if ever, call up the Secretaries of any of the major departments and question them and examine them like we do the heads of agencies."[40] He contended that the reorganization would tend to insulate the RFC from the committee's supervision and place "between us and the RFC a member of the president's cabinet who is given supervision and policy guidance over that Board. I think the tendency would be to look upon it as not our responsibility anymore."[41] Senator Fulbright's views were confirmed by the committee in its report recommending disapproval of the reorganization plan. The report observed the following:

> This proprietary attitude of the Congress toward the Reconstruction Finance Corporation was emphasized time after time during the course of the hearings, invariably coupled with the fear that, were the corporation to be placed within the framework of an executive department, the affinity between the corporation and the Congress would increasingly become a thing Of the past.[42]

The Congress does not concede, however, that a secretary's right to reign over a department necessarily carries with it the power to rule. Herbert Hoover discovered as secretary of commerce that the Congress "while giving us generous support for our new activities . . . refused to add to my personal staff."[43] Secretary Hoover employed two secretaries and three assistants at his own expense.

Limitations on congressional access to cabinet members do not extend to their principal bureau chiefs. At one time, many bureau chiefs, for all practical purposes, were immune to secretarial authority. These chiefs were appointed by the president subject to Senate confirmation, often for fixed terms of office, and statutory powers were vested in them, not in the secretary. The first Hoover Commission found that "statutory powers often have been vested in subordinate officers in such a way as to deny authority to the president or a department head."[44] Since 1949, the number of autonomous bureaus has been reduced by a series of reorganization plans, but by no means wholly eliminated. The plans transferred the statutory functions of all subordinates to the department head.

Even the Executive Office of the President has not been wholly immune from infiltration by the Congress. What some in Congress have termed a "congressional agency," the Office of Federal Procurement Policy (OFPP) was established within the Office of Management and Budget in 1974 The OFPP administrator is appointed by the president, by and with the advice and consent of the Senate, and the office's functions are vested in him, not in the

OMB director. The administrator is required to keep the Congress and its committees "fully and currently informed" and to transmit, at least thirty days prior to the effective date, proposed policies and regulations to the Oversight Committees of the House and Senate. The bill's Senate sponsor, Senator Lawton Chiles, emphasized that the law made the administrator independently responsible for carrying out the office's duties and keeping the Congress informed.[45]

Congress has been somewhat less successful in its attempts to exert its influence by limiting the president's power to appoint and remove federal officers, other than by indirect means. The Tenure of Office Act of 1867 provided that certain civil officers, appointed by and with the advice and consent of the Senate, should hold office during the term of the president who appointed them and one month thereafter. This act was declared unconstitutional.[46] Congress provided that members of the Tennessee Valley Authority Board could "be removed from office at any time by concurrent resolution of the Senate and House of Representatives," but this power has never been exercised and is of doubtful constitutionality. Congress has gone so far as to vest removal power exclusively in the hands of an agency, thus presumably taking it away from the president. Board members of the Legal Services Corporation may be removed "by a vote of seven members" for specified causes.[47]

Executive power also may be offset by specifying terms of office coterminous with or exceeding that of the appointing official. Such was the congressional intent when it specified nine-year overlapping terms for members of the Postal Service Board of Governors.

Efforts by the Congress to assume the appointing power have been rebuffed by the Supreme Court. The Court held unconstitutional a 1974 statute authorizing the Congress to appoint four members of the Federal Elections Commission. All six voting commission members (including two to be nominated by the president) were to be confirmed by both Houses of the Congress. The Court ruled that administrative functions had to be carried out by "officers of the United States" appointed in the manner prescribed by the Constitution.[48]

The U.S. Supreme Court held unconstitutional the Board of Review composed of nine members of Congress "serving in their individual capacities" established to oversee the Washington Metropolitan Airports Authority.[49] Comparable constitutional questions are raised by the Social Security Advisory Board consisting of seven members appointed by the president, Speaker of the House, and president *pro tem* of the Senate. While the law provides that the board "will not become involved in management of the agency," the detailed functions vested in the board, including making recommendations to the Congress with respect to program coordination, nominees for the position of administrator and deputy administrator, quality of service, evaluation of research, etc., exceed those normally placed in a wholly advisory body.[50]

Congress may bypass the established chain of command either by providing independent lines of communication to the Congress or by subjecting specified executive actions to veto by a congressional committee or by one or both houses of the Congress. Examples of dual reporting requirements are those applicable to inspectors general and certain regulatory commissions. The Inspector General Act of 1978 requires inspectors general to keep both their administrative superiors and the Congress fully and currently informed about any deficiencies detected by their offices. The Commodity Futures Trading Commission and the Consumer Product Safety Commission are directed by law to transmit concurrently to the Congress copies of budget estimates and any legislative recommendations submitted to the president.

Congressional determination to influence or control administrative decisions was illustrated most dramatically by the proliferation of statutory provisions requiring the president or his subordinates to submit proposed orders, regulations, and plans to the Congress for review and potential veto. In effect, by this device the Congress was giving itself the power to preaudit executive branch proposals. Since 1932, about 210 laws containing some 320 separate veto provisions were enacted, most since 1970.[51] The Supreme Court, in its historic Chadha decision of June 23, 1983, in one stroke invalidated as unconstitutional virtually every variety of congressional veto enacted in the last fifty years.

Congress is now exploring constitutional alternatives to the legislative veto. These include *report-and-wait* provisions requiring that proposed regulations or actions be reported to Congress for a specified period before implementation; joint resolutions of approval or disapproval that would have to be adopted by a majority of both houses and submitted to the president for his approval; and nonbinding concurrent resolutions expressing the views of the Congress on pending matters.[52]

Statutory interdepartmental committees are condemned by James Rowe Jr. as another device "striking directly at the jugular of presidential responsibility."[53] These and statutory advisory committees can be used to limit presidential and secretarial discretion by controlling their sources of advice. Rowe correctly concludes that once an interdepartmental committee or advisory body "is given a statutory floor with defined powers and a separate staff, it too begins to look toward its creator, the Congress, for sustenance."

Multiheaded agencies are classified indiscriminately by the Congress as "agencies of the Congress" without regard to nice distinctions between executive functions and quasi-judicial and quasi-legislative functions. Boards and commissions are unloved by everyone but the Congress.

Plural executives may be inefficient administrators, but the Congress is generally more concerned with responsiveness than efficiency. A proposed reorganization to replace the Consumer Products Safety Commission with a single administrator was rejected in spite of overwhelming evidence that political infighting among the then commissioners prevented effective action. The General Accounting Office was highly critical of the commission and noted that "the commission structure is more appropriate for an agency with a significant adjudication function, which is not a large part of CPSC's responsibility."[54] Chairman James J. Florio, of the Committee on Energy and Commerce, Subcommittee on Commerce, Consumer Protection and Competitiveness, argued that there is a "value in democratic disarray."[55]

Congressional support for a single administrator for an independent Social Security Administration was an exception. The Senate committee concluded that the administration under a single head "would increase the ability to obtain and retain the most experienced and capable leadership for the agency, and enhance the agency's stature within the executive branch."[56]

Almost every member of Congress feels obliged at times to rise above principle. The urge is overwhelming when the issues involve the location or relocation of federal field offices or delegations of decision-making authority to the field.

Wrangling over proposed locations of U. S. Customs' regional headquarters came close to defeating Reorganization Plan No. 1 of 1965 abolishing the offices of collector of customs, comptroller of customs, surveyor of customs, and appraisers of merchandise. The plan itself did not specify regional headquarters locations, but an independent study by a group of management experts had recommended Boston, New York, Miami, New Orleans, San Francisco, and Chicago. To salvage the plan, Treasury bowed to congressional pressures and added regional offices in Baltimore, Houston, and Los Angeles—districts represented by influential members of the Committee on Government Operations and Appropriations Committee. The Government Operations Committee has jurisdiction over reorganization plans.

Members are experts at earmarking appropriation bills to protect field and regional offices and to obtain their fair share of the pork. Speaker Gingrich established a policy against earmarking unauthorized projects, but this did not prevent him from approving such projects when necessary to help a vulnerable Republican member. As expressed by an aide to staunch conservative Senator Larry E. Craig (Idaho), "there will always be room for items that lubricate the political process."[57]

Decentralization makes an excellent theme for campaign speeches, but those who take campaign promises seriously run the risk of incurring congressional displeasure. Governors and mayors are competitors of senators and representatives. Once decisions are made outside the nation's capital, local officials can deal directly with federal field staff, and members of Congress are excluded from a key role in the decision-making processes.

Franklin Roosevelt became painfully aware of senatorial jealousy of governors when he bypassed the Senate delegations and dealt directly with his former colleagues in the Governors' Conference. He told Frances Perkins, "Every governor, particularly in states where the governor's salary is about $3,000, looks forward to being a United States Senator. No United States Senator, even if he belongs to the same party, likes to be ousted by the superior prestige and patronage which the expenditure of federal money may get for the governor. Well, *that* is something to remember."[58]

If we persist in treating separately those things that are inseparable, we will seek in vain the improvements in government structure and processes that must be accomplished to maintain the effective functioning of our democratic system. More studies of executive branch organization in isolation from the Congress are likely to be unproductive. These interrelationships are beginning to be recognized. The Senate Committee on Governmental Affairs, in its report recommending enactment of legislation to establish a Commission on More Effective Government, made clear that the proposed commission's mandate would include executive-legislative relations. It cautioned, however, that the commission would not have a roving charter "for the study of congressional organization and operations per se."[59]

In proposing reorganization of the congressional committee structure, the Senate and House Select Committees on Committees largely ignored interrelationships with executive organization. Roger H. Davidson and Walter Oleszek, who served on the staff of the House Select Committee, report that the committee "though not adverse to promoting better legislative-executive relationships, never gave the matter high priority."[60] The members of the house committee deliberately rejected the concept of developing a structure parallel to that of the executive branch. Committee structure was viewed by both committees as something almost exclusively concerned with distribution of power within the Congress.

Admittedly, reform of congressional organization presents a unique complex of difficult issues that are not raised by executive reorganization. Every member of the Congress constitutes an independent sovereign entity subject to no authority other than the Congress as a whole or the voters in his or her constituency. Congressional structure must be capable of reconciling the needs of members and the needs of the Congress as an institution.

Existing arrangements result from compromises and historical accidents, not from conscious organizational philosophy or planning to achieve identified purposes. Committee jurisdictions reflect a series of pragmatic decisions designed mainly to provide an acceptable division of the workload and to secure committee assignments that enhance an individual member's ability to represent and serve his or her constituency. Inadequate attention has been given to the implications of these decisions for government policies, program-administration, and relationships with the executive branch.

In determining committee jurisdictions, the Congress should be aware that the kind of constituency that is being created can significantly influence policy outcomes and encourage or discourage alliances with executive agencies and interest groups. Constituencies can be established in such a way that a committee will be uninterested in or actually hostile to certain program objectives. Care must be taken to ensure that committees have reasonably consistent sets of program responsibilities and that no single function is so dominant that it will determine committee membership and outlook.

Committee assignments should be viewed as something more than a means for distributing power within the Congress. If the government is to function effectively, congressional organization also must be compatible with that of the executive branch. Speaker Carl Albert was of the view that "up to a point" legislative committee jurisdictions should reflect the organization within the executive branch.[61] This does not imply that executive and legislative organization structures must be identical. A legislative body has different requirements from the executive.

Obviously any committee structure that fails to serve the needs of individual members and their constituents will be unacceptable. But compensating features should be built into the present system to balance the strong centrifugal forces representing the particular interests of professional and economic groups and regions. Such urgent problems as energy, rural poverty, and urban transportation should not be permitted to fall within the cracks of the present committee and subcommittee structure. If the Congress is to be something more than a representative and advocate of the diverse interests in our society, it must be capable of examining problems from a national perspective and reviewing and appraising the results of executive operations.

Former Congressman James R. Jones has warned that distrust and outright confrontation between the executive and legislative branches has a high cost. He stressed that to restore confidence in government "both branches urgently need to adapt their behavior and institution to address critical demands."[62]

3

Executive Branch Organization: View from the White House

Andrew Jackson saw it as the president's "special duty to protect the liberties and rights of the people and the integrity of the Constitution against the Senate, or the House of Representatives, or both together."[1] As the elected representative of all the American people, the president alone has the power and the responsibility to balance the national interest against the strong centrifugal forces in the Congress for the special interests of subject matter or region. His effectiveness in performing this pivotal role within our constitutional system depends in no small measure on his instinctive grasp of the political and strategic uses of organization type and structure.

Such insight is not likely to be gained within the halls of the Congress, the military service, or by serving as governor of a small state. Perspectives, attitudes, and behavior patterns developed on Capitol Hill, or in the Pentagon or a statehouse become a way of life. They are a key to understanding the style, values, and administrative habits of recent presidents, particularly those who have come from the Congress. Five of our last ten presidents earned their public reputations in the Congress.

Whatever its other virtues as a breeding ground for presidents, the Congress is a poor school for executives and managers. The emphasis in a legislative body is on individuals, not institutions or organizations. Legislators do not think in institutional terms, except when some immediate constituency interest is threatened. The skills needed are those of the tactician, not the long-range strategist. Congress cannot respond to problems, other than with speeches, press releases, investigations, and, ultimately, enactment of laws and appropriation of money.

Some senators are critical of what John Gardner calls "the vending-machine concept of social change. Put a coin in the machine and out comes a piece of candy. If there is a social problem, pass a law and out comes a solution."[2] Senator Abraham Ribicoff acknowledged that "because we rely so heavily on the programmatic approach—passing a program whenever we discover a problem or a part of the problem—and rely so little on a systematic approach that would treat our major problems in a comprehensive manner—our efforts often are marked by confusion, frustration, and delay."[3] But the critics are unable to offer clear alternatives. The diffusion of power within the Congress and the inherent constraints of the legislative process do not foster concentration on long-range goals or allow anything other than a piecemeal approach to problem solving.

Within the Congress, words are sometimes equated with deeds. Votes represent final acts. There is concern with administration, but it is focused principally on those elements that directly affect constituency interests or committee jurisdictions. Legislative proposals are seldom debated from the viewpoint of their administrative feasibility. Grubby details of planning, organizing, staffing, and developing the administrative system to translate laws into working programs are for someone else to worry about. It is assumed that the executive branch or, in the case of grants-in-aid, state and local governments have or can obtain the necessary competence to devise and install efficient delivery systems. If things go wrong, failure can always be attributed to the incompetence or stupidity of the administrators.

Congress is weak on follow-through, even though it has been devoting increasing attention to legislative oversight. Laws on the statute books are not news, except when investigations disclose scandals or serious abuses in their administration. The political payoffs from measures to improve administrative efficiency or to promote administrative reform are minimal. To capture the headlines, studies must be launched into problems of the moment and new legislative proposals thrown into the hopper. An ambitious senator with an eye on the White House has an insatiable appetite for "ideas" that will keep him or her on the front pages and contribute to his or her national image.

For a president, long service in the Senate or House carries with it special disabilities. President Johnson saw the outside world through the eyes of the Congress, particularly the Senate. Congressional reaction on major issues was, for him, the most accurate and reliable expression of the national will. As a result, his sensitivity to evolving trends in public opinion and national concerns was markedly reduced.

The Johnson "system," which functioned admirably in the Senate, had fundamental weaknesses when installed in the White House. The essence of the Johnson system was a network of loyal henchmen who could be counted on to furnish timely information and help when needed, bilateral negotiations, and meticulous head counts before action. You moved when you had the votes, not before. Effective operation of the system placed a premium on secrecy. Premature disclosure of the majority leader's position would seriously impair his ability to harmonize the contending forces and arrive at a consensus.

Presidential leadership demands something more than the talents of an expert congressional power broker. People want to know where the president stands and what he stands for. Secrecy cuts off the communication flow within the executive branch and blurs the president's public image. Presidential greatness is not measured by his legislative batting average or his standing in the public opinion polls. A true gauge is his capacity for leadership—his ability to anticipate and articulate the nation's needs, hopes, fears, and aspirations. In the words of the first president: "For the more combined and distant things are seen, the more likely they are to be turned to advantage."[4]

Unlike a legislator, a president should view the passage of a law as a beginning, not an end. His responsibility does not cease when he has decided *what* to do. The less politically rewarding and often more complex task of determining *how* to do it must be undertaken by the executive, if programs are to produce results. Training in the Congress does not equip a president to deal with the *how* to, and he is predisposed to downgrade its importance. The tendency has been, as noted by Louis Brownlow, "to elevate the political consideration, the *what* to do, above the administrative consideration of how to do it," and "even on the rare occasions when administrative questions do rise to a level where they are subject to general and popular discussion, very frequently that discussion will go off at a tangent whose direction is determined by some political, even some partisan or pressure group, interest."[5]

Brownlow made this observation some thirty years ago. In the interim, the strengthening of the staff resources available to the president has not noticeably enhanced White House appreciation or understanding of administrative management. If anything, the growing preoccupation with the legislative program and legislative and political tactics reinforce the disposition to dismiss administrative and organization problems as annoying trivia.

Martha Derthick has observed that, "if the agencies repeatedly fall short, the flaw may be in the source of instruction rather than in the objects of it—or, more precisely, in the relation between the two. . . . Policy making neglects administration. Policy makers, who define administrative tasks with their choices, act with limited understanding of administrative organizations and without attaching high priority to anticipating the consequences of their choices for the agencies performance."[6]

Responsibility for reminding the president and his immediate staff of the importance of the "how to" was assigned to the Bureau of the Budget. But the bureau's effectiveness as the advocate of management planning declined as budget directors became more preoccupied with fiscal and economic policy.

Reorganization Plan No. 2 of 1970 was designed to reemphasize the management role of the Office of Management and Budget (the successor to the Bureau of the Budget) and provide the president with substantially enhanced institutional staff capability in areas of executive management other than the budget—"particularly in program evaluation and coordination, improvement of executive branch organization, information and management systems, and development of executive talent."[7] Whatever its intentions, the reorganization plan has not restored the Office of Management and Budget, as an organization, to its position as the "President's principal arm for the exercise of his managerial function." The office has not reestablished the monopoly the Bureau of the Budget once exercised as the "unique supplier of presidential services" and adviser on legislation and government organization.[8]

President George Bush's deputy director of the Office of Management and Budget, William M. Diefendorfer III, described OMB's management oversight of the executive branch as "moribund." We had one person looking at the management side for all government."[9] President Bush declined to activate the National Commission on Executive Organization authorized by the 1991 Act creating the Department of Veterans Affairs.

Under Presidents Reagan and Bush, all that was left of the "M" in OMB, like the Chesire Cat in *Alice in Wonderland*, was the smile. Under President Clinton the smile was gone.[10] Congress in 1990 had created a deputy director for management to give the "M" equal status with the "B." As a result of the OMB 2000 review the management functions were integrated with and wholly subordinated to the budget functions. Most of the deputy director for management's staff were transferred to five Resource Management Offices.[11]

Based on an in-depth investigation and extensive subcommittee hearings chaired by Congressman Steven Horn, the House Committee on Government Reform and Oversight severely criticized the Executive Office of the President for abrogating "its responsibility to oversee and improve the government's management structure." The committee found:

- The capacity available to the president in the Office of Management and Budget to reform or improve management has steadily declined and now barely exists.
- The National Performance Review in its ad hoc and episodic approach to management issues, reveals the weakened state of management capacity of the executive office of the president.[12]

The committee recommended establishment of an office of management within the Executive Office of the President. Such an office had been recommended by nonpartisan organizations such as the National Academy of Public Administration.[13]

The distinction between institutional staff in the executive office of the president serving the presidency and the White House staff serving the president has been seriously eroded. OMB's director functions more as an assistant to the president than as the head of an independent office. At its senior levels, the OMB has been almost completely politicized and career staff rarely have direct access to the principal policymakers in the OMB and the White House.

President Roosevelt recognized that the White House staff is not immune to Parkinson's disease. Work will expand in proportion to the number of people available to do it. The president needs help, but he does not need helpers who monopolize his time and try to interpose themselves between him and his department heads. President Ford was estimated to have spent 50 percent of his time with White House staff, even though he desired to maintain an open office.[14] When James H. Rowe Jr., one of the original assistants with a "passion for anonymity," asked President Roosevelt for an assistant, his request was politely but firmly denied. Roosevelt told him that if he was unable to do his job without assistance, he was not doing what the president wanted him to do.

Rowe was impressed by Roosevelt's deep understanding of government organization and "what in it was good for Presidents," and his insistence that "the White House not do everything." He pushed as much on the departments as he could and wanted only vital matters to come to him and then only for a last quick look.[15]

Roosevelt drew a sharp distinction between staff who served him as president and those whose first duty was to the presidency. Rowe was assigned responsibility to assist in the process of reviewing and developing recommendations on enrolled bills, but with precise instructions that his job "was to look after the President," and the Budget Bureau's job was to protect the interests of the presidency.[16] The personal, political interests of an incumbent president and the interests of the presidency as an institution are by no means identical, although it may be hard at times for White House staff to see the difference. Continuity is essential for protection of the institution, and this is something no White House staff can provide.

Roosevelt emphasized that his administrative assistants were to be "personal aides to the President and shall have no authority over anyone in any department or agency, including the Executive Office of the President." Executive Order No. 8248, September 8, 1939, establishing the divisions of the Executive Office of the President, directed: "In no event shall the administrative assistants be interposed between the President and the head of any department or agency or between the President and any one of the divisions in the Executive Office of the President." The executive order reflected the President's Committee on Administrative Management's view that assistants to the president "would not be Assistant Presidents in any sense" and should remain in the background, "issue no orders, make no decision, emit no public statements."[17]

President Nixon did not rescind or modify Executive Order No. 8248. Shortly after his inauguration he explained that his personal staff would function exclusively as "information gatherers," not as major policy advisers or "freewheeling" operators.[18]

The contrast between the White House office prescribed by executive order and envisaged by President Nixon in 1969 and that described by H. R. Haldeman, John Ehrlichman, John Dean, and other witnesses before the Senate Select Committee on Presidential Campaign Activities could not be more dramatic. From analysis of the testimony and evidence, it would appear that President Nixon's principal assistants acted on the following assumptions:

- The president's constitutional powers, including his inherent powers, are delegable and may be legitimately exercised by his principal assistants acting in his name.
- The president must operate on the basis that staff come to him only when called.

As surrogates of the president, the principal assistants must be "self-starters" because "in the Nixon White House there is no one else who is going to have the time to supervise, make assignments, decide what should be looked into. It would be impossible for the President, or any one person in his behalf, to keep informed of everything being done by the staff, even in areas of major current interest or concern."

Department and agency heads must obey orders from the White House even in those areas in which statutory powers are vested in them and they are legally accountable for the actions taken. Agency heads should understand that when a request comes from the White House, they must accomplish it without being told how to do it.[19]

No development in the past quarter century has been more significant than the transformation of the White House from a personal office to a bureaucratic organization. The 1996 budget provided for a White House complement of 400 permanent positions. Thomas E. Cronin, among others, has noted that "the presidency has become a large bureaucracy itself, rapidly acquiring many dubious characteristics of large bureaucracies in the process: layering, overspecialization, communication gaps, inadequate coordination, and an impulse to become consumed with short-term operational concerns at the expense of thinking systematically about the consequences of varying sets of policies and priorities and important long-range problems.[20]

Tensions between political "dilettantes" and "civil service" experts are inevitable, as observed by Max Weber in his classic essay on bureaucracy, but these tensions are heightened when the competing White House bureaucracy is staffed with young and inexperienced outsiders with little knowledge of the way in which the federal government works. President Clinton surrounded himself with cronies from Arkansas—Thomas McLarty (chief of staff), Vincent Foster, and Bruce Lindsey—and others rewarded for their service in the campaign. About one in seven of Clinton's aides was under twenty-four.[21] Perhaps the most difficult task for an incoming president is to shift from campaigning to governing. Some questioned whether the Clinton staff was able to make the transition.[22]

What has come into being is a presidential court with all the trappings and intrigues associated with an ancient monarchy. The Johnson court is vividly characterized in George Reedy's book *The Twilight of the Presidency* as a "mass of intrigue, posturing, strutting, cringing and pious commitment to irrelevant windbaggery. Members of the White House staff possess no power in their own right and depend for status, prestige, and influence on the favor of the president. Consequently, staffs compete with each other, other units in the Executive Office of the President, and cabinet secretaries for information and presidential access.

No one will quarrel with the need for some growth in the size of the White House staff. The world of Bill Clinton is not the world of Franklin D. Roosevelt. Some would argue that the centralization of power in the White House is a necessary and inevitable response to the incompatible and contradictory demands made on the government, the consequences of the technological revolution, the increasing number of federal programs cutting across established jurisdictional lines and the frequency of jurisdictional disputes, the need to control departmental and bureau satrapies that are responsive only to their constituencies, the decline of the cabinet as an institution, and the supineness of the Congress.

But there are dangers. One of the prime lessons of Watergate is that large "do-it-yourself" staffs can isolate the president and, if they mirror his personality too closely, accentuate rather than compensate for his weaknesses. Most important, a large, ambitious, and able staff can create for the president an illusion of self-sufficiency where none exists. Congressman Morris K. Udall summed it up well in the following words:

> Certainly no loyal American would begrudge any President the expertise or manpower needed to cope with the pressing problems of the nation and the world. But a serious problem does arise when the White House staff begins to replace both the functions of the Cabinet and the career civil service.

Few studies of the presidency have failed to quote with approbation Charles G. Dawes's statement that "Cabinet members are the natural enemies of the President." They rarely, however, quote the first budget director in full. What Dawes said was that "Cabinet members are vice presidents in charge of spending, and as such they are the natural enemies of the President."[23] Dawes obviously was speaking from the perspective of budget director. Cabinet members may be the natural enemies of the budget director, or White House staff, but they are the president's natural allies. A president may not like his cabinet members; he may disagree with them and suspect their loyalty; but he cannot destroy their power without seriously undermining his own.

Sudden awareness of his dependency on the executive establishment and the bureaucracy can produce severe cultural shock in a president fresh from the Congress or, for that matter, from the Pentagon or a statehouse. A president is not self-sufficient. The Congress can perform its constitutional functions without the executive establishment and the bureaucracy. A president cannot.

It is the agency heads, not the president, who have the men, money, material, and legal powers. With a few exceptions, such as foreign assistance, disaster relief, and economic stabilization activities, funds are appropriated to the agencies and authority to execute the programs is vested by law in agency heads. As a general rule, the president cannot enter into a contract, make a loan or grant, initiate a public works project, or hire and fire federal employees other than those appointed by him. The president's authority to approve or modify regulations issued by agencies has been challenged on the grounds that such power has not been expressly granted to him by law.[24] To work his will in the Congress and outside community, a president must have at his disposal the trade goods controlled by the agencies and be able to enlist the support of their constituencies.

The occupant of the "most powerful office on earth" quickly learns the harsh truth. His executive power has a very frail constitutional foundation—the power to appoint officers of the United States. Appointing authority may be so hedged about with restrictions as to limit severely his discretion. He can fire officers performing administrative duties, but here again his power is limited. Dismissal of a high official is a measure of last resort, which can be used only under extreme provocation.

A president does not enforce his will by dictate. His instructions are not obeyed automatically. Jesse Jones admitted that when the president "asked me to do something which in my opinion we could not or should not do—and that happened only a few times—we just did not do it."[25] Harry Truman believed that the principal power possessed by a president was "to bring people in and try to persuade them to do what they ought to do without persuasion. That's what I spend most of my time doing. That's what the powers of the President amount to."[26]

An alliance—which is what the executive branch really is—is by definition a confederation of sovereigns joined together in pursuit of some common goal. Some members may be more powerful than others, but they are nonetheless mutually interdependent. Individual purposes and goals are subordinated only to the extent necessary to hold the alliance intact. Each member will find it necessary at times to act contrary to the interests of the alliance when compelled to do so to protect its own vital interests. Unless a president is able to convince his departmental allies that they need him as much as he needs them, they will inevitably gravitate to another power base.

The executive branch is no more a monolith than the Congress. There are multiple power centers, and the president must employ all of the authority and ingenuity at his command "to evoke the prime loyalty of the divers parts of the great governmental machine, each part being also animated by loyalty to its particular purpose."[27]

Intellectually, presidents recognize that their own power is not entirely separable from that of their department heads. But presidents operate under rigid time restraints. What they want, they want now. They are impatient with solutions that go beyond the next congressional election, and their maximum time span is four years. They say they welcome disagreement and dissent, but cannot understand why cabinet members do not share the presidential perspective. The fiefdoms are fractious, and the machinery of government moves too slowly to suit their purposes. Their experience in the Congress or statehouse has given them neither the knowledge nor the aptitude to energize the executive establishment, so as far as possible they attempt to bypass and neutralize it.

Executive departments and the bureaucracy are called on to behave in a way that is contrary to their very nature. McGeorge Bundy reflected a typical White House view when he said, "Cabinet officers are special pleaders" and "should run their part of the government for the Administration—not run to the Administration for the interests of their part of the government."[28] One might as well repeat Professor Henry Higgins's plaint in *My Fair Lady*, "Why can't a woman be more like a man?" as ask "Why can't Cabinet members act more like presidents?" Those who accept the differences can enjoy them and put them to proper use.

The bureaucracy is damned as "uncreative" because it is unable to satisfy the White House appetite for immediate solutions to complex social and economic problems and dramatic imaginative proposals for the legislative program. "Slow moving," "unresponsive," "disloyal" are among the milder epithets used to describe the bureaucracy. Bundy is dismayed because "the contest between the President and the bureaucracy is as real today as ever, and there has been no significant weakening in the network of triangular alliances which unite all sorts of interest groups with their agents in the Congress and their agents in the bureaucracy,"[29]

As an entity, the bureaucracy is no better equipped to manufacture grand designs for government programs than carpenters, electricians, and plumbers are to be architects. But if an architect attempted to build a house, the results might well be disastrous. What the White House identifies as bureaucracy's inherent deficiencies are often its strengths. Effective functioning of the governmental machine requires a high degree of stability, uniformity, and awareness of the impact of new policies, regulations, and procedures on the affected public.

The bureaucracy all too frequently is not asked for its advice on the "how to," for which it does have the knowledge and experience to make a contribution. Senior career managers attribute the government's "loss of credibility" to the "gap between federal policies and their implementation." In their judgment, "better means are needed to draw the experienced program manager into the processes of drafting legislation or developing administration policy so that practical problems of implementation are faced as a regular part of those processes."[30]

Although the White House may not consider a Cabinet member's participation in the development of a legislative proposal essential, the president will hold him to account for ensuring its enactment by the Congress. As far as the president is concerned, a cabinet member's primary responsibility is to mobilize support both within and outside the Congress for presidential measures and to act as a legislative tactician. Major questions of policy and legislative strategy are reserved, however, for decision by the White House staff.

To perform in this role, a department head must maintain the loyalty of his subordinates and strengthen his alliances with congressional committees and interest groups, which in turn raises questions about his allegiance to the president and confirms White House distrust. John Ehrlichman complained that cabinet officers "go off and marry the natives."[31] Senior Carter staff maintained that cabinet secretaries were given too much leeway at the start of the administration and had to be put on notice that "we expect them to work with the President in a positive way."[32] "Loyalty" and "ability to work with White House staff" were the primary tests employed by President Carter in determining who would be retained in his cabinet. The net result was that more and more, those responsible for carrying out policies were excluded as "special pleaders" from the development of the policies they were to administer. The ill-concealed unhappiness of several Carter Cabinet members was not surprising.

Joseph W. Bartlett, former undersecretary of commerce, noted the difficulties posed for cabinet officers by the "baffling ambivalent" White House attitude. White House staff demand "unquestioning obedience" to orders, but the president expects secretaries to maintain "at least the public image of independence" and the capability to enlist their constituencies in support of presidential proposals. Bartlett observed: "In short, a Cabinet officer who is loyal to the President and his deputies but feels constrained to retain some independence must anticipate trouble in carrying water on both shoulders."[33]

No president can afford to allow his cabinet, the Congress, or outside constituencies to restrict his choice of counselors or the devices he employs to obtain advice. He must be no less zealous in preventing his own staff from doing so.

Each component of the governmental system has its own special function. Each has its strengths and each its weaknesses. The White House staff is no exception. The most critical and difficult job facing a president is to learn the system and to ensure that each component is properly used and exploited to its full potential.

Perhaps a president's most important lesson is to learn the strengths and limitations of his personal staff. There are many things the White House staff cannot do or will do poorly. The do not have technical competence and do not have the time to acquire it. Errors may occur when staff usurps the functions of technicians. These errors can be embarrassing, as dramatically demonstrated by the Clinton staff's ineptitude in the Travelgate affair.

Authorship of a proposal necessarily narrows the staff's vision and judgment. The advice they give the president and their evaluation of conflicting opinions will inevitably be colored by their own biases. They are disposed to discount objections and to exaggerate potential benefits. The president cannot rely on them to report accurately and promptly on their projects that go sour. A president has too many advisers who are protagonists of special interests; he does not need them in his own household.

Members of the staff do not have to explain or justify their proposals before the Congress. White House staff members do not testify. The fact that one ultimately has to undergo cross-examination by the Congress is a healthy tempering influence and compels an officials to anticipate the questions that are going to be asked. It is too easy for a staffer to gloss over the unanswered questions.

Unless decisions are fed into the institutional machinery, there will be no effective follow-through. President Johnson's senior aide, Joseph Califano, conceded, "We are not equipped to maintain day-to-day relationship with only one program—no matter how important."[34] If a White House aide picks up the ball and runs with it, no one will be around to retrieve the ball when it is dropped.

Bill Moyers is right when he observes that power is the president's greatest resource and "is not something that he is likely to invest in people whose first allegiance is not to him."[35] Moyers does not seem to appreciate, however, that a president can conserve his power by delegating decision-making *authority* to agency heads. The distinction between power and authority is vital. When authority is delegated, the president can employ his power selectively and let others absorb the heat of the initial contact.

Presidential power is a precious commodity and is not inexhaustible. It retains its potency only as long as it is applied to issues of immediate presidential importance. White House staff members have no power of their own, and whenever they exercise power they drain the president's limited resources. The Watergate record graphically demonstrates the consequences of allowing the presidency to speak with many voices. Furthermore, the president cannot disavow acts by White House aides even when they are acting on their own. All their mistakes become the president's mistakes.

The answer does not lie in having the presidency secede from the executive branch and constituting it as an independent branch of the government. The Nixon administration moved in this direction by attempting to run the whole government from the White House. The bureaucratization and institutionalization of the White House as a separate branch has continued under Bill Clinton.

What a president *does not do* may be as important as what he does do. It was Reagan's strategy to avoid the mistakes of his immediate predecessors by limiting the subjects with which the President becomes personally identified. Overcentralization of decision-making in the White House inevitable encourages buck-passing and stifles initiative by executive agencies. Clinton did not learn this lesson.[36]

White House involvement inevitably produces a chain reaction that has repercussions through the executive establishment. Decisions are sucked up to the top, with the result that department heads may be compelled to deal with matters that might best be left to their bureau chiefs, and Washington bureau chiefs are left with matters that ought to be delegated to the field. Cabinet members are reluctant to delegate authority when their actions are subject to close White House scrutiny.

A president should carefully pick and choose the issues that merit his personal participation in the give and take of policy formulation. This does not imply that he should allow himself to become the captive of completed staff work to the point that his only option is to say yes or no. It does imply a need for a keen sense of timing as to when presidential participation will not cut off debate at too early a stage and discrimination to avoid overexposure and dilution of presidential influence.

President Truman deliberately limited his attendance at National Security Council meetings because he believed that his presence would inhibit frank and open discussion.[37] If a president says at a council meeting, "I think thus and so," the others will take their cue from him.

A president's most important challenge is to harness the energy produced by diversity in support of the national good, not to try to eliminate it. The bureaucratic bastion cannot be reduced by bombarding it with a fusillade of White House directives ordering it to be more creative and more efficient. The perspectives of the president's chief lieutenants cannot be broadened or redirected by concentrating more and more power in the president's own household. More effective means for meeting the challenge are at a president's disposal, if he has the knowledge to use them and is willing to pay the cost.

A president should be as alert to safeguarding the powers and prestige of his department heads as to safeguarding those of his own office. To the extent that any department head's status and authority are downgraded, he is less able to resist the pressures brought on him by his constituencies, congressional committees, and the bureaucracy.

Frontal assaults on the bureaucracy and entrenched constituencies can yield, at best, temporary gains, and the cost may well be excessive. A president is not powerless to bring about significant transformations in the bureaucracy and in the balance of power among constituencies, but his approach must be indirect. To secure lasting results, a president has to take positive action to alter the bases of bureaucratic and constituency power administrative systems and organization structure—so as to adapt them to the nation's long-range goals and requirements. The task is fraught with hazards, but it can be done if the president exercises leadership and exploits fully the powers at his command. The likelihood of success is enhanced if actions are planned within the context of a well-conceived and realistic organization strategy. It is in the development of a sound and realistic organization strategy that recent presidents have failed most conspicuously.

In the words of Morton H. Halperin: "Every President needs to know how bureaucratic interests interact, in order to be the master rather than the prisoner of his organization, and also in order to mold the rational interests of the bureaucracies into the national interest as he sees it."[38]

Personnel systems are the nerve center of bureaucracy. It is idle for presidents to complain that the State Department is a "bowl of jelly," and then do nothing to reform the Foreign Service system, which makes the State Department what it is. The department's career professionals have condemned the recruitment and promotion system for stifling "the creative dissent and responsible questioning of alternatives which could have helped the organization adapt to changing times."[39]

Control of the nonfederal agents on whom the government increasingly relies for service delivery demands a different strategy and set of tactics. Federal influence over these third parties—state and local governments and various private entities—is exercised mainly through the regulatory process. President Reagan was perhaps the first to recognize the need for procedures to ensure that regulations accord with administration policies.

Organization and reorganization can be used to change program emphasis and to modify the power balance among constituencies. But as Hugh Heclo has observed, reorganization plans or techniques like management by objectives and zero-based budgeting are all executive proclamations that presume rather than create changes in subordinates' behavior. Instituting new management techniques and making them part of the bureaucracy's standard operating procedure lie at the end of state-craft, not the beginning.[40] If he is to be successful in promoting desired change, a president must have an organization strategy. A miscellaneous collection of reform proposals such as those contained in the report of the National Performance Review does not constitute an organization strategy.

James Webb demonstrated in the National Aeronautics and Space Administration what could be done with organizational restructuring as an "element of Leadership.[41] In his efforts to maintain management initiative and drive, Webb "deliberately employed fairly frequent organizational restructuring. . . ."

Reorganization and restructuring are important, but they can be overemphasized. Califano exaggerates the difficulties when he asserts that "any President may have one or two shots at it in his career, but that's all, maybe one that's already under way when he comes in and one he gets up himself.[42] There is no contesting the fact, however, that major reorganizations do call for a heavy investment of presidential capital. The same results can sometimes be achieved at considerably less cost by building sound organizational concepts into the design of new programs. It is here that the lack of organizational strategy has hurt the most. Without agreed upon organizational concepts and goals, policies will be related solely to short-term tactical objectives.

When Franklin D. Roosevelt was president, he had a personal organization strategy. Roosevelt played with federal agencies as if they were pawns in a chess game, moving them wherever it would best strengthen his strategic position. He delighted in violating the organizational commandments laid down by the orthodox theorists. Organization for him was "fun," something that could not be said of any of his successors. Only Roosevelt could have written to his budget director:

> I agree with the Secretary of the Interior. Please have it carried out so that fur-bearing animals remain in the Department of the Interior.
>
> You might find out if any Alaska bears are still supervised by (a) War Department (b) Department of Agriculture (c) Department of Commerce. They have all had jurisdiction over Alaska bears in the past and many embarrassing situations have been created by the mating of a bear belonging to one Department with a bear belonging to another Department.
>
> F.D.R.
>
> P.S. I don't think the Navy is involved but it may be. Check the Coast Guard. You never can tell![43]

Roosevelt relied heavily on competition among agencies and checks and balances to keep final authority in his own hands.[44] Innovative programs were cultivated with care so they could grow strong roots before being transferred to old-line agencies that might stunt their development. Staff for the New Deal agencies was recruited from outside the civil service. At the same time, Roosevelt knew how to use his department heads and encouraged rather than deplored their dedication to departmental programs.

In fostering competition, Roosevelt was not organizing to produce conflict. Competition and conflict are not the same thing. One is constructive; the other is destructive. This difference is misunderstood by those who believe incorrectly that Roosevelt was promoting conflict for its own sake.

Roosevelt's organization strategy was formulated before he entered the White House. As assistant secretary of the navy, he advocated strongly a national budget system under the president's direction and urged that department heads should be given complete authority in all matters over bureau chiefs. Rexford G. Tugwell cited this Roosevelt statement as providing something of a preview of his sophistication, as he entered the presidency, in such matters. As many still living can testify, one of the most obsessive preoccupations of Roosevelt as president was to be reorganization of the government.[45]

Roosevelt knew in general terms what he wanted from his Committee on Administrative Management. The committee's primary focus was to be on "what gives the President more effective managerial control," rather than on the traditional goals of economy and efficiency.[46] Roosevelt instructed the committee to "not get lost in detail" and waste its time on constructing a neat and orderly organization chart. When Brownlow and Gulick discussed the committee's draft report with the president, they found that their recommendations were in accord with Roosevelt's own thinking. The president's Committee on Administrative Management performed an indispensable service, but its contribution consisted mainly in providing a conceptual framework for the president's organization strategy. Unless a president has an organization strategy, he runs a considerable risk in establishing an outside commission on federal organization that may devise its own strategy without regard for the president's interests and objectives.

President Truman had an organization strategy, but it was that supplied to him by the first Hoover Commission. The Hoover Commission reports provided a conceptual framework for the organizational philosophy developed by Herbert Hoover during his years as president and secretary of commerce, and did not stem from Truman's own thinking There is no evidence, however, that the return to orthodoxy symbolized by many of the commission's recommendations was in conflict with Truman's views.

Of the forty-one reorganization plans transmitted by President Truman under the Reorganization Act of 1949, nine dealt with relatively minor matters and had little if any strategic significance. Most of the others did have a unifying theme that tied together the recommendations of the first Hoover Commission and made them a consistent whole. Though expressed in terms of the orthodox dogmas, they complemented the recommendations of the President's Committee on Administrative Management and were Rooseveltian in their concepts of presidential power. The fourteen reorganization plans vesting in department heads the functions previously vested in subordinate officers, and transferring "executive functions" to regulatory commission chairs designated by the president were calculated to eliminate some of the impediments to the effective exercise of presidential and secretarial power. The Congress reacted by disapproving the plans reorganizing the Treasury Department, Interstate Commerce Commission, Federal Trade Commission, and Federal Communications Commission.

Truman did accomplish the first restructuring of executive departments since 1913. At his initiative, steps were taken toward unification of the armed services, and this led to formation of the National Military Establishment in 1949. The powers of the new secretary of defense as head of the establishment were compromised seriously in order to accommodate the deep-seated and often bitter differences among the army, navy, and air force Truman twice failed in attempts to elevate the Federal Security Agency to cabinet rank. The idea for a Department of Welfare or Department of Health, Education, and Security did not originate with Truman but with the president's Committee on Administrative Management.

Truman was not given to theorizing about organization, but, as in other areas, his intuitive responses exhibited a keen understanding of the issues. He was quick to sense threats to the powers of the presidency. His adroit maneuvers scotched the schemes of those who wanted to assure Defense Department domination of the National Security Council by housing the council in the Pentagon, where office space already had been prepared, and by designating the secretary of defense as chairman in the president's absence.[47] Truman's forthright veto of the bill creating the National Science Foundation took courage and his veto message forecast the problems that would result if public powers were yielded to private institutions.

President Eisenhower shared Truman's orthodoxy, but not his intuition or convictions about the powers of the presidency. A President's Committee on Government Organization, composed of Nelson Rockefeller, Milton Eisenhower, and Arthur Flemming, was organized before the inauguration and remained more or less active throughout the Eisenhower administration. Neither Eisenhower nor the committee produced a coherent organization doctrine.

Except for the 1953 reorganization of the Department of Defense and the establishment of the Department of Health, Education, and Welfare, Eisenhower's fourteen reorganization plans either represented follow-up on Hoover Commission recommendations or dealt with minor items. President Eisenhower passed on the most controversial proposals coming from his Advisory Committee—a First Secretary of Government, an Office of Executive Management, a Department of Transportation, and transfer of the Army Corps of Engineer's civil functions to the Department of the Interior—as a legacy to President Kennedy.

President Eisenhower was willing to say the right things, but he was less willing to act. Draft veto messages occasionally became signing statements, as is evidenced by signing statements deploring legislation requiring executive agencies "to come into agreement" with congressional committees, or circumventing the president's veto authority.[48] He did veto a few of these so-called encroachment bills. President Eisenhower hailed the Farm Credit Act of 1953, which for all practical purposes made the farm credit system independent of the president, as "another milestone in our march toward an agriculture which is productive, profitable, responsible and free from excessive regulation."[49] He had some second thoughts when the board later defied his instructions, but, nonetheless, approved "despite some misgivings" the Farm Credit Act of 1956, which relaxed the few remaining controls over the farm credit institutions.[50]

President Eisenhower warned about the growing influence of the military-industrial complex, but apparently he did not recognize the role of institutional arrangements in fostering that influence. In any event, he did nothing to curb the power of the industry advisory committees that flourished and multiplied during his administration and sometimes arrogated to themselves effective decision-making authority.

President Kennedy evinced little interest in organization structure and administration; his orientation was almost entirely toward individuals and programs. He appointed a panel of advisers on government organization but never used them collectively, and rarely as individuals, except for Neustadt. The main thesis of Sorensen's book, *Decision-Making in the White House*, which stems from his experience in the Kennedy administration, is that there is too much preoccupation with "form and structure" and too little with "the more dynamic and fluid forces on which Presidential decisions are based."[51]

Kennedy was unwilling to send forward a reorganization plan unless he was assured that it was noncontroversial. His reaction to the letter from the Atomic Energy commissioners proposing their own demise was that he would support a bill if introduced by the chairman of the Joint Committee. President Kennedy chastised the Budget Bureau when a 1963 amendment to the Reorganization Act prohibiting the use of reorganization plans to create executive departments was construed as a defeat for the president and advised the bureau in no uncertain terms that he had never asked for extension of the act. The reorganization authority was allowed to lapse and was not restored until Lyndon Johnson took office.

Kennedy sent forward ten reorganization proposals, four of which relating to regulatory commissions were disapproved. None were designed to strengthen the president's powers, and the creation of the Office of Science and Technology was in the main a response to pressures from the Congress for access to the president's science adviser. His one major reorganization effort, establishment of a Department of Urban Affairs and Housing, met with a crushing defeat.

Lyndon Johnson's all-encompassing concern with every aspect of government policies, programs, and operations included government organization and reorganization along with everything else. For him, important reorganization measures—such as those establishing the Department of Transportation and the Department of Housing and Urban Development, and reorganizing the District of Columbia government—were trophies to be hung on his wall next to the other landmark bills enacted during his administration. Johnson could react boldly to attempts by the Congress to encroach on the president's constitutional powers and did not shrink from direct confrontations over such issues. His position on provisions requiring committee consent to executive actions or bypassing the president's veto authority was unequivocal, and he was less inclined to compromise than any of his predecessors.

President Johnson's thinking about government organization was traditional. His messages invariably made proper obeisance to the gods of "economy and efficiency" and overlapping and duplication. He stressed that he would take steps to "modernize and streamline" the government with the objective of ensuring that federal programs are "administered effectively and at minimum cost to the taxpayer."[52]

Johnson's reorganization program and decisions on organization issues reflected little if any unity of purpose. His approach was episodic and pragmatic, and sometimes gave the appearance of being improvised on the spur of the moment.

Emmette S. Redford and Marlin Blissett's in-depth analysis of President Johnson's efforts to reorganize the executive branch found that "the president's actions—though measured for political effectiveness—did not reflect an overall organizational strategy. In the main they were piecemeal and reactive."[53] Lyndon Johnson was a master legislative tactician, not a strategist. To facilitate passage of an administration measure in the Congress, he was quite prepared to rise above organizational principles and was not disturbed in the least by inconsistencies.

Several Johnson reorganizations did have a significant strategic impact. The transfer of water pollution control responsibilities from Health, Education, and Welfare to Interior was motivated by a desire to obtain a change in program emphasis and to wean Interior away from its narrow western orientation. The reorganization of the District of Columbia made its government somewhat less susceptible to domination by the House and Senate district committees. The plans relating to the Public Health Service, customs, locomotive inspection, statutory interagency committees, mass transit, and narcotics accomplished subtle alterations in the balance of power with respect to the affected programs and afforded an opportunity to reexamine and reorient program objectives.

Opportunism can be self-defeating, as shown by Johnson's controversial proposal to merge the Commerce and Labor departments—probably his worst fiasco. A combination of circumstances, the impending resignation of Secretary of Commerce Connor, White House irritation with both the Commerce and Labor departments, and, perhaps most of all, the search for a "surprise" to liven up the 1967 State of the Union Message inspired the idea. White House staff had unearthed the 1964 task force recommendation for a Department of Economic Development, which would absorb the Department of Commerce, Office of Economic Opportunity, Small Business Administration, and at a later date, the Department of Labor. The president agreed to the merger, but not the rationale. By recommending simply the consolidation of the two departments and preserving the words *Labor* and *Commerce* in the title, the president hoped to avoid alienating the two constituencies involved.[54] The Budget Bureau was told that it could not refer to economic development or economic planning and had to develop a new justification out of whole cloth *after* the recommendation had gone to the Congress.

Neither the justification nor the details had been thought through before the State of the Union Message. Labor and business opposition probably would have been sufficient by itself to doom the proposal. Defeat was guaranteed by an indiscriminate dragnet operation to identify functions that could be transferred to the Commerce and Labor Department. This triggered immediately the powerful defensive mechanisms within the departments and the bureaucracy.

Consolidation of the Labor and Commerce departments had a superficial logic, but not much more. Absent an intention to create a Department of Economic Development, the arguments for the reorganization were strained indeed. It is certainly open to doubt that merger of his organized labor and business constituencies would have been to the president's advantage. Interlocking arrangements between organized labor and organized business have rarely been in the public interest. Some within the administration feared that the proposed merger represented a step toward a new mercantilism.

At the very time when government programs increasingly called for a high degree of teamwork and unity in program design and execution, the Johnson administration did not oppose and sometimes supported measures that stimulated the powerful centrifugal forces working within the federal structure. Its principal institutional innovation was the twilight zone agencies—the Urban Institute, the private Federal National Mortgage Association, and the National Housing Partnerships—which are insulated against effective public control and diminish the president's powers.

President Johnson devoted more personal time and attention to government organization than any president since Roosevelt. Measured by customary standards, his accomplishments were fantastic—two new executive departments and the first reorganization of the District of Columbia in almost a century, all within the space of two years. The times, however, called for strategy adapted to a radically different mix of organizational problems, and this Lyndon Johnson was unable to provide.

4
Nixon's New American Revolution

For Richard M. Nixon the major cause of ineffectiveness of government was not a matter of men or money. It was "principally a matter of machinery."[1] Government reorganization was to be the means for bringing about "a new American Revolution." President Nixon's concept of government as a machine was at odds with that of Franklin D. Roosevelt, who stressed that "reorganization is not a mechanical task, because government is not a machine, but a living organism."[2]

President Nixon apparently did not believe that accomplishment of the "new American Revolution" called for the development of revolutionary doctrines. The forging of "new institutions to serve a new America" was to be achieved by strict application of the orthodox dogmas. As in the case of the "New Federalism," the new, in fact, represented a return to the old.

What President Nixon described as "the most comprehensive and carefully planned . . . reorganization since the executive was first constituted in George Washington's administration 183 years ago"[3] professed to be a nonpartisan measure without political implications and to contain nothing that would offend the fundamentalists. In his several reorganization messages, President Nixon repeatedly reaffirmed his faith in the orthodox doctrines: economy and efficiency as the objective of organization and administration; organization around major goals or purposes; policy administration dichotomy; rigid separation of powers; limited span of control; and straight lines of authority and accountability with each subordinate expected to obey the orders of his superior.

President Nixon argued that the organizational principles he advocated had been "endorsed" by the Brownlow and Hoover commissions, but the underlying philosophy has its roots in Max Weber's ideas about bureaucracy and power relationships. Weber is concerned with the special type of power relationship he calls domination. As explained by Nicos P. Mouzelis, "domination refers to a power relationship in which the ruler, the person who imposes his will on others, believes that he has a right to the exercise of power; and the ruled consider it their duty to obey his orders. . . . Domination, when exercised over a large number of people, necessitates an administrative staff which will execute commands and which will serve as a bridge between the ruler and the ruled."[4]

With respect to the career civil service or the bureaucracy, to use Nixon's code word, Nixon parted company with Brownlow. The President's Committee on Administrative Management recommended that "the merit system be extended upward, outward and downward to include all positions in the Executive Branch of Government except those which are policy determining in character."[5] President Nixon considered that President Eisenhower had committed a major error in failing to clean out the "Democrat-infested" federal bureaucracy. He was resolved to replace Democratic civil servants with Republican civil servants.[6] Nixon's viewpoint is reflected in an internal White House memorandum, which complains that "the lack of key Republican bureaucrats at high levels precludes the initiation of policies which would be proper and politically advantageous."[7]

Distrust of the bureaucracy was a recurring theme in almost all of Nixon's public statements. "Ossified" and "obstructive" are typical of the adjectives applied to the civil service. When he signed the legislation establishing the Special Action Office for Drug Abuse, the president threatened that "heads would roll" if "petty

bureaucrats" thwarted the efforts of the office director.[8] John Ehrlichman was not exaggerating when he described relationships
with the bureaucracy as "guerrilla warfare."[9] As it ultimately
evolved, the major objective of Nixon's organization strategy was
to contain and neutralize the bureaucracy. This became clear
in his March 1972 reorganization message, which included the
following:

> Notwithstanding the famous sign on President Truman's desk—
> "the buck stops here"—there will be no stopping of the buck,
> no ultimate clarification of blame and credit, and no assurance
> that voters will get what they contracted for in electing presi-
> dents, senators, and members of congress until the present con-
> voluted and compartmentalized Washington bureaucracy can
> be formed anew and harnessed more directly to the people's
> purposes.

President Nixon did not come into office with a preconceived
organization strategy. He did not see in organizational and procedural reform—reorganization, decentralization, and revenue sharing—a vehicle for achieving his political goals. Government reorganization was something that could be left to businessmen who
would solve the government's management problems by applying
sound business techniques. In 1969 he established an Advisory
Council on Executive Organization, chaired by Roy L. Ash, then
president of Litton Industries, to study and recommend reform of
the government structure. All the council members, except former
Texas governor John B. Connally, were businessmen without significant government experience. Evans and Novak reported that
the president's eyes would glaze during the council's periodic reports. Only a strong protest from Ash gained an appointment with
the president to discuss the council's proposals for reorganization
of the Executive Office of the President.[10]

Management of domestic affairs was something that Nixon at
first thought could be left to the cabinet. He told an interviewer:
"All you need is a competent cabinet to run the country at home.

You need a president for foreign policy; no secretary of state is really important; the president makes foreign policy."[11] There was to be no Sherman Adams or Joe Califano in the Nixon White House. All the president had to do was put the right people in charge and let them do the job.[12]

Reorganization Plan No. 2 of 1970, which changed the name of the Bureau of the Budget to the Office of Management and Budget and established the Domestic Council, reflected the thinking of the Ash Council and Haldeman and Ehrlichman, not that of the president. Ehrlichman reacted negatively to the Ash Council draft, but changed his mind after he secured modifications designed to enhance his power.[13] The Ash Council intended that the Domestic Council be a small agency with a highly qualified professional staff that would (1) help define national goals and objectives; (2) synthesize policy alternatives into consistent domestic programs; (3) provide policy advice on pressing domestic issues; and (4) consider policy implications on ongoing programs. To avoid the necessity of Senate confirmation, it was recommended that the council's executive director be an assistant to the president, but it was expected that the designated assistant would testify before congressional committees in his capacity as executive director.

John Ehrlichman wanted the Domestic Council to be a part of his personal apparatus, a power base comparable to Henry Kissinger's National Security Council staff. He insisted that (1) the plan be revised to eliminate the provision for staff appointments within the career civil service and (2) the Congress be advised that under no circumstances would the executive director be available for questioning. The latter qualification came close to defeating the plan.

Congressman Chet Holifield objected bitterly to the "90-man faceless, formless group" made up of "a group of people that apparently are political appointees, they have not been confirmed, and they can do many things and can remain hidden in the things that they do."[14] The House Committee on Government Operations voted against approval of the reorganization because, among other objections, the executive director of the Domestic Council and his staff would not be accountable to the Congress and would be "beyond the power of the Congress to question."[15] The plan survived on a close House vote. Reorganization Plan No. 2 of 1970 is significant mainly because it marks the beginning of the trend toward formalizing the transfer of power to the president's personal staff. The director of the OMB also was given a status comparable to that of Ehrlichman when he was housed in the White House and designated as assistant to the president.

With the 1971 State of the Union Message, structural reform moved from the wings to center stage. In defining his "six great goals," President Nixon stated: "I shall ask not simply for more new programs in the old framework, but to change the framework itself—to reform the entire structure of American government so we can make it again fully responsive to the needs and wishes of the American people." Included among the major goals were revenue sharing and a bold plan, modified from the blueprint prepared by the Ash Council, for abolishing the constituency- and clientele-oriented departments of Agriculture, Commerce, Labor, and Transportation and distributing their functions among four "goal-oriented" superdepartments of Community Development, Economic Affairs, Human Resources, and Natural Resources.

Herbert Roback, staff director of the House Committee on Government Operations, explained the shift in emphasis from substantive programs to structural reform as the logical outgrowth of fiscal conservatism. According to Roback, "reorganization fits nicely with fiscal conservatism since it requires no significant budgetary outlays. In that sense, reorganization is policy on the cheap, an inexpensive commitment to progress."[16]

A desire to promote "progress" without significant budgetary costs obviously made the reorganization plan attractive. But the strategic objectives of the proposal were far more subtle and aimed at nothing less than a fundamental change in the balance of power within the federal system. It is something of a measure of Nixon and his advisers' naivete and administrative inexperience that they assumed initially that cabinet officers were mere extensions of the presidency and had no competing loyalties. Discovery of the triangular alliance among departments, congressional committees, and clientele groups, known to any reasonably sophisticated observer of the Washington scene, came as a rude and nasty shock. Obscured within the sixteen pages of full-blown rhetoric and theoretical justification contained in the March 25, 1971, reorganization message is the following key sentence: "When any department or agency begins to represent a parochial interest, then its advice and support inevitably become less useful to the man who must serve *all* of the people as their President." Administration spokespersons conceded privately that a major purpose was to break "the linkages of professional groups and bureaucracies."

Given the political difficulties of enacting any single departmental reorganization, the very dimensions of the Nixon plan raised serious problems of credibility.[17] Some members of congress viewed it as a "grandstand play," which was not to be taken seriously. Nixon's legislative tacticians miscalculated in thinking it "easier to win large wars than small ones." By uniting in opposition such unlikely allies as farmers, labor unions, highway contractors, poor people's organizations, and congressional committee chairmen fearing loss of jurisdictions, the "New American Revolution" faced almost overwhelming odds.

Compromises had been incorporated in the Nixon grand design in an effort to placate the U.S. Army Corps of Engineers and the protectors of the pork barrel. Presidents Harding, Hoover, and Eisenhower and the Hoover Commission Task Force recommended that the civil functions of the Corps of Engineers be transferred as an integral unit to the Department of the Interior.[18] On the pretext of retaining an essential training capability in the corps, an argument disputed by President Eisenhower among others, Nixon provided for only a partial transfer to the proposed Department of Natural Resources. He recommended that the Corps retain responsibility for project construction. operation, and maintenance.[19] Further concessions to the corps and the Department of Agriculture incorporated in the 1973 proposal for a Department of

Energy and Natural Resources cannot be reconciled with President Nixon's stated purpose of establishing "a center of responsibility for natural resources, energy and water policies" and "a single key official" on whom the president could rely to carry out natural resource policies and programs.[20] The Corps of Engineers and the Soil Conservation Service would retain responsibility for preparation of feasibility reports, project design, construction, operation, and maintenance, but the secretary of energy and natural resources would be made responsible for project approval, budget requests, and justifications. The proposed reorganization did not eliminate but perpetuated fragmentation of executive responsibilities for energy and natural resource programs.

The solicitude shown for pork barrel programs did not extend to the social and economic programs identified with the New and Fair Deals and President Johnson's "Great Society." If the bureaucracy was the primary target of the "New American Revolution," certainly the "Great Society" programs and comparable measures designed to assist and provide access for the disadvantaged were a secondary target. The poverty agency, the Office of Economic Opportunity, was to be retained as a symbol but stripped of its major programs, which would be transferred to the departments of Community Development, Economic Affairs, and Human Resources. The Small Business Administration was to be abolished and responsibility for loans to small businesses and minorities lodged, along with services to big business, in an Administration for Business Development in the Department of Economic Affairs. Also to be abolished was the Farmers Home Administration, whose programs to assist small farmers were to be split up among the departments of Community Development, Natural Resources, and Economic Affairs.

The House Committee on Government Operations conceded a need for executive branch reorganization but expressed doubts about the feasibility of superdepartments modeled on corporate conglomerates. It noted that the organizing principle for conglomerates is profitability, not functional similarity or common goals.[21] In the committee's view the attempt to organize around "basic goals" presented serious difficulties because: "Such goals, characteristically, are broad, overlapping and open-ended. Furthermore, they can be formulated in different ways, so that alternative or additional organizational patterns could be readily devised."[22]

Administration witnesses were hard pressed to identify the basic goals for the disparate programs (business loans, labor management relations, transportation, etc.) to be lodged in the Department of Economic Affairs. The department looked like a last-minute creation to accommodate the pieces left over from the other reorganizations. George P. Shultz, then OMB director, acknowledged that "to a certain extent it is true that everything is related to everything else. . . . So some sort of breakdown within the total picture is necessary, and the problem is to design a reasonably small number of packages and to find dividing lines that make sense in terms of their effectiveness in generating policy in managing the results of the legislative process."[23]

The ultimate defeat of the "New American Revolution" could not be blamed entirely on its enemies, powerful as they were. Administration support was at best lukewarm. On the very day that the Undersecretary of Agriculture J. Phil Campbell was dutifully testifying before the House Committee on Goverment Operations that the Department of Agriculture ought to be abolished as a constituency and clientele-oriented department, the president, disturbed by the political repercussions of declining farm prices, announced that the plan had been abandoned and that the Department of Agriculture would be retained as the representative for farmers. The position that what was good for farmers was not good for organized labor or other interest groups could not be logically sustained. The president's failure to veto the Rural Development Act of 1972 placed the supporters of the bill to create a Department of Community Development in an awkward position and made it easier for the Rules Committee to kill the legislation.

Enthusiasm may have cooled because of growing awareness that the sources of bureaucratic power would not be reduced significantly by rearranging the big boxes on the organization chart. The real power centers in the federal structure are the bureaus. Break-

ing up the constituency-oriented departments might make the secretaries more responsive to the White House, but not necessarily
the bureaus. Most secretaries today have difficulty in managing
and controlling their departments, and without a strong, relatively
cohesive constituency their power would be reduced further.

Even if it had succeeded, the "New American Revolution" never
would have amounted to more than a paper revolution. This could
not be said of the new cabinet and White House staff relationships
established by President Nixon on January 5, 1973, "to revitalize
and streamline the federal government in preparation for America's third century." As a panel of the National Academy of Public
Administration reported to the Senate Select Committee on Presidential Campaign Activities, if it were not for the accidental discovery of the Watergate break-in, the American state might well have
been transformed into "Max Weber's ideal type of monocracy,
ruled from the top through a strictly disciplined hierarchical system" with impeachment the only means of holding a president accountable.[24]

By White House press release, the president created a corporate
type of structure with a rigid hierarchy in which:

1. Access to the president was limited to five assistants to the
    president (a more accurate description would be assistant
    presidents).
2. Four assistants to the president would act as presidential
    surrogates with responsibility "to integrate and unify poli-
    cies and operations" in the following areas: domestic affairs
    (Ehrlichman); foreign affairs (Kissinger); executive man-
    agement (Ash); and economic affairs (Shultz).
3. Access to the assistants to the president would be limited
    with some exceptions, to three counselors (to be housed in
    the Executive Office Building) for human resources (secre-
    tary of HEW), natural resources (secretary of agriculture),
    and community development (secretary of HUD). An
    anonymous "think-piece" supplied by the administration to
    the Senate Committee on Government Operations indi-

cated that within his assigned area a counselor would be informed and make judgments on budget matters; control key personnel positions and staff strength; provide policy direction on legislation and legislative strategy; and review speeches, testimony, press releases, and internal policy statements.

In effect, the president had converted the executive branch into a three-tiered structure with the assistants to the president at the top and department and agency heads (other than those designated as counselors) at the bottom. The clear intent was to transfer to the president's immediate staff effective control over executive branch policies and programs and to reduce cabinet officers to an essentially ministerial role. In the words of John Ehrlichman: "There shouldn't be a lot of leeway in following the president's policies. It should be like a corporation, where the executive vice presidents (the cabinet officers) are tied closely to the chief executive, or to put it in extreme terms, when he says jump, they only ask how high."[25]

White House control over the departments would be maintained directly through key deputies appointed by and reporting to assistants to the president. The *Washington Post* disclosed that over a hundred people formerly employed by the White House, Office of Management and Budget, and Committee to Re-elect the President had been reassigned to departments and occupied such strategic positions as undersecretary (HEW, Interior, Transportation), deputy director of OMB, Federal Aviation administrator, and director of the National Parks Service.[26] Politically endorsed appointees recruited by the deputy director of OMB and operating under his general supervision replaced the departmental assistant secretaries for administration, most of whom had been career civil servants. Assistant secretaries for administration, with their control of budgets, management services, and personnel, were regarded as potentially powerful instruments of control—"an instant bush telegraph into the jungle."[27] President Ford's transition advisers, headed by Secretary of the Interior Rogers C. B. Morton, were highly critical of the OMB role and recommended that steps be taken to prevent the OMB from boring holes "below the waterline in the departments."[28]

No doubt as a result of the Watergate disclosures and the resignation of top White House aides, the press was advised in a very low-key announcement on May 10, 1973, that the president was reinstituting "a direct line of communication with the cabinet" and discontinuing the "experiment" with counselors, except on an informal basis.[29]

President Nixon's organization strategy stemmed from certain ideological biases and his unique interpretation of the president's role within our constitutional system. Although he never precisely articulated his philosophy of government, if one puts the bits and pieces together certain basic premises emerge:

1. As "the president of all the people," the president does and should occupy a superior position to that of the Congress, which represents narrow parochial interests.
2. As the sole definer and protector of the "national interest," the president has the implied constitutional authority and moral obligation to take such actions as he deems necessary to carry out his responsibilities.
3. Protection of the national interests, as defined by the president, requires undivided loyalty to the president and unquestioning obedience to his orders.
4. Department and agency heads function as presidential delegates and powers vested in them by law are, in fact, powers stemming from the president as chief executive.
5. Loyalty to the office of the presidency and loyalty to the incumbent are indivisible.
6. The bureaucracy or civil service represents the principal threat to presidential power. Members of the civil service cannot be trusted because they are either disloyal or have divided loyalties.

Richard M. Nixon was a self-proclaimed Gaullist. Aaron Wildavsky pointed out that Nixon shared with de Gaulle "a plebiscitary view of the presidency," one in which the presidency exists wholly apart from other institutions and is at one with the people.[30] This plebiscitary view was reinforced by the "mandate" of November 1972.

The organization strategy developed after the 1972 election was aimed squarely at the vitals of bureaucratic power. Political appointees too narrowly identified with programmatic and constituency interests, or with an independent power base, were purged. The transition between the first and second terms was as extreme as most transitions from one political party to another.[31] The bureaucracy was neutralized and isolated by (1) leaving major departments "headless" by co-opting the secretaries as assistants to the president and White House counselors, thus preventing "capture" by the natives; (2) depriving it of resources through revenue sharing and impoundment; and (3) cutting lines of communication by interposing regional councils under White House and OMB control between departments and their agents in the field. The departments were to be allowed to wither away, with the White House assuming direct operational responsibility.

The testimony and evidence presented to the Senate Select Committee on Presidential Campaign Activities underscore the serious and disturbing constitutional questions raised by the centralization of power in the White House, the fractionalization of presidential power among assistants to the president, and the assumption that statutory powers of executive agencies automatically vest in the president and his principal assistants.

The Nixon strategy reflected a profound misunderstanding of the executive establishment and its culture and personality. Emmet J. Hughes observed most perceptively: "And the President who dreads this legion of careerists, as a conspiracy bent on his embarrassment or frustration, fails to perceive the realities as completely as the President who wastes dreams on a vision of mobilizing them in an army eager to do battle for his own political success."[32]

5

Carter's "Bottom-Up" Reorganization

If nothing else, President Jimmy Carter shared with Richard M. Nixon a profound distrust of the bureaucracy and faith that bureaucrats can be brought to heel through structural change. As used by President Carter, reorganization appeared to be a code word symbolizing citizens' hostility toward intrusive government and frustration with the bureaucratic system. President Carter again stressed this antibureaucracy theme in his 1979 State of the Union message in which he stated, "With the support of the Congress, we have begun to reorganize and get control of the bureaucracy."

Jimmy Carter ran for president on a platform of government reorganization. He promised that he would duplicate the success he had had in Georgia by drastically reducing the number of agencies and by making the bureaucrats more efficient and responsive. He told the Democratic Platform Committee: "Our government in Washington now is a horrible bureaucratic mess. . . . We must give top priority to a drastic and thorough reorganization of the Federal bureaucracy, to its budgeting system and to the procedures for analyzing the effectiveness of its services."[1] In New Hampshire he advised voters: "Don't vote for me unless you want to see the executive branch of government completely reorganized."[2]

Outsider Jimmy Carter was at a serious disadvantage in debating fundamental issues of foreign and domestic policy with his more experienced rivals for the Democratic nomination. Government reorganization was a safe issue, as long as he avoided specifics, and it was an advantage not to be identified too closely with the existing "bureaucratic mess."

Except for one lapse when he pledged to reduce 1,900 federal agencies to 200, Carter refused to go into the details of his reorganization proposals. Jules Witcover, who covered Carter's primary campaign, concluded that "he was unable or unwilling to be more specific."[3] The 1,900 figure remained an unexplained mystery for some time and apparently included 1,189 advisory committees.

Jimmy Carter as a candidate appeared to recognize that he ran grave political risks by talking about reorganization in other than general terms. As Vice President Walter F. Mondale said at a later date: "Organizing the government is very much like cutting the Federal budget. Everyone is for it in principle, but the difficulties and controversies arise when you get specific."[4]

If candidate Jimmy Carter had a well-articulated organization strategy and precise reorganization objectives, these were never revealed by president Jimmy Carter. In his book *Why Not the Best?* Carter argues against an incremental approach and concluded that reorganization proposals are doomed unless "they are bold and comprehensive."[5] President Carter's approach to government reorganization was not bold or comprehensive. Instead, the president's Reorganization Project adopted "an incremental, people-centered, bottom-up approach."[6] The "bottom-up approach" was proclaimed as an innovative method of analyzing organization structure as it affects people directly, and not looking at it from the top down, as was done in previous reorganization studies.[7]

The reorganizers appeared to assume that the people would be able to tell them what should be reorganized, or at least give them clues on the trouble spots. In a letter dated June 24, 1977, Richard A. Pettigrew, assistant to the president for reorganization, invited citizens to submit comments on reorganization issues to "assist both in guiding initial studies and in identifying additional reorganization priorities." Approximately 2,000 replies were received. According to staff, none was useful and a number were typical crank letters. Few citizens are concerned with or directly affected by the structure of federal agencies or the subtleties of bureaucratic politics.

Jimmy Carter was called, perhaps unfairly, "the first process president."[8] But the President's Reorganization Project clearly emphasized the *how* above the *what* and *why*. Innovations were limited to the methods and tactics of conducting reorganization studies.

No unifying theme or set of innovative organizational principles can be discerned from analysis of Carter's proposals for departments of Energy, and Education, as well as for civil service reform and consumer protection. The same can be said for his reorganization plans for the Executive Office of the President, International Communication Agency, Equal Employment Opportunity Commission, Federal Emergency Management Agency, and Employment Retirement Income Security Act. Except for civil service reform, none can be related specifically to Carter's goal of energizing and controlling the bureaucracy.

Overall reorganization objectives were described in almost meaningless generalities—streamlining the government and making it more competent to serve the people. Specific proposals were justified mainly by reference to orthodox doctrines: elimination of overlapping and duplication, consolidation of related functions, improved economy and efficiency, and more effective planning and coordination.

Absence of organization "principles" was regarded as a virtue, not a vice, by the Carter reorganizers. Harrison Wellford, executive associate director of the Office of Management and Budget for reorganization and management, emphasized, "We're not operating under the assumption that the government is so simple that it can be reorganized according to one or two basic principles."[9] The pragmatic and ad hoc approach to reorganization was explained by OMB Director James T. McIntyre Jr. as (1) concentrating on solving problems, (2) looking for the least disruptive remedies to identified problems, and (3) following a process committed to openness and public and congressional involvement.[10]

Congressmen John W. Wydler, Thomas N. Kindness, and Arlan Strangeland were highly critical of the absence of a "defensible administrative theory" in objecting to President Carter's first reorganization plan restructuring the Executive Office of the President.[11] In their dissent they wrote, "Aside from this highly dubious 'shell game' of showing more or fewer employees in any particular part of an organization chart, a reader will search in vain for any indication of a basic premise underlying the plan. This is one of its most serious shortcomings."

Without a well-conceived presidential organization strategy and agreed upon organization concepts, reorganization proposals are highly vulnerable to attack on political grounds. Reorganizations attract many enemies and almost no friends. A major mistake of Carter was to deal with reorganization as if it were a purpose in itself, divorced from policy and program development.

Peter S. Szanton, who was responsible for the Carter reorganization studies, reported that the "President's predilections to reorganize were steadily resisted by the officials closest to him, especially his domestic policy adviser and Vice President Mondale. The result was that although great effort and substantial time were expended at high levels in the planning of ambitious change, the only substantial reorganizations proposed by the Carter administration were those made unavoidable by either explicit campaign commitments or powerful congressional pressure."[12]

The plans for a Department of Development Assistance, a Food and Nutrition Department, and a Trade Department were dropped altogether. The plan for a Department of Natural Resources emerged in an emasculated form, without the water resource functions, and it finally was abandoned because of strong opposition by key members of the Congress,

In the light of the political heat generated by congressional committees, clientele groups, and others whose turf was threatened by proposed reorganizations, President Carter was advised "to point to civil service reform, declare victory in reorganization and withdraw from the field."[13]

Organizational errors made in the initial program design can be undone by subsequent reorganizations only rarely or at considerable cost. Presumably, the expertise developed by the President's Reorganization Project would have been useful to the White House staff concerned with program development, but it was seldom utilized. As in past administrations, decisions were dictated by political expediency. HEW Secretary Joseph A. Califano Jr. admitted that when he served in the Johnson White House "often we didn't know where to put a program . . . and we didn't particularly care where it went; we just wanted to make sure it got enacted. That's one reason why the government is disorganized now."[14]

The incremental, people-centered, bottom-up approach to reorganization implied an absence of presidential direction and leadership. For President Carter reorganization appeared primarily to represent fulfillment of a campaign commitment, not an opportunity to alter the distribution of power within the government in ways that would support accomplishment of his long-range programmatic goals and strengthen the institution of the presidency.

The President's Reorganization Project was a project, or series of projects, not a program. No one was assigned responsibility for examining the total government system and identifying problems cutting across functional lines or common to all agencies. Consequently, critical issues were ignored by the project staff. The implications of the drift toward third-party government with the increasing reliance on nonfederal instrumentalities for service delivery were neither seen nor understood. The piecemeal incremental approach inevitably yielded piecemeal results.

Measured against President Carter's expressed goal of energizing and controlling the bureaucracy and making a substantive change in the government's behavior and outlook, his reorganization program must be judged a failure. Four years of intensive and highly publicized efforts, in the opinion of Ronald C. Moe, specialist in American national government, Congressional Research Service, "resulted in more, not fewer departments and agencies and in more agencies and programs being considered outside of direct accountability to the president. To his critics, therefore, the net effect of this reorganization exercise has been to further undermine the president's managerial authority and influence over the administrative instrumentalities of the federal government."[15] President Carter's own evaluation of his reorganization program is perhaps indicated by the fact that he devotes fewer than three pages of his 596-page memoir to a discussion of his much-vaunted campaign promise.[16]

6

Reagan: From the Positive to the Regulatory State

If Franklin Roosevelt's "New Deal" marks the birth of the positive state, Ronald Reagan's "revolution" symbolizes its end. The evolution from the positive to the regulatory state began in the 1960s, but President Reagan was the first to redefine the federal government's role as limited, wherever possible, to providing services without producing them.[1] This theme is echoed in the 1984 Republican platform, which proclaimed the following:

> To benefit all Americans, we support the privatization of government services whenever possible. This maximizes consumer freedom and choice. It reduces the size and cost of government, thus lessening the burden on the taxpayers. It creates jobs. It demonstrates the primacy of individual action which, within a free market economy, can address human needs most effectively.

In its embrace of privatization, the Reagan doctrine represented not so much the beginning as the culmination of a trend in federal administration and management of domestic programs. As noted by Lester M. Salamon, "While political rhetoric and a considerable body of academic research continue to picture the federal government as a rapidly expanding behemoth growing disproportionally in both scope and size relative to the rest of society in order to handle a steadily growing range of responsibilities, in fact something considerably more complex has been underway."[2] Except for programs such as social security, there has been a shift from direct to what Salamon calls "indirect or 'third party' government," with responsibility for service delivery delegated to quasi-government or nonfederal entities such as government-sponsored enterprises, nonprofit corporations, states, cities, counties, special districts, and a wide variety of private businesses. The preferred means for carrying out federal programs are grants-in-aid to states and local governments, contracts, loan guarantees, or subsidies, and regulation.

The General Accounting Office has highlighted as a major management issue the extent to which the federal government relies "on states, localities, nonprofit agencies, and profit-making contractors to deliver its services." It estimated that the federal government grants over $180 billion a year to third parties and contracts for another $190 billion in goods and services.[3] An investigation undertaken by Sen. David Pryor showed that the basic work of the Environmental Protection Agency "is being performed not by federal employees but by an invisible bureaucracy of contractors and consultants."[4] The Department of Energy operates with 149,000 contract employees and 17,000 civil servants.[5]

Employment of contractors to manage and operate government facilities and "captive" corporations such as Rand and Aerospace to provide analytical services began shortly after World War II, but use was confined to the defense and atomic energy programs. The 1960s and 1970s witnessed not only an increasing reliance on contractors to manage and operate government facilities and programs, but also a proliferation of agencies outside the normal executive branch framework such as the Legal Services Corporation, Corporation for Public Broadcasting, and Synthetic Fuels Corporation.

Federal assistance for housing, agriculture, exports, students, veterans, and small businesses is provided through private financial institutions, although some or all of the risk is assumed by the federal government, which guarantees the loans. The guaranteed loan has the same economic effects as a government direct loan, but it is the private lenders who negotiate the terms and conditions. Commitments for guaranteed loans are estimated at $727 billion for 1995.

The reasons for bypassing the established government apparatus and utilizing third parties to administer federal programs are complex. The trend, in part, reflects a widespread antigovernment and antibureaucratic bias. Typical is President Reagan's statement in his first inaugural address: "Government does not solve problems, it is the problem." Most recent presidents have considered growth in the number of federal civilian employees to be a major political liability. President Clinton echoed republicans in proclaiming that the era of big government was over.

Perhaps more important, the trend reflects political expediency because third-party arrangements permit the president and the Congress to take credit for acting without assuming responsibility for program design, administration, and results. For example, if the law enforcement assistance program does not curb crime, the feds can blame the state and local program administrators for the failure. New York City Mayor Edward Koch argued that "nonaccountability" motivated Mayor John Lindsay to turn over administration of the city hospitals to a third party. According to Koch, Lindsay formed the Health and Hospitals Corporation so that he could say, "Don't blame me. I don't have anything to do with hospitals."[6] Politicians are also by no means unaware of the political payoffs for obtaining federal grants and contracts for constituents—what has sometimes been described as the "social pork barrel."

It has reached the point that distinguished scholars such as Bruce L. R. Smith believe distinctions between the "public" and "private" sectors have ceased to be an operational way of understanding reality."[7] Peter Drucker goes so far as to contend that governing has become "incompatible with doing" and that "any attempt to combine governing with doing on a large scale paralyzes the decision making capacity."[8]

Whatever other reasons may be cited, the primary, and often the determining factor in resorting to third parties or proxy agencies is the need to escape controls that government has imposed on itself. Implicit in the arguments advanced by proponents of privatization is an assumption that is no longer possible to design and staff government institutions that can function with flexibility, speed, and independence. Existing controls, whether rational or irrational, are accepted as fixed and immutable.

The General Accounting Office has criticized the Departments of Defense and Energy for contracting out basic management functions that should be performed by government personnel, including the determination of national energy policies and development of plans and organizational responsibilities in the event of mobilization.[9] Military officers are hired by private contractors to do the same thing they did when directly employed by government. Some of the defense contractors are organized and staffed by retired military personnel.[10] Personnel ceilings and personnel freezes have made it impossible for these agencies to obtain staff necessary to perform essential tasks mandated by the president and the Congress and funded in the budget.

The National Performance Review report agrees with federal managers that "red tape and regulation are so suffocating that they stifle every ounce of creativity. It found that "the federal government is filled with good people trapped in bad systems. . . . When we blame the people and impose more controls, we make the systems worse."[11]

The National Performance Review urged that the government "cast aside red tape, shifting from systems in which people are accountable for following rules to systems in which they are accountable for results" thus "liberating organizations to pursue their missions."[12]

Few practitioners or scholars have attempted to analyze the causes or the consequences of the massive shift from direct to indirect government. Frederick C. Mosher was one of the first to recognize that the fundamental change in the role and responsibilities of the federal government and the way it conducts its business called for rethinking of orthodox theories and development of new strategies and approaches to public administration.[13] We have yet to develop a theory or theories that reflect the rise of grant and contract administrators, regulation writers, and auditors as the new generation of public administrators. Today, management inevitable tends to be identified with control of the third parties who provide the goods and services rather than with responsibility and accountability for service delivery.

Lester M. Salamon accurately described the "reshaped landscape of federal operations" when he wrote the following:

> What is involved here, moreover, is not simply the contracting out of well-defined functions or the purchase of goods and services from outside suppliers. The characteristic feature of many of these new, or newly expanded tools of action is that they involve the sharing of a far more basic governmental function: the exercise of discretion over the spending of federal funds and the use of federal authority. They thus continually place federal officials in the uncomfortable position of being held responsible for the programs they do not really control. . . . Instead of a hierarchical relationship between the federal government and its agents, therefore, what exists in practice is a far more complex bargaining relationship in which the federal agency often has the weaker hand.[14]

Theories positing the establishment of clear lines of authority and accountability from the president down through department heads to every employee with no subordinates possessing authority independent from their superiors are no longer relevant for many federal programs. A strategy that assumes presidential primacy within the system can be maintained by manipulating the boxes on the organization chart is certain to be unproductive. Although the outer executive branch structure retains symbolic importance and may influence policy positions and allocation of resources, in most instances altering the structure is not calculated to enhance the president's ability to direct the third parties who administer federal programs.

A National Academy of Public Administration study made clear that "privatization does not eliminate the need for public management; it only changes its character. As long as public funds or authority are involved, public accountability and control are essential." Federal managers need to be more precise in defining the work to be undertaken by a contractor and to learn how to negotiate and create incentives for optimum performance.[15]

In many respects Ronald Reagan was unique among recent presidents. His agenda was highly selective and was established before he was inaugurated. His goal was to reverse the federal government's direction by cutting domestic programs and spending, reducing taxes, and limiting federal regulations. To gain control of the vast federal establishment and harness it to his purposes, he had to devise a new approach and a radically different organization strategy.

Reagan learned from the mistakes made by Jimmy Carter. Organizational change in the traditional sense of departmental restructuring ranked at the bottom of his priorities and was regarded as something concerned with mere housekeeping and not with matters of fundamental importance.[16] Attempts by prior administrations to reform government management were criticized because they "dealt more with structure than with process."[17] Congress in November 1984 extended the president's reorganization authority until the end of the year, which did not allow the president sufficient time to submit reorganization plans before the Reorganization Act expired, even if he had desired to do so.

Reagan made gestures toward old-style reorganization, but there was little if any follow-through. As promised during his campaign, he proposed dismantling the Departments of Energy and Education. The very existence of these departments was considered to symbolize "the progressive intrusion of the federal government into the educational system" and federal intervention with the workings of the free market, which should determine energy development. Claims that abolition of the Department of Energy would produce $250 million in savings over a three-year period were found to be without substance by the General Accounting Office.[18] Faced with strong congressional opposition to the reorganizations, President Reagan made no effort to push his proposals. At

the beginning of his second term, President Reagan informed the
Congress that he had "no intention of recommending abolition of
the Department of Education at this time,"[19] and plans for combining the Interior and Energy departments never emerged from
the discussion stage.

Though not indulging in old-style reorganization, the Reagan
administration devised a strategy for centralizing unprecedented
decision-making power in the White House and reorganizing the
executive branch without a significant change in the organization
chart. It was a strategy focused on command relationships and
processes rather than on formal structure; it was a strategy that, for
the most part, could be implemented administratively and that was
not dependent for success on enacting legislation.

The Reagan strategy consisted of four main elements: (1) centralization of the budgetary process, (2) centralization of the appointments process, (3) centralization of decision making, and (4)
centralized control of regulations.

The first step was to restore the budgetary process as an instrument of presidential policy As noted by Allen Schick, budget
preparation had been "mostly bottom up, with agencies preparing
their requests with little policy guidance from the White House."[20]
Reagan reversed the process and instituted a system whereby budgetary decisions are made at the top, with the agency role reduced
to complying with White House orders. Budgets are now developed by the White House and the Office of Management and
Budget, not by the spending agencies.[21]

Next, tight control was established over the appointments process. Presidents Nixon and Carter had permitted department heads
some discretion in appointing their principal subordinates. Reagan's cabinet secretaries were allowed no such leeway and were
told bluntly that the White House was going to handle the appointments process.[22] The primary selection criteria were loyalty to the
president and support of his goals; a majority of appointees had no
prior government experience whatsoever.[23]

Decision making was centralized in the White House through establishment of seven cabinet councils: Economic Affairs; Natural

Resources and Environment; Human Resources; Food and Agriculture; Legal Policy, Commerce and Trade, and Management and Administration The councils "served more as communicators and enforcers of centrally determined policy positions than as mechanisms for active deliberation over priorities."[24] As described by Edwin Meese III, Reagan used the cabinet council system "so that cabinet members feel closer to him than they do to their departments—and he gives them a lot of opportunity to remember that."[25]

In April 1985 the cabinet councils were abolished and replaced with an Economic Policy Council and a Domestic Policy Council, chaired by Secretary of the Treasury James Baker and Attorney General Edwin Meese. This action was proclaimed by President Reagan as embracing his "commitment to Cabinet government," but it was interpreted generally as further centralizing of power in the White House.

Government by regulation is the inevitable concomitant of government by proxy. If the government wishes to control or influence the nonfederal agencies that administer federal programs, it must do so either by grant and contract provisions or by regulations. Interpretation and application of rules and regulations are also the only available means for controlling the so-called entitlement programs, which account for $750 billion in the 1993 budget, or 50 percent of federal outlays. These programs permit minimal administrative discretion. In her study of public assistance grants in Massachusetts, Martha Derthick concluded that, to the extent federal administrators attempt to realize substantive ends, they are "likely to do so indirectly, through the use of administrative conditions" or regulations.[26] If one cannot control the players, then the next best thing is to dictate the rules of the game.

In the past the contest between the president and the Congress for power to direct executive policies and actions focused mainly on issues related to executive branch structure. The contest has shifted to a new arena with jurisdiction over the review and control of regulations providing the major source of conflict. The 1970s witnessed a concerted campaign by the Congress to obtain the dominant position. Executive and independent agency rules and regulations were increasingly subjected to veto by one or both houses of the Congress. Twenty-three bills calling for legislative veto of rules and regulations were introduced in the 96th Congress (1979–80), In 1982 the Senate voted to make almost all agency regulations subject to a veto procedure. The Congress temporarily lost the battle when the Supreme Court held the legislative veto to be unconstitutional.[27] The Congress is actively exploring alternative methods for reasserting its control.

Beginning with the so-called Quality of Life Reviews initiated in 1971 under Richard Nixon, presidents began to take an interest in reviewing agency regulations. The Quality of Life Reviews were aimed at all agencies having regulatory jurisdiction over environmental, occupational safety, and consumer protection matters. In practice, review was limited almost exclusively to regulations of the Environmental Protection Administration. President Gerald Ford tried another approach by directing his Council on Wage and Price Stability to analyze the inflationary impact of proposed regulations. The Inflation Impact Statement and its successor, the Economic Impact Statement, were credited with little more than stimulating agency economic and policy analysis of their regulatory outputs.[28]

A highly complex system for "improving" and reviewing regulations was established by Executive Order No. 12044, March 23, 1978, promulgated by President Carter. The Carter order required agencies to review and revise procedures for developing significant regulations with a view to minimizing paperwork. Agency procedures were, at a minimum, to provide for a semiannual agenda of significant regulations, agency head oversight, opportunity for public participation, and compliance with criteria specified in the order, including an evaluation of alternative approaches, direct and indirect effects, and potential costs. Agencies were also required to submit a paperwork budget to the Office of Management and Budget. Administration of the Carter directives was vested in a regulatory council, the Council on Wage and Price Stability, and a regulatory analysis review group.

One result of the Nixon, Ford, and Carter measures was to broaden somewhat the president's authority over the regulations, but it is evident that the central objective was to stem the mounting flood of regulations and to reduce the burden on the private sector. No one yet perceived that review of regulations would take its place with budgetary review as one of the principal management tools available to the president.

Reagan had the insight to sense the significance of regulations in a government that depended increasingly on outsiders to do its job. He stressed that, "Hamilton's admonition that the executive 'produce a good administration' requires careful, continuous attention to regulatory and managerial reform."[29] It was no coincidence that President Reagan referred first to regulatory reform. In establishing review and control of regulations by Executive Order No. 12291, February 17, 1981, and Executive Order No. 12498, January 4, 1985, Reagan underscored that it was his intent to "increase the accountability of agency heads for the regulatory actions of their agencies" and to "provide for presidential oversight of the regulatory process." He argued that his authority to review and control regulations derived directly from his constitutional power to "take care that the laws be faithfully executed."[30]

Although some in the Congress complained that Executive Order No. 12291 raised serious constitutional issues,[31] the Congress itself unwittingly created the foundation on which President Reagan built when it enacted the Paperwork Reduction Act of 1980 establishing a statutory Office of Information and Regulatory Affairs in the Office of Management and Budget. President Reagan abolished Carter's Council on Wage and Price Stability and Regulatory Council and transferred responsibility for reviewing regulations to his principal management arm, the Office of Management and Budget.

The guidelines contained in Executive Order No. 12291 made it unequivocally clear that a cost-benefit test would be applied to all rules and regulations. The thrust of the order was directed at "major rules," those having an economic impact of $100 million or more annually, but the OMB was given authority to prescribe criteria for determining what was "major." The OMB's hand was further strengthened by Executive Order No. 12498, which requires each agency to submit "an overview of the agency's regulatory policies, goals and objectives for the program year and such information concerning all significant regulatory actions of the agency, planned or underway. . . as the director [OMB] deems necessary to develop the administrations's regulatory program." The order's announced purpose is to "assure consistency with administration policy" and to "enable the president to guide and supervise the implementation of administration policy."[32]

There can be little doubt that the Reagan administration was in charge of the regulatory process. President Clinton also prescribed principles that should guide federal agencies in writing regulations and maintained OMB review of regulations to assure that regulations "are consistent with applicable law and the president's priorities."[33]

Reagan's organization strategy was custom tailored to his distinct operating style and conservative agenda. It worked because of his ability to remain above the battle and his willingness to delegate authority to a chief executive officer or officers in the White House—Donald Regan, Howard Baker, and Kenneth Duberstein in his second term, and the triumvirate of James Baker, Edwin Meese, and Michael Deaver in the first. It is doubtful that it would work as well for a president with a different role concept who wanted to promote new programs—the approach is not well adapted to building coalitions in support of innovative program initiatives.

The tightly controlled decision-making process installed by President Reagan bore a striking resemblance to Richard Nixon's abortive plan for fundamentally altering the chain of command within the White House and executive branch. It again raised the question of whether or not undue centralization of power in the White House would upset the delicate constitutional system of checks and balances deemed by the founding fathers to be essential for protection of our liberties.

Privatization is certain to multiply the number of federal corporate dependents who look to Washington for sustenance and whose economic welfare depends more on political skills than on entrepreneurship and managerial ability. The U.S. government has become the "major philanthropist," outstripping foundations, private individuals, and corporations as provider of revenues to nonprofit corporations. Through grants and service contracts, nonprofit service corporations now receive the largest share of their income from the federal government.[34]

When it is acting through third parties, the federal government is not subject to some of the constitutional limits on its powers. Provisions included in grants and contracts may be used vastly to expand the federal outreach and intrusiveness. The Advisory Commission on Intergovernmental Relations correctly observed that "he who pays the piper calls the tune."[35] The Supreme Court held that conditions attached to grants are a legitimate exercise of Congress' power to fix the terms by which federal funds are expended, although Justice Benjamin Cardozo foresaw that the point "at which pressure turns into compulsion and ceases to be inducement" is "a question of degree—at times, perhaps, of fact."[36] Consolidation of categorical grants into massive block grants has made it even more difficult for state and local governments to resist federal pressure.

Indirect administration vastly complicates the problems of establishing accountability for program results, not to mentionmaintaining simple honesty and integrity. More than twenty years ago the Bureau of Budget stressed the following in a report to the Congress on contracting for research and development:

> No matter how heavily the government relies on private contractors, it should never lose a strong internal competence in research and development. By maintaining such competence it can be sure of being able to make the difficult but extraordinarily important program decisions which rest on scientific and technical judgments. Moreover, the government's research facilities are a significant source of management personnel.[37]

Federal agencies have not been able to maintain adequate in-house competence to supervise and evaluate contractor performance. According to a Brookings study, "in most agencies. . . contract management exists on a hope and a prayer." It points out that schools of public administration do not include contract management in their curricula and "if the civil service were to attempt to recruit specifically for contract managers, knowing where to look would be difficult." It warns that "failure to put highly skilled and motivated workers into these jobs literally puts two hundred billion federal dollars at risk."[38]

Most disturbing are the implications of current trends for the quality and character of the federal career service. A majority of senior career executives would advise talented young people to seek careers outside the federal government. College recruiters find it increasingly difficult to interest the best students in federal careers.[39]

In the past, the senior career service has been distinguished from classic bureaucracies by its identification with program and professional objectives. With some exceptions, it has attracted "do-ers" rather than careerists seeking status and prestige. Opportunities for doers are becoming increasingly restricted in the regulatory state.

Administration through third parties has converted the role of many senior career executives to that of grant and contract administrators, paymasters, and regulation writers and enforcers.

Emphasis inevitably has shifted from delivering services and evaluating results to complying with rules and regulations. David Lilienthal, over thirty-five years ago, posed the crucial issue:

> I can think of few things that. . . . can be more demoralizing to the dignity and strength of the federal career service: the creation and proliferation of a body of super civil servants, men who perform government functions, yet who are independent of government and its obligations as carried by federal employees, men recruited and paid and supervised as if they were in private employment but who are in fact doing the public's work.[40]

Conservative rhetoric portrays federal civil servants as masters of red tape who do not care what you do, as long as you comply with the rules and complete the necessary paperwork. Unless present trends are reversed, this image may become fact in the United States. In the regulatory state there will be fewer career civil servants but more bureaucrats. In the Reagan administration, under the supervision of a centralized and deeply politicized managerial structure in the OMB and elsewhere,[41] these trends were accentuated by design.

Perhaps the most important consequence of the growth of the regulatory state is the increasing involvement of the courts in administrative decision making and execution. Up to now public administration literature and theories have almost totally ignored the role of the judicial branch. This is no longer possible when substantially less than 10 percent of the federal budget is spent on domestic programs performed directly by federal employees and the lion's share of federal programs are administered by independent third parties through grants, contracts, and transfer payments. Such arrangements not only invite litigation, but since disputes among parties in these relationships cannot be resolved authoritatively within the executive branch, they virtually command a litigation strategy by third parties and their supporting interest associations as vital means of dealing effectively with federal monitors, rulemakers, and enforcers. In addition, Congress has added commands of its own in the form of direct requirements for public participation in and judicial review of administrative decision making and appropriations for attorneys' fee awards. Once judges accepted the appropriateness of their courts as sites for the resolution of such disputes, they became significant, sometimes the most significant actors in the administrative process.

7

Amputation Before Diagnosis

If the Clinton reinventors or the Gingrich revolutionaries had an organization strategy, it was a well-kept secret. For example, enhancement of the executive branch's capacity to govern or achievement of priority program goals were never advanced as arguments for abolishing the Departments of Education, Energy, Commerce, and Housing and urban development. How individual citizens or groups would benefit from reducing the number of executive departments was never explained. The approach was aptly described by Peter Drucker as "Amputation before diagnosis."[1]

The Department of Commerce was targeted as the first department to be eliminated because it was perceived to have a weak constituency incapable of mobilizing an effective defense. This proved to be a serious miscalculation. Commerce's supporters both within the Congress and in the business community had sufficient power to save the department from extinction. Measures to eliminate the other executive departments never emerged from committee.

Abolishing executive departments may provide the illusion of a smaller federal government, but not the reality. Unless specific programs are also terminated, a decrease in departments inevitably will be off-set by a substantial increase in the number of independent federal agencies. Nonetheless, the 1996 Republican platform again advocated "as a first step in reforming government" elimination of the commerce, housing and urban development energy and education departments and agencies that are "too regional in focus," without also listing the programs to be ended.

Republican presidential candidate Bob Dole promised to "eliminate the Internal Revenue Service (IRS) as we know it." Dole and those in the Congress who would privatize many of IRS's functions ought to heed the advice of Adam Smith who, devoted as he was to laissez-faire, drew the line at the prevalent eighteenth-century practice of contracting out the collection of public revenues to tax farmers. Adam Smith wrote:

> Taxes upon consumable commodities may either be levied by an administration of which the officers are appointed by government and are immediately accountable to government, of which the revenue must in this case vary from year to year according to the occasional variations in the produce of the tax, or they may be let in farm for a rent certain, the farmer being allowed to appoint his own officers, who, though obliged to levy the tax in the manner directed by the law, are under his immediate inspection, and are immediately accountable to him. The best and most frugal way of levying a tax can never be by farm. Over and above what is necessary for paying the stipulated rent, the salaries of the officers, and the whole expense of administration, the farmer must always draw from the produce of the tax a certain profit proportioned at least to the advance which he makes, to the risk which he runs, to the trouble which he is at, and to the knowledge, and skill which it requires to manage so very complicated a concern. Government, by establishing an administration under their own immediate inspection of the same kind with that which the farmer establishes, might at least save this profit, which is almost always exorbitant.[2]

The Clinton/Gore reinventors engaged in their own form of numbers game with boasts about ending "the era of big government."[3] The Clinton/Gore administration claimed to have made the federal government smaller by nearly a quarter of a million jobs—the "largest, swiftest government-wide cut in the history of the United States."[4] It is significant that in his introduction to "The Best Kept Secrets In Government," Vice President Al Gore cites reductions in federal employment as the National Performance Review's principal accomplishment. Cutting red tape and improving government performance receive only passing mention.

Downsizing has been accomplished by across-the-board cuts in supervisors, personnel specialists, budget analysts, procurement specialists, accountants, and auditors—the very staff required to oversee the contractors, state and local governments, and others who provide federal services. Most federal agencies do not provide services directly to customers.

The best-kept secret in government is not the numbers of those on the federal civilian payroll, but the number of those working for and being paid, directly or indirectly, out of the U. S. treasury. The number on the federal payroll may be maintained constant or reduced by contracting for services or devolving functions to state and local governments through grants and contracts. Reductions in federal personnel may well be offset by increases in state and local government and contractor employees. It is significant that federal civilian employment as a percentage of all government employment has decreased from 20.9 percent in 1962 to 13.6 percent in 1995.[5] The number of contract employees is unknown, but in some agencies they greatly out number civil servants. The Federal Workforce Restructuring Act of 1994 instructs the president to prevent the increase in service contracts, except when "cost comparison demonstrates such contracts would be to the financial advantage of the federal government."

Enthusiasm about reducing federal employment has not extended to political appointees. Paul C. Light has characterized the period since 1960 as one of "thickening government."[6] He notes that there has been a 430 percent increase in the number of presidential appointees and senior executives marked by a proliferation of deputy secretaries, undersecretaries, deputy undersecretaries, assistant secretaries, deputy assistant secretaries, associate deputy assistant secretaries, and chiefs of staff.[7] The number of political appointees were reported by the General Accounting Office as increasing from 2,022 in 1981 to 2,436 in 1991. The House Committee on Government Reform and Oversight found that "short-term political appointees have layered and thickened the upper echelons of organization to a point where productivity, management, and continuity of operation have become seriously affected."[8] Legislation to limit the number of political appointees received a frigid reception from both Republicans and Democrats.

Playing the numbers game diverts attention from the fundamental issues that ought to be addressed. Decisions about federal goals and program priorities ought to precede and not follow decisions with respect to restructuring and downsizing. First of all, we should reexamine the federal government's role and determine what changes would best enable it effectively to perform its constitutionally mandated functions in the twenty-first century. As noted by Donald F. Kettl, if we continue playing the numbers game the legacy of reinvention could be "an even more hollow government with far less capacity to do its job and managed by employees with even less incentive to do their jobs well."[9]

The budget has become the principal arena for playing the numbers game. A series of laws to place limits on federal spending have provided an incentive for creating off-budget agencies. Organizations are designed to reduce the amounts of government spending reported in the budget and to circumvent the arcane scoring rules established by the Budget Enforcement Act of 1990. The act imposes caps on discretionary spending and requires that increases for one program be balanced by decreases for others.

President George Bush was adamantly opposed to any method other than off-budget borrowing to pay for the bailout of the savings and loan institutions.[10] His elaborate scheme to keep the estimated $80 billion in tax payer money off-budget would never have survived scrutiny by the Securities and Exchange Commission if presented by a private corporation. The bailout was to be administered by the Resolution Trust Corporation, which was falsely classified as mixed ownership corporation so as to exempt it from budget review. The Corporation's Oversight Board composed of the secretary of the treasury, attorney general, and chairman of the Federal Reserve Board was defined by law as nongovernment corporation for purposes of Title 5 of the U. S. code applicable to federal employees.

The Resolution Trust Corporation was to be financed by thirty-year bonds sold by the Resolution Funding Corporation, a shell corporation without employees. The Resolution Funding Corporation was also classified as mixed-ownership, although the nonvoting capital stock held by the Federal House Loan Banks conferred none of the normal rights of ownership. Because of its implicit government guarantee, the Resolution Funding Corporation was able to market its obligations in spite of the fact that it had a substantial negative net worth. President Bush threatened to veto the legislation, if expenditures were to be on-budget. Subsequent legislation enacted by the Congress was necessary to simplify the confusion and conflict resulting from the Bush plan.

Preference is given to programs that will be self-funding from user fees. It has been proposed that the Bonneville Power Administration, Naval Petroleum Reserves, Patent and Trademark Office, Federal Aviation Administration, and Federal Housing Administration be converted to revenue producing and potentially self-sustaining government corporations. Vice President Al Gore announced that legislation incorporating the Patent and Trademark Office was to be the model for a new type of "performance-driven customer-oriented" organization.[11]

Performance-based organizations (PBOs) are intended to replicate the "next steps" agencies introduced by Margaret Thatcher in Great Britain, which in turn are based on the Swedish government model. PBOs would be accorded flexibility, where necessary, in human resources management, budget, procurement and other administrative functions. The president's 1997 budget sets forth criteria for performance-based organizations:

- The performance-based organization must have a clear mission with broad support from stakesholders.
- It must focus on ends (and customers) rather than means.

- It will function under a three to five year framework agreement that sets goals and specific exceptions from administrative and financial laws and regulations.
- Operations must be separated from policy making and regulatory activities that will be conducted outside the PBO.
- The chief executive will be appointed for a limited term, compensated at market rates, and held accountable for results.

Self-financing has not been made a condition for establishing a PBO, but it is significant that the first group of agencies recommended for conversion are all expected to be self-financing. These include the Patent and Trademark Office, St. Lawrence Seaway Development Corporation, National Technical Information Service, and Department of Defense Commissaries.

There is some doubt that organizations that work in governments with parliamentary systems can be successfully imported into the United States. Appointment of highly qualified chief executives selected exclusively for merit, a key to a PBO's success, would require the president to ignore political considerations and the Senate to forego confirmation. Such forbearance by the president and the Senate is unlikely. Some in the Congress might interpret PBOs as an attempt to weaken congressional control and further concentrate power in the executive.

President Bill Clinton is not and has never claimed to be an organization strategist or manager. He can no longer rely on the Office of Management and Organization for advice on organization policy and planning. His failure fully to appreciate the importance of a sound and politically marketable organization design contributed to defeat of health care reform. The proposed organization was so complicated that it was almost impossible to explain, much less defend.

Government reform has been relegated to a sideshow managed by the vice president. Except for downsizing the federal bureaucracy, the president has left it to the vice-president to sell the report of the National Performance Review and to create a government that "works better and costs less."

We run a considerable risk if we continue a wholly political and nonprincipled approach to organizing and managing the federal government. Ronald C. Moe and Robert Gilmour stated it well when they wrote:

> Law-based principles of public administration are not quaint proverbs, nor are they impediments to sound management practices. They provide the necessary foundation for a growing and evolving administrative system. The principles not only protect the citizenry from an overbearing, arbitrary and capricious use of government power, they permit substantial public involvement in processes of developing rules and regulation.[12]

8

The Executive Establishment: Culture and Personality

Until the Congress declared by law in 1978 that all presidential records were federal property, a president's office files were deemed to be his private property and were taken with him when he left the White House.[1] In theory at least, an incoming president started with a clean slate. Obviously a president's freedom is circumscribed by the need for continuity, political commitments, tradition, and accepted norms of presidential behavior. But within these limits he retains considerable discretion to organize and staff his household as he sees fit, determine his work priorities, and develop his own style and interpretation of the presidential role. In Woodrow Wilson's words, each president has the freedom "to be as big a man as he can."[2]

Department heads seldom start with a clean slate. Generally they must adapt to the institution rather than the institution to them. There are likely to be daily reminders that they are merely temporary custodians and spokespersons for organizations with distinct and multidimensional personalities and deeply ingrained cultures and subcultures reflecting institutional history, ideology, values, symbols, folklore, professional biases, behavior patterns, heroes, and enemies. The individual style of department heads must not do violence to the institutional mystique, and the words they speak and the positions they advocate cannot ignore the precedents recorded in the departmental archives. Most department heads are free only to be as big as the president, the bureaucracy, the Congress, and their constituencies will allow them to be.

A cabinet member is confronted with all the problems of an actor typecast to take over the lead role in a long-running classical drama. The audience expects the part to be played in a certain way and will react hostilely to departures from the main lines of characterization set by generations of previous actors. Responses different from those in the prepared script are highly disturbing to the bureaucracy and the principal constituencies in the Congress and the outside community on whom a department head must rely for support. It would be as unthinkable for a secretary of agriculture to question the innate goodness of the rural way of life and the inherent virtues of the family farm as it would be for a Office of Management and Budget director to be against economy and efficiency.

Whatever his background and individual bent, a secretary of the treasury, for example, is obliged to play the part of a "sound" money man. Given the setting in which he performs, it would be very difficult for him to do otherwise. One has only to walk into the ancient Treasury Department building adjoining the White House to sense the atmosphere of a conservative financial institution. The money cage at the main entryway, the gilt pilasters, the gold-framed portraits on the walls all reinforce the treasury "image." As the leader of a rugged "outdoors-type" department, a secretary of the interior is not out of character when he climbs mountains, shoots the Colorado River rapids, and organizes well-publicized hiking and jogging expeditions. Identical conduct by the secretary of the treasury would shake the financial community to its core.

Program transplants that are alien to the institutional culture and environment seldom take root and are threatened with rejection. Franklin Roosevelt recognized this risk when he vetoed the Brownlow Committee's suggestion that federal loan programs be placed under the Treasury Department. Roosevelt advised Brownlow: "That won't work. If they put them in the Treasury, not one of them will ever make a loan to anybody for any purpose. There are too many glass-eyed bankers in the Treasury."[3]

A department head who cannot adapt to the institutional environment also runs the risk of rejection. Appointment by the president and confirmation by the Senate are no guarantee of institutional loyalty. Former attorney general and later Chief Justice Harlan F. Stone is reported to have said of FBI Director J. Edgar Hoover, "If Hoover trusted you, he would be absolutely loyal; if he did not, you had better look out; and he had to get used to his new chief each time."[4] Among bureau chiefs, Hoover was unique in power and influence, but not in his attitude toward his nominal political superiors.

Cabinet members have much in common with the university president who observed ruefully, "Universities may have presidents, but presidents don't have universities." The plain truth is that such powerful subordinate organizations as the Federal Highway Administration, Army Corps of Engineers, National Park Service, and Forest Service constitute the departmental power centers and are quite capable of making it on their own without secretarial help, except when challenged by strong hostile external forces. Often they can do more for the secretary than he or she can do for them.

Institutional loyalty is not as crucial when the secretarial role is discrete and separable from that of department head. The secretaries of state, treasury, and at times, defense and the attorney general tend to function more as staff advisers to the president than as administrators of complex institutions. Their effectiveness and influence are only coincidentally related to their access to institutional resources. On occasion, presidents have utilized cabinet officers essentially as ministers without portfolio, notably the postmaster general and attorney general, offices that have been occupied by political party chair, campaign managers, legislative strategists, or others who were appointed to serve in a noninstitutional capacity as presidential advisers.

For the secretaries of agriculture, commerce, energy, health and human services, education, housing and urban development, interior, labor, veterans, and transportation, as well as the heads of the major independent agencies, the secretarial or agency head and institutional roles cannot be divorced. Without the loyalty, or at least neutrality, of their principal bureau chiefs, these officials can be little more than highly ornamental figureheads. As such, they are powerless to advance the president's objectives either within their agencies or with their constituencies. The paradox is that a president ultimately may be best served by an agency head who is willing to risk occasional presidential displeasure to defend his agency's territory and vital interests. Once he has established his credibility within his agency, he can be much more effective in achieving his own goals and mobilizing support for the president's program.

The political executive is the proverbial man in the middle-what James E. Webb identifies as "the main point of impact in the relationships between the endeavor and its environment."[5] Based on his experience as NASA administrator, Webb recognizes that a department head has twofold and sometimes conflicting responsibilities:

> . . . he has to represent within the endeavor the outside environmental factors—the federal government, the President and the administration in all its facets, the Congress, and the national public; he has to make sure that the endeavor's goals and activities are responsive to the requirements and desires of the environment under conditions of rapid change and uncertainty.
>
> At the same time, the executive represents the entire endeavor as against the environment. He has the ultimate responsibility for securing from the environment the support necessary for gaining and sustaining momentum, for safeguarding against dysfunctional forces seeking control and influence, for—in short—keeping the endeavor viable and on course toward its goals.
>
> The executive can do none of these inside or outside tasks alone. He must bind his associates to his objectives and to his team, even though they may hardly understand all the forces that are at work.[6]

The restraints applicable to cabinet appointments are of two kinds. Custom still requires that the secretary of the interior be from the west and that the secretary of agriculture, if not a "dirt farmer," be from an agricultural state and have a farm background. The secretaries of commerce, labor, and treasury must be individuals who have the confidence of their respective constituencies — organized business, organized labor, and the financial community.

President Clinton pledged to have a cabinet that "looks like America," but he conformed to custom when he named a Wall Street investment banker secretary of the treasury; a former Arizona governor secretary of the interior; a former Kansan member of the House Agriculture Committee secretary of agriculture; and a former mayor secretary of housing and urban development.

Generally speaking, in making appointments, presidents attempt to find individuals who are simpatico and subscribe to the basic institutional outlook, goals, and values. There may be bitter disagreements about methods and policies, but these tend to resemble family differences and do not threaten institutional survival. To appoint a known critic of an agency's program, as President Reagan did in naming Anne Gorsuch Burford as administrator of environmental protection, is the equivalent of a presidential vote of no confidence.

As one descends the hierarchical scale, the distinctive departmental colorations come into focus even more sharply. Deputy secretaries, undersecretaries, and assistant secretaries are less likely than secretaries to be generalists or people with broad political background. Subcabinet appointments tend to mirror the diverse clientele groups, dependencies such as defense contractors, construction companies, educational institutions, and professional organizations that constitute an agency's constituency.

Hubert Humphrey may have complained with some justice that "Every once in awhile one gets the view down here in Washington that the respective departments are members of the United Nations, and that each has a separate sovereignty."[7] But if all department heads were cast from the same mold and always spoke in unison with the president, could our pluralistic political system as we now know it survive? It may be doubted that either the national interests or, in the final analysis, those of the president himself would be best served if departments were headed by agnostics who did not believe in the goals and values of the institutions they administered.

Admittedly there are dangers in the present system. Institutional myths and symbols may be worshiped for their own sake long after they have lost their original meaning. Institutional loyalties may be internalized with the result that programmatic goals are displaced and institutional, professional, or bureaucratic survival and aggrandizement become the overriding objectives, These dysfunctional influences are latent in almost all organizations. Most susceptible are agencies with obsolete, static, or contracting programs or those that are highly inbred, such as the military and Foreign Service.

Former chairman of the joint chiefs of staff, General David C. Jones, acknowledged that the military services "find it difficult to adapt to changing conditions because of understandable attachments to the past. The very foundation of each service rests on imbuing its members with pride in its mission, its doctrine and its customs and discipline—all of which are steeped in traditions."[8]

Organizational behavior can be modified and redirected by substituting new program goals, redesigning administrative systems, altering standards for recruitment and promotion, reorganization, training, and indoctrination. To be effective as a "change agent" takes what few secretaries possess: leadership, a profound knowledge of institutional mores and programs, and, above all, time. Turnover among secretaries is high, and few serve for a full presidential term. One fact is clear, however—presidents seldom evaluate cabinet appointees in terms of their potential as agents of change. As we have seen, appointments generally go to conformists.

In selecting their cabinets, presidents tacitly acknowledge what the orthodox organization theorists ignore—each major agency and its component elements symbolize certain widely held social values and bring a unique perspective to the councils of government. What has been described as the "machinery of Government" is not a machine with interchangeable parts.

Attempts to reinvent government without knowledge or understanding of the institutional psyche or the environmental factors that condition organizational behavior are bound to fail and may produce severe traumas. Reorganizations are major surgery and should not be prescribed as a cure for personality problems. If reorganizations are indicated, under no circumstances should a physician trained only in anatomy be allowed to operate.

James Q. Wilson has observed, "Every organization has a culture, that is, a persistent patterned way of thinking about the central tasks of and human relationships within an organization. Culture is to an organization what personality is to an individual. Like human culture generally, it is passed from one generation to the next. It changes slowly, if at all."[9] Such common expressions as "the military mind" and the "navy way" recognize that institutions do have individual personalities and outlooks, but we rarely associate this phenomenon with civilian agencies. Although each of the major departments has its own special character, these personality traits may or may not be shared fully by its principal subordinate bureaus. Attorney General Robert Kennedy's failure to understand the unique culture and language of the FBI, what Victor Navasky calls "Bureau-speak," constituted a major obstacle to achieving Kennedy administration goals of promoting civil rights and combating organized crime.[10] Deviations occur most frequently among the professional officer corps and in bureaus with limited missions and narrow constituencies. The Bureau of the Budget once was advised bluntly that the "Secretary of State does not necessarily speak for the State Department" when it cited conflicts between the secretary's views and those advocated by a foreign service representative. There is a Department of Agriculture culture, but there are also Extension Service, REA, Soil Conservation Service, and Forest Service cultures. These are not always compatible and sometimes produce conflicts.

According to social psychologists, "social systems are anchored in the attitudes, perceptions, beliefs, motivations, habits, and expectations of human beings."[11] A major unifying force in any organization is what Chester Barnard terms "associational attractiveness."[12] People seek favorable associational conditions from their viewpoint and tend to gravitate toward organizations that share their personal values and norms and where they can work comfortably with colleagues of the same professional, educational, and social backgrounds. For this reason, career executives do not transfer freely from one department to another. Whatever movement there is normally takes place within the foreign affairs, science, intelligence, and budgeting communities, where interagency relationships are particularly close, or within the established professions such as law, engineering, and accounting.

The American Civil Service emphasizes loyalty to one's profession, program, bureau, and department, probably in that order, and not to the Civil Service career system. The exceptions, again, are the Foreign Service, Public Health Service, and Environmental Science Service, which adhere more closely to the classic bureaucratic pattern. In those cases, loyalty is given to the service rather than to the program or to the department. The corps systems are characterized by individual ranks (Civil Service grades, except for the senoir executive service, depend on job classification), entry at junior levels with a commitment to a career within the service, periodic rotation in job assignments, and, perhaps most important, selection and promotion based on the judgment of one's senior officers. Like the military officers corps, these are "closed systems." Interference by politicians or other outsiders in the selection and promotion processes is viewed as the "gravest impropriety."[13]

To speak of the federal bureaucracy as if it were a homogeneous entity is obviously most misleading. About the only thing that some federal employees have in common is that they are paid by the U.S. Treasury. Each group or subgroup has identifiable characteristics that motivate its behavior. A congenial or tolerable organizational environment for one group may be highly repellent to another. Limited movement among the groups exists, but this is partly because of people seeking their right niche, as well as promotion opportunities. A small number have transferred by lateral entry from the Department of Agriculture and defense establishment to the Foreign Service, but we doubt that any diplomat has ever seriously considered transfer to such agencies as the Postal Service or Soil Conservation Service.

Most agencies conduct "orientation" programs for new employees, and several, notably the Forest Service and Marine Corps, have devised sophisticated techniques for making true believers out of their recruits.[14] Formal indoctrination is seldom necessary, however. Professional employees who remain with an agency for any length of time partly "co-opt" themselves. It is true that people shape an institution but an institution also shapes its personnel.

The kinds of people an agency attracts, its organization, policy positions, and responses to environmental influences are conditioned by a complex of tangible and intangible forces. To understand an agency's organization and behavior, one must first know its history, program patterns, administrative processes, professional hierarchies, constituencies, and budget structure.

Many agency traits are acquired; others are inherited. For example, the Atomic Energy Commission's internal organization structure was modeled on that of the Tennessee Valley Authority, which furnished the commission's first chairman, David Lilienthal. The policy of hiring private concerns to manage and operate atomic energy facilities was initiated by the U.S. Army Corps of Engineers when it ran the Manhattan Project and could have been reversed by the commission only at the risk of major disruptions to the program. While the Atomic Energy Commission subsequently developed an elaborate rationale to justify the policy of contracting out its work, the Corps of Engineers was doing nothing more than conducting its business as usual when it began the practice.[15] The corps traditionally has performed its civil functions through contractors, who provide much of its political muscle, and was not organized and staffed to construct and operate atomic energy facilities with its own personnel, even if it had believed that direct operations would be preferable.

Government officials have an instinctive drive to reproduce the organizations, systems, and procedures with which they are most familiar. When asked to develop a self-financing plan for the rural electrification program, the Agriculture Department inevitably proposed an exact duplicate of the farm credit banks. The regulatory commissions invariably insist that new regulatory programs be administered by multiheaded bodies. Sometimes the motivation is self-protection. David Lilienthal believed that the Tennessee Valeey Authority (TVA) would be vulnerable as long as it remained the only institution of its kind and, therefore, he wanted the TVA model to be duplicated in other parts of the country. Organizational eccentricities are often directly traceable to the institutional biases of the legislative drafters and first administrators.

It does not take much digging for an organization archaeologist to uncover evidence of prior civilizations and cultures within the executive branch. The Department of the Interior was once the catchall department of internal affairs before it was transformed into a natural resources and conservation agency, and its Bureau of Indian Affairs and Office of Territories represent vestiges of this earlier period.

The Naval Petroleum Reserves have ceased to be maintained as a reserve oil supply for the U.S. Navy. The program was transferred to the Department of Energy from the navy and its mission changed from keeping oil in the ground for future navy use to increasing domestic production and producing revenues for the treasury. Nonetheless, the law still requires that active-duty navy officers be assigned to key management positions, including that of program director.

Organization structure may provide clues to dimly remembered public controversies and catastrophes. The Forest Service might well be in the Interior Department today if the historic dispute between Secretary Ballinger and Gifford Pinchot had not left conservationists with a nearly pathological distrust of the department. A collision of two commercial airliners over the Grand Canyon brought about the removal of the Federal Aviation Agency from the Department of Commerce. Organization location may stem from such ephemeral factors as the personality or background of a former secretary. President Kennedy wanted a southerner to administer the Community Relations Service and enforce the public accommodations laws and mainly for this reason gave the job to Secretary of Commerce Luther Hodges, who was from North Carolina. It was only with some difficulty that President Johnson was able to transfer the Community Relations Service to the Department of Justice after Secretary Hodges was succeeded in office by Secretary Connor, a northerner.

There are discernible differences between departments created in response to outside pressures (Agriculture, Commerce, Education, Vetrans and Labor) and those established primarily at executive initiative (Health and Human Services, Housing and Urban Development, and Transportation). Clientele groups have a somewhat less proprietary interest in the latter departments. They are more concerned with protecting their pet bureaus from departmental domination, as evidenced by statutory provisions according special status to the Federal Housing Administration, Federal Highway Administration, and Federal Aviation Administration.

Labor unions also have a proprietary interest in certain agencies and bureaus and will oppose reorganizations that threaten union jurisdictions. Lars H. Hydle, president, American Foreign Service Association, objected to Reorganization Plan No. 2 of 1977, creating the Agency for International Communications, because it would transfer State Department employees represented by his organization to a bargaining unit represented by another union.[16] Proposed transfer of immigration and naturalization service inspectors to the customs service raised comparable jurisdictional issues. The implications of public service unions and collective bargaining for government organization and reorganization are only beginning to be recognized.

The influence on organization structure of historical memory, clientele, and union pressures cannot be wholly eliminated. Greater discretion exists with respect to the choice of tools for accomplishing program objectives. There is yet insufficient awareness that "different tools of government have their own distinctive dynamics, their own 'political economics,' that affect the content of government action" and institutional behavior.[17]

Regardless of where they are located on the organization chart or their program objectives, agencies engaged in common types of activities, such as lending and insurance, regulation, or public works, require people with comparable professional skills and backgrounds and share much the same professional and institutional values.

Lester Salamon has observed, "each distinctive form of government action is really a complex system of action with its own personality, actors, and dynamics. Because of this, different instruments can be expected to impart their own distinctive twists to the operation of public programs."[18]

Government loans and insurance probably would be employed less frequently than they are to accomplish basic social and economic objectives if it were known that these programs have built-in conservative bias. The professional elites in a lending agency are bankers or those with banking or financial experience. Bankers judge their success by the number of loans made and the repayment record, not by what they have contributed to the achievement of vague goals. Congress and the president are disposed to apply the same standard because it is very difficult to measure whether and to what extent government loans have, in fact, improved the relative position of small business in our economy, fostered regional development, or assisted developing nations.

The U.S. District Court of the District of Columbia reminded the Department of Housing and Urban Development that it was "not simply a banker." It held that HUD "before it acts because of default on a project clearly otherwise meeting housing objectives it must consider national housing policy and decide what further steps authorized by Congress it will take to assure continuity of the decent, safe, sanitary low cost housing then being provided."[19]

A quite different set of professional norms is introduced by the regulatory process. The financing institution is the banker's domain, but the lawyer reigns supreme over the regulatory agencies. Lawyers approach problems as "cases" and rely primarily on precedent and highly formalized adversary proceedings to produce fair and just solutions. The lawyer's criterion for success is the number of cases won or the decisions sustained on appeal and, more recently, the correctness and completeness of the rulemaking process. The regulatory approach has obvious limitations, if what is called for is positive government leadership and initiative in protecting the public interest and maintaining the economic health and vigor of the regulated industries.

Public works also have drawbacks as a means for accomplishing social and economic objectives because of the dominance given to the engineering profession. Project approval may depend more on sound engineering design than on extraneous social values. Under the accelerated public works program, projects tended to be awarded to communities with well-drafted plans on the drawing boards rather than to those that needed them the most. By nature, engineers like to build things and are not social and economic planners.

Each profession seeks to mold and shape the decision-making process so that issues will be presented and resolved in accordance with its professional standards. Harold Orlans has found that "once a particular profession becomes entrenched in agency or institute, it is not easily dislodged. Thus, research programs and institutes often concentrate on the methods and theories of one profession (even of one school within a profession) rather than employing whatever methods and theories are most pertinent to the problems at hand."[20]

In every organization there is likely to be an elite profession whose values tend to determine institutional behavior. The roles and mission of the General Accounting Office are no longer mainly limited to audit and investigations, but it continues to be dominated by an audit culture. It is said that "auditors feel that they can say something only if they gather all the information and verify it by adding it up twice. They would rather be 99 percent accurate and two months late than 90 percent accurate and on time." The National Academy of Public Administration criticized GAO's quality control process as "hierarchical, expensive, time consuming, homogenizing, and uneven in it's effectiveness."[21]

Inspector general offices dominated by audit culture differ significantly from those where investigators are the elite. Unlike cautious auditors, investigators prefer action and are less observant of rules. The combining of audit and investigating functions in the same office is bound to produce a culture clash.[22] To shift the inspector general's focus from "strict compliance auditing to evaluating management control systems," as recommended by the National Performance Review, would demand a basic change in professional outlook and values of both auditors and investigators.[23]

Robert A. Katzmann graphically portrays how disagreements among professionals—lawyers and economists—within the Federal Trade Commission led to conflicts about antitrust policy. Each group is motivated by different professional norms and personal goals. Katzmann notes that "by training the economist is wary of interference with the market mechanism, he perceives his task as the prevention of unwarranted government action. . . . In contrast to the economist, the lawyer is trained to be prosecution-minded; his career prospects depend upon his securing trial experience."[24]

Professions are characterized by their "relative insularity" and "imperial proclivities."[25] Jockeying for position among various professions or for position among sects within professions is a prime cause of structural disequilibrium. Each profession wants to be represented at the apex of the departmental structure, preferably with its spokesperson reporting directly to the secretary. Scientists propagandize for assistant secretaries for science or science advisers; accountants for comptrollers; lawyers for general counsels at the assistant secretary level; archivists for autonomous archival services. None wants to be subject to officials trained in alien disciplines.

Arguments for status and autonomy are rationalized by an appeal to a "higher loyalty." Government lawyers are by no means the only professionals to claim that members of their profession are answerable to the people of the United States and their professions as well as to their immediate administrative superiors. Lawyers contend that "they must have a degree of independence from administrative control which will enable them to serve as lawyers in Government and not merely as employees of Government."[26]

Scientists argue that national policy for science is a matter to be determined primarily by scientists themselves. Alan T. Waterman, former director of the National Science Foundation, testified as follows: "In any recommendations . . . concerning a research effort of the country, any agency, public or private, should defer to the judgment of the active and capable research scientists in the field."[27]

A Brookings Institution study opposed a Department of Health, Education, and Welfare because it doubted "whether power over professional matters should be vested in a lay department head."[28] The fact that health, education, and welfare were separate professions, each with its distinctive body of knowledge and techniques, and that the bureau chiefs were leaders in their respective professions, meant for Brookings that anything other than a housekeeping and coordinative role for the secretary would be inappropriate. If a secretary attempted to do something to which the organizations of state, federal, and local professionals were opposed, he or she would have a difficult fight on his hands.[29] The Brookings Institution was correct in anticipating that establishment of a Department of Health, Education, and Welfare would not diminish significantly the power of the professional guilds.

Most HEW secretaries preferred not to get involved in disagreements among professional groups. Such modest legislative proposals as one giving a secretary discretion to waive the singlestate agency provision on a governor's request were approached with extreme caution. Under these provisions, state agencies other than those designated by federal law were ineligible to administer grant-in-aid funds. The designated agency was generally a "professional" agency such as the Health or Education Department.

Wilbur J. Cohen, at the time assistant secretary of HEW, testified in 1965 that the proposal was undesirable because "it did not protect a secretary or a governor from being pressured by professional or other groups" and would expose the secretary to "these kinds of sharp differences of opinion, which provoke strong feelings of professional personnel in the health, education, and welfare field." Cohen concluded that, "If you want good administration you have ultimately to get the support of the professional people, the state people, and the local people, or it makes little sense to change the administrative structure and lose the support of the people whom you actually have to count on to administer something."[30] Contrary to the advice from many of his principal subordinates, Secretary Gardner withdrew HEW's objection to this legislation and it was enacted in 1968.

Professional guilds are by no means confined to the Department of Health and Human Services. No less powerful guilds include the National Conference on State Parks, Society of American Foresters, American Association of State Highway Officials, National Association of Housing and Redevelopment Officers, Interstate Conference of Employment Security Agencies, and the Society of American Archivists. Federal officials are very active in these organizations. The guilds constitute a form of private government and are regularly consulted about proposed federal policies and regulations, often before the policies and regulations are discussed with the secretary. Secretaries have almost no option but to approve when presented with pacts reached after several months of negotiations with a guild.

Organization issues may be sensitive because they spring from jurisdictional disputes among professional guilds or splinter groups within professions. Engineers and biomedical specialists vied for control of the environmental health program. The debate over organization was, at its root, a debate over whether environmental health was primarily a disease problem or an engineering problem. It was the surgeon general's view that, "it is an engineering job to get pollutants out of the environment, but it is a biomedical job to know how much lead in the environment will not cause harm to human beings."[31] Business economists demanded that the Council of Economic Advisers be reconstituted so as to break the virtual monopoly that was held by academic economists over council appointments.[32]

Few developments have had more significance for public administration than the rapid growth in the proportion of professional and technical employees since World War II. This trend is not limited to the federal government. Frederick Mosher estimates that about one-third of all government employees are engaged in professional and technical pursuits, more than three times the comparable proportion in the private sector.[33] Mosher defines profession to include both the general professions (law, medicine) and the predominantly public service professions (foresters, social workers, educators).

The consequences of increasing professionalization for federal organization structure are only beginning to be perceived. Professional concepts of status and autonomy are difficult to reconcile with orthodox doctrines of economy and efficiency, hierarchy, span of control, and straight lines of authority and accountability. The most sacred tenets of the orthodox theology are being openly challenged. Educators insist that "education is a unique activity—so different in its essential nature that it withers in an atmosphere of control to which most state activities can accustom themselves."[34] Archivists argued that "no mere concept of administrative efficiency could be permitted to deflect the object for which historians had labored so long," an independent National Archives.[35] From time to time scientists, lawyers, doctors, and other professionals have voiced similar heresies.

Mosher warned of the danger that, "the developments in the public service of the midcentury decades may be subtly, gradually, but profoundly moving the weight toward the partial, the corporate, the professional perspective and away from that of the general interest."[36] In and of itself, professionalization is a major force for dividing the executive branch into separate narrow compartmentalized units. When professionalization is mixed with the centrifugal forces generated by clienteles, dependents, congressional committees, the politics of fund raising, and collective bargaining, the pressures for further balkanization of the executive branch become nearly irresistible.

Clientele groups and dependencies fear agencies with divided loyalties. They want agencies to represent their interests and theirs alone. Some years ago, rumors of a pending reorganization of bank supervisory agencies inspired this banner front-page head-

line in the United States Investor: NATIONAL BANKS NEED
SPOKESMAN: OFFICE OF THE: COMPTROLLER OF CUR-
RENCY SHOULD BE PRESERVED.[37] It is clear from positions
taken on banking legislation that the comptroller of currency still
speaks for the national banks, although few present-day comptrollers would express it as baldly as the comptroller's annual report in 1923: "The Comptroller of the Currency should, in the governmental organization, be the representative and partisan of the
national banks."[38]

Chief Justice Rehnquist commented to attorneys representing
Citibank (South Dakota), on April 24, 1996: "I have been on the
court for twenty-three or twenty-four years and heard a number of
these cases and I've never heard of a case in which the Comptroller ruled against the banks."

Certain agencies are admittedly partisans and representatives of
particular interests within our society, and some were deliberately
established for that purpose. President Truman thought it entirely
proper that the Department of Commerce should be "a channel to
the White House for business and industry" and regretted that organized labor did not use the Department of Labor in the same
way.[39] President Nixon cited the need for preserving the Department of Agriculture as a "vigorous advocate" of farm interests
when he abandoned his plan to abolish the department in order to
divide its functions among the proposed departments of Community Development, Economic Affairs, Human Resources, and Natural Resources.[40]

Clientele interests rarely focus, however, at the departmental
level. The department is valued mainly as a symbol. Departmental
constituencies, even for acknowledged partisans such as Agriculture, Commerce, and Labor, represent a diversity of interests and
may speak with conflicting voices. That there is a contest for access
and power among the diverse elements in each constituency is
demonstrated by the struggles between the Farm Bureau, the
Grange, and the Farmer's Union, and, before the merger, the
American Federation of Labor and the Congress of Industrial
Organizations.

Pressures are most intense when constituencies are narrowly based and united by a common interest in preserving tangible economic privileges granted to them by federal law. It is the independent agency or the bureau that is most likely to be seized upon as the vehicle for safeguarding and advancing these interests.

These groups are very jealous of the special relationship with their government sponsor. Interlopers are not treated kindly. Programs that may dilute the sponsor's single-minded concern with their interests are vigorously opposed. The Farm Bureau attempted to throttle at their birth the agricultural adjustment, farm security, and soil conservation programs that threatened the Extension Service–land grant college monopoly consummated by a 1914 agreement with the secretary of agriculture. Unless courted continually with suitable favors, an interest group may turn on its patron. The Department of Agriculture learned, to its sorrow, that the price of Farm Bureau allegiance was complete subservience.

Administrative systems are no more neutral than organization arrangements. Professional, dependency, and bureaucratic interests may be as much affected by *how* a program is administered as by *where* it is administered. The far-reaching policy implications of TVA's decision to channel its agricultural programs through the land grant colleges are brilliantly documented in Philip Selznick's *TVA and the Grass Roots.* TVA became firmly locked into the Farm Bureau-Extension axis.

Federal agencies may be more responsive to the middleman or their administrative agents than they are to the ultimate consumers of goods and services. The Department of Health and Human Services, which channels most of its funds through state agencies, is subject to quite a different set of influences from the Small Business Administration and Veterans Department, which provide services directly to the people. The Department of Housing and Urban Development, which deals with urban agencies, responds differently than the Department of Agriculture, which administers its programs through land grant colleges, chosen instruments such as soil conservation districts, and elected farmer committees.

Difficulties occur when agencies and their clienteles develop a vested interest in the way things are done. New approaches are resisted for no other reason than that they require major modifications in existing administrative patterns or complicate constituency relationships. John Gardner has observed that if agencies become prisoners of their systems and procedures, "the rule book grows fatter as the ideas grow fewer. Almost every well-established organization is a coral reef of procedures that were laid down to achieve some long-forgotten objective."[41] The Atomic Energy Commission was practically incapable of operating anything except by contract, and went so far as to contract out administration of the city of Oak Ridge. This has become a major problem for the Department of Energy, which has had to assimilate the AEC functions.

Original purposes may be submerged in an overlay of myths, sentiment, and slogans. The farmer committee system is venerated as the most perfect expression of the principles of "grassroots" democracy. Forgotten are the system's humble beginnings as the offspring of a marriage of convenience between New Deal idealism and old-fashioned agricultural politics. The system was inaugurated at a time when the Farm Bureau and its state and local government allies were making a determined effort to capture the new action programs providing cash benefits to farmers. Whatever his public explanations, it is clear that Secretary Wallace was motivated as much by a desire to establish an effective counterweight to the Farm Bureau's political power as he was by ideological considerations. Soil conservation districts under elected boards were organized with much the same objective in mind.[42] Secretary of Agriculture Mike Espy's plan to reform the committee system so as to provide greater diversity in committee membership was overwhelmingly rejected by the Congress.[43] In 1992, of 9,069 county committee seats available only 169 were held by ethnic minorities and 453 by women.

Clientele-oriented policies also may be engraved in stone. Devotion to these "historic" policies endures in the face of changing circumstances and challenges by presidents and prestigious study commissions. The U.S. Army Corps of Engineers adheres rigidly to the policy first enunciated in 1987 that inland waterways should be regarded "as public highways open to use of the public generally without restriction," although every president since Franklin Roosevelt has recommended the imposition of user charges. It was the corps' unswerving dedication to this policy, rather than admiration for its engineering skills, that caused user organizations to lobby for Corps of Engineers' control of the St. Lawrence Seaway. The campaign did not succeed, but the house committee report directed that the St. Lawrence Seaway Corporation use the services of the Corps of Engineers for design, construction, maintenance, and operation of the seaway and emphasized that in approving tolls it was "not digressing from the firm and long-standing toll-free policy established with respect to inland waterways."[44]

Interest groups have fascinated a generation of American scholars.[45] Political pluralists consider competition among interest groups as an integral and indispensable element in the democratic process. Those who deem all interest groups by definition to be evil and picture government agencies as marionettes dangling from strings manipulated by "special interests" are indulging in gross oversimplifications. The relationship between an agency and its constituency is based on a mutuality of interests—a mutuality generally established by the provisions of laws enacted by the Congress. The government agency often does the manipulating, not the reverse. The Forest Service, for example, maintains a roster of "key men" who can be called on in time of need for succor.[46] Other agencies maintain similar networks of individuals and organizations.

Interest groups are not monoliths. Their power is essentially negative. They are most effective in blocking actions—modification of the interest rate on Rural Electrical Administration (REA) loans, transfer of the Maritime Administration to the Department of Transportation, imposition of user charges. These issues do not generate internal disputes. It is far more difficult to obtain unanimity when new proposals are being advanced, for then the sharp differences that exist in any organization quickly come to the surface.

Once systems are developed and patterns of organization behavior are established, in most instances they cannot be altered significantly by interdepartmental reorganizations. This is particularly true when bureaus, such as the U.S. Employment Service, are moved intact from one department to another. Reorganizations may result in scarcely more than a new name on the letterhead. Where changes are produced, they are seldom those anticipated or intended by the proponents of reorganization.[47] *Vin ordinaire* cannot be transformed into champagne merely by shifting the location of the bottle in the wine cellar.

The behavior of adult institutions can be altered. But this generally requires a combination of organization and nonorganizational measures, which enlarge the agency's constituency, compel redesign of the administrative system, and call for a different mix of professional skills. Important as it was, the transfer of the U.S. Coast Guard from the Treasury Department to a more compatible environment in the Department of Transportation would not by itself have been sufficient to bring about the dramatic change in the service's self-image and concept of role and mission. For the first time in the Department of Transportation, the coast guard was asked to participate in the formulation of departmental policies. By legislation and executive action the coast guard's mission was enlarged to include new regulatory activities, such as boating safety and environmental protection, which transferred "Coast Guard men and women from deck to desk."[48] The end result was, according to Lieutenant Commander Lawrence I. Kiern, to compel the coast guard "to abandon its traditionally apolitical character in regard to departmental affairs."[49]

The *first* organization decision is crucial. The course of institutional development may be set irrevocably by the initial choice of administrative agency and by how the program is designed.

Unless these choices are made with full awareness of environmental and cultural influences, the program may fail or its goals may be seriously distorted.

Herbert Hoover believed that the simple physical grouping of functions cheek-by-jowl in departments organized by major purposes would automatically make it possible to eliminate overlaps and produce coordinated policies. This hypothesis assumes that department heads are or should be chief executives, as the term is used in business or military organizations, with authority reaching down through every step of the organization.

Luther Gulick defined the work of a chief executive by the acronym POSDCORB: planning, organizing, staffing, directing, coordinating, reporting, and budgeting.[50] In major or minor degree, department heads do perform all of these functions, but POSDCORB by itself provides an inadequate and unrealistic description of a secretary's job. Statutes that contemplate that a department head will "control" his agency are equally unrealistic.

A department head's job is akin to that of a major university president and is subject to the same frustrations. His principal duties involve matters that are unrelated to the internal administration and management of the institution. As far as his subordinates are concerned, he is the institution's ceremonial head, chief fundraiser, and protector of institutional values and territory. A department head may spend 25 percent or more of his time in meetings with members of the Congress and appearances before congressional committees, and probably an equivalent amount of time in public relations work such as speech-making and cultivating agency constituencies. One administrator reported that he was required to keep thirty-five full committees and seventy-five subcommittees informed of his agency's activities.[51] Another block of time is devoted to White House conferences and meetings of interagency and advisory committees. Minimal time is left for managing the department, even if a secretary is one of the rare political executives with a taste for administration.

A department head's managerial role is primarily that of a "mediator-initiator." In the words of Clark Kerr, former president of the University of California, who was referring to university presidents, "he must be content to hold the constituent elements loosely together and to move the whole enterprise another foot ahead in what often seems an unequal race with history."[52] He has opportunities to set directions and exercise significant influence only when new programs are being developed or when major increases in expenditures are being requested for old programs. Normally a department head has neither the time nor the inclination to concern himself with ongoing operations that appear to raise no problems.

The prime quality required of a department head, and most often lacking, is political leadership. Hugh Heclo correctly diagnosed the problem when he wrote the following:

> A political executive who does not know what he wants to accomplish is in no position to assess the bureaucracy's performance in helping him to do it. Likewise, an executive whose aims bear little relation to the chances for accomplishment is in an equally weak position to stimulate help from officials below. By trying to select goals in relation to available opportunities, political appointees create a strategic resource for leadership in a bureaucracy.[53]

Too often department heads equate management with control. Instead of providing positive policy leadership and coordination, departments may have a negative influence and impose restraints that hamper operating agencies in carrying out their missions. An independent industry panel condemned the Department of Energy for its failure to distinguish between nuclear sites, research facilities, and production and sale of oil and gas in imposing what it termed "nonvalue added" regulations on the Naval Petroleum Reserves.[54]

Almost forty-six years ago the Bureau of the Budget found that "the outstanding weakness in federal administration today lies in deficiencies in administrative leadership, coordination and control at the top of federal departments and agencies.[55] Since then the number of chiefs of staff, undersecretaries, assistant secretaries, and special assistants have multiplied, staff resources available to a secretary has been augmented, and sophisticated systems have been installed to enhance a secretary's decision-making powers. However, department heads remain the weakest link in the chain of federal administration. Unless departmental management can be improved, reorganization and reinvention cannot be counted on to yield more than marginal benefits.

If we are to do something meaningful about the organization and management of the executive branch, we must start first with department and agency heads. New approaches are needed—approaches based on what the political executives' functions really are not on obsolete concepts of what they should be.

9

Coordination: The Search for the Philosopher's Stone

In ancient times alchemists believed implicitly in the existence of a philosopher's stone, which would provide the key to the universe and, in effect, solve all of the problems of humankind. The quest for coordination is in many respects the twentieth-century equivalent of the medieval search for the philosopher's stone. If only we can find the right formula for coordination, we can reconcile the irreconcilable, harmonize competing and wholly divergent interests, overcome irrationalities in our government structures, and make hard policy choices to which no one will disagree.

When interagency committees such as the Economic Opportunity Council fail as coordinators, the fault is sought in the formula, not in deeper underlying causes. The council's inability to perform its statutory duties as coordinator of the federal government's antipoverty efforts was attributed to the fact that the law (1) placed coordinating responsibility on a body of peers who could not be expected voluntarily to relinquish decision-making control over planning for or operation of programs, and (2) designated the director of the Office of Economic Opportunity, then a non-Cabinet-level official, as chairman with coordinative authority over officials of greater status. The formula was changed to provide that the council have an independent chairman and staff, but with no better results. The original council at least met a few times; the re-structured council was never convened at all. Again, revision of the formula was prescribed as the remedy. The comptroller general proposed that the council's functions be transferred to an Office of Community Resources in the Executive Office of the President, which would provide staff support for President Nixon's interdepartmental Urban Affairs Council.[1]

Whether we are dealing with poverty, science, telecommunications, AIDS, drugs, or international and national security programs, the search for a coordinating formula seems to follow almost a set pattern: (1) establishment of an interagency committee chaired by an agency head and with no staff or contributed staff; (2) designation of a "neutral" chair and provision for independent staff; and (3) transfer of coordinating functions to the White House or Executive Office of the President, establishment of a special presidential assistant, and reconstitution of the interagency committee as a presidential advisory council.

Defective machinery may contribute to the difficulties of coordinating multifaceted federal programs, which cut across traditional agency jurisdictions, but it is seldom, if ever, at the root of the problem. The power to coordinate does not normally carry with it the authority to issue binding orders. Executive orders customarily confer broad powers "to facilitate and coordinate" federal programs and direct each department and agency to "cooperate" with the official designated as coordinator. However, buried in the boiler plate at the end of the order there is usually a section reading, "Nothing in this order shall be construed as subjecting any function vested by law in, or assigned pursuant to law to, any federal department or agency or head thereof to the authority of any other agency or officer or as abrogating or restricting any such function in any manner."[2]

Neither the president nor a coordinator appointed by him can perform the functions vested by law in the heads of departments and agencies. When conflicts result from clashes in statutory missions or differences in legislative mandates, they cannot be reconciled through the magic of coordination. Too often organic disease is mistakenly diagnosed as a simple case of inadequate coordination.

If agencies are to work together harmoniously, they must share at least some community of interests about basic goals. Without such a community of interests and compatible objectives, problems cannot be resolved by coordination. Senator Frank Moss ascribed the conflict between the National Park Service and the Army Corps of Engineers over the Florida Everglades to "uncoordinated activities." Park service officials complained that the engineers drained the Everglades National Park almost dry in their efforts to halt wetlands flooding and reclaim glade country for agriculture. The Army Corps Engineers argued that wetlands were "for the birds" and flood control for the people.[3] Coordinating devices may reveal or even exacerbate the conflict, but they cannot produce agreement among the agencies when a choice must be made as to whether a single piece of land should be drained for flood control and reclaimed for agriculture or maintained as wetlands to preserve unique and valuable forms of aquatic life.

Coordination is rarely neutral. To the extent that it results in mutual agreement or a decision on some policy, course of action, or inaction, it inevitably advances some interests at the expense of others or more than others. Coordination contains no more magic than the philosopher's stone. In does, however, contain a good deal of the substance with which alchemists were concerned: the proper placement and relationship of the elements to achieve a given result.

Coordinators are seldom judged objectively or evaluated by realistic standards. Coordination may influence people, but it makes few friends. The tendency is to consider that coordination most effective which operates to one's own advantage. Few coordinating systems have worked as successfully as the Office of Management and Budget's procedures for clearing proposed legislation and reports on legislation and advising agencies as to the relationship of legislative proposals to "the administration's program," but the legislative clearance process is by no means universally admired. By doing its job well, OMB has gained few friends among members of

Congress and interest groups whose pet bills have been held "not in accord with the administration's program."

The term *coordination* is used in laws and executive orders as if it had a precise, commonly understood meaning. Yet probably no word in our administrative terminology raises more difficult problems of definition. For James D. Mooney, coordination is no less than "the determining principle of organization, the form which contains all other principles, the beginning and the end of all organized effort."[4] Coordination is also defined as concerted action, animated by a common purpose, responding to recognized signals and using practiced skills. Coordination describes both a process—the act of coordinating—and a goal: the bringing together of diverse elements into a harmonious relationship in support of common objectives. The power to coordinate in and of itself confers no additional legal authority, but merely provides a license to seek harmonious action by whatever means may be available under existing authorities.

In current usage, coordination has come to be identified primarily with the formal processes by which we attempt to adjudicate disagreements among agencies. Mooney would regard the proliferation of coordinating mechanisms, such as interagency committees, as prima facie evidence of "lack of coordinated effort" resulting from inexact definitions of jobs and functions.[5] Coordinating machinery becomes necessary only when coordination cannot be achieved by sound organization, good management, and informal cooperation among agencies engaged in related and mutually supporting activities.

Formal coordinating processes are time-consuming and the results are generally inconclusive. True coordination sometimes may be obtained only by going outside the formal processes.

By overemphasizing coordinating machinery, we have created the false impression that most federal activities are uncoordinated. This is by no means the case. Without informal or so-called lateral coordination, which takes place at almost every stage in the development and execution of national programs and at every level within the federal structure, the government probably would grind to a halt. Skilled bureaucrats develop their own informational networks. Managers who are motivated by a desire to get something done find ways and means of bridging the jurisdictional gaps. Informal coordination is greatly facilitated when people share the same goals, operate from a common set of legal authorities and information assumptions, agree on standards, have compatible professional outlooks, and can help each other. Where these conditions exist, there is no need for the intervention of third parties to secure harmonious action.

Politicization of the senior career service inevitably disrupts the networks and impedes lateral coordination. It is argued by some that the networks are instruments of bureaucratic ideologies that must be controlled if an administration is to achieve its political objectives.[6]

Coordination does not necessarily require imposition of authority from the top. State and local governments have the crucial role in the process of administering and coordinating federal assistance programs. The functions of establishing state, regional, and local goals, developing comprehensive plans, and determining priorities among grant proposals in terms of these goals and financial restraints is a local responsibility. Effective performance of these functions by state and local governments can reduce or eliminate need for coordinating arrangements at the federal level.

Complete reliance on voluntary cooperation is not feasible, however, except in Utopia. The goals of our pluralistic society, as reflected in federal programs, are frequently contradictory. No matter how the government is organized, it is impossible to define jobs and design programs in such a way as to eliminate all overlaps and potential conflicts among agencies. Even when the will to cooperate is present, good intentions may be thwarted by the size of the federal establishment, the growing complexity and compartmentalized character of federal programs, differences among professional groups, and the absence of a clear sense of direction and coherence of policy either in the White House or in the Congress. We cannot produce harmony by synthetic substitutes when the essential ingredients are lacking within the governmental system.

The much maligned interagency committees are the result, not the cause, of our inability to agree on coherent national objectives and to find a workable solution to our organizational dilemma.

Interagency committees are the crabgrass in the garden of government institutions. Nobody wants them, but everyone has them. Committees seem to thrive on scorn and ridicule and multiply so rapidly that attempts to weed them out appear futile. For every committee uprooted by Presidents Kennedy, Johnson, Carter's, and Clinton's much publicized "committee-killing" exercises, another has been born to take it place.

Interagency committees as a general institutional class have no admirers and few defenders. Former Secretary of Defense Robert Lovett ascribed the proliferation of interagency committees to the "foul-up factor," or the tendency of every agency with even the most peripheral interest to insist on getting into the act. According to Lovett, committees have now so blanketed the whole executive branch as to give it "an embalmed atmosphere."[7] From his observation, committees are composed of "some rather lonely, melancholy men who have been assigned a responsibility but haven't the authority to make decisions at their levels, and so they tend to seek their own kind. They thereupon coagulate into a sort of glutinous mass, and suddenly come out as a committee."[8] Lovett concluded that "two heads are not always better than one, particularly when they are growing on the same body."[9]

Nelson Rockefeller, W. Averell Harriman, and Lyndon B. Johnson were no less critical. Rockefeller contended that interagency committees "reduce the level of government action to the least bold or imaginative—to the lowest common denominator among many varying positions. In such circumstances, policy may be determined not for the sake of its rightness—but the sake of agreement."[10] Harriman condemned committees as organs of "bureaucratic espionage" employed by agencies to obtain information about the plans of other departments that could be used to "obstruct programs which did not meet with their own departmental bureaucratic objectives."[11] In a memorandum to the heads of departments and agencies, President Johnson cautioned that "improper use of committees can waste time, delay action, and result in undesirable compromise."[12]

Interagency committees cannot be discussed rationally without distinguishing among the distinct types of committees and the varied purposes they serve. These differences relate primarily to method of establishment, duration, chairperson, membership, staff, financing, and functions.

Statutory committees financed by separate appropriations and employing their own staff are nothing more or less than an independent agency headed by an interagency board. The president may be authorized to designate the chairperson, or the law may designate a cabinet officer or agency head as chair. The president may be given some discretion in selecting committee members, or membership may he determined by statute.

Difficulties occur when the law endows these agencies with something more than advisory functions. Budget Bureau Circular No. A-63 observed that "committees should be used for such functions as advising, investigating, making reports, exchanging views, etc." As a matter of executive branch policy, the circular instructed agencies that "responsibility for performance of operating or executive functions, such as making determinations or administering programs should not be assigned to committees." This admonition is repeated in the Federal Advisory Committee Act of 1972, which declares that "committees should be advisory only, and that all matters under their consideration should be determined, in accordance with law, by the official, agency, or officer involved."

By far the largest number of interagency committees deal with highly technical problems and provide a convenient vehicle for exchanging information and bringing the technical people together on a regular basis to discuss problems of mutual concern. There are many professional "communities" in the federal government that cut across jurisdictional lines, and the committees in part serve as a forum and meeting place for the "law enforcement," "intelligence," "foreign affairs," "scientific," and "educational" communities, among others.

To provide a forum for sharing experiences, ideas, and processing practices, President Clinton by executive order established a Chief Information Officers Council composed of the chief deputy information officers in the major departments and agnecies.[13]

Controversy centers principally on a relatively limited number of interagency committees that have become, in the words ofthe Jackson Subcommittee, "the gray and bloodless ground of bureaucratic warfare—a warfare of position not of decisive battles."[14] The battle for position is never-ending and grows more intense as agencies seek to gain control or at least exercise influence over the growing number of new and important programs that cut across established jurisdictional lines. Sometimes a stalemate is evidenced by co-chairpersons or rotating chairs. Occasionally, the stalemate is resolved by making the vice president or some other "neutral" the chair.

Members of these committees act as instructed delegates of their agencies. They judge their effectiveness by how many points they win for their side. With this emphasis on gamesmanship, agency staff assigned to the committee become highly expert in identifying and escalating interagency differences, even when the issues are insignificant or nonexistent. Staff of the National Security Council Planning Board, before the board was abolished by President Kennedy, were among the leading exponents of this art.

Whatever their other drawbacks, interagency committees can be useful in setting the metes and bounds of agency jurisdictions and areas of legitimate interest. Without them, or a reasonable substitute, we would have no criteria for discriminating claims in such areas as education, water resources, science, poverty, economic and trade policy, and manpower. Agencies vie for membership on committees established by the Congress or the president, not necessarily because they expect the committee to play a decisive role, but to establish their right to request information and to be consulted about matters that concern them. Otherwise their colleagues could charge them with "meddling." The fact that the committee may never meet, or, if it does, only third- and fourth-echelon officials might attend, becomes a matter of relatively little importance.

Chairmanship of a committee establishes primacy within a given program area but confers no authority, other than that which the chairman already possesses by law. Membership in an exclusive club such as the National Security Council carries with it a certain amount of prestige but, in and of itself, little influence.

Membership can provide greater access if the president or senior White House staff chair meetings. Under Clinton, membership on the National Economic Council and Domestic Policy Council afforded an opportunity to influence White House decision making.

Much of the criticism of interagency committees is directed at the wrong target. Committees can perform effectively when they are assigned appropriate tasks that are within their competence. The Alaska Reconstruction Commission was successful because each of the committee members had the statutory authority and motivation to do things that were necessary to assist Alaska's recovery from the disastrous Good Friday earthquake. The committee was not called on to revise basic government policies, except for a few modifications it recommended to meet the special circumstances in Alaska, but to obtain agreement among the agencies on the work that needed to be done and to see that it was carried out on a phased time schedule.

On the other hand, the federal executive boards proved totally ineffective in dealing with critical urban problems because they were given a job that they were inherently incapable of accomplishing and that was wholly alien to the purpose for which they were organized. President Kennedy established federal executive boards in ten of the largest cities in 1961. The number was, by the end of 1969, increased to twenty-five. Board membership was limited to the principal federal civilian and military officials who happened to be located within the designated geographic area. Unless the agencies most concerned with critical urban problems—the Departments of Housing and Urban Development, Health, Education, and Welfare, and Labor, and the Office of Economic Opportunity—had offices in a city, they were not represented on the federal executive board. When they were represented, it might be by someone from a specialized bureau, such as the Food and Drug

Administration, who was not competent to discuss departmental programs.

The objectives in creating the boards were reasonably modest and attainable: improvement of communications between Washington and the field and among federal officials in the field; encouragement of cooperation among federal agencies in areas where cooperation might be to their mutual advantage; support of community activities such as blood donor drives and community chest campaigns. In each of these areas, members of the boards had the authority to act. As long as the boards confined their activities to such programs as equipment sharing, joint training, and improved public services, they were able to make a valuable contribution.

The boards failed when they were directed in 1965 to identify unmet urban needs and to devise and carry out interagency and intergovernmental efforts to help solve critical urban problems. A 1969 Bureau of the Budget–Civil Service Commission evaluation identifies three principal reasons for this failure, all of which should have been anticipated before the assignment was made: (1) interagency committee have no decision-making authority and cannot resolve fundamental conflicts about agency priorities; (2) collaborative efforts among members of the boards could not be effective because of the weaknesses in the boards' composition and the disparity among the boards' members in the powers delegated to them by their respective agencies; and (3) members of the boards with full-time jobs elsewhere could not be expected to devote the necessary time to activities that were extraneous to their official duties.[15]

The federal executive boards' manifest failure as coordinators did not deter efforts to assign comparable functions to a somewhat differently constituted group of interagency committees, the ten federal regional councils. It should have come as no surprise that the councils also proved incapable of reconciling "conflicting policies and practices among their member agencies."[16]

The deficiencies associated with interagency committees can be avoided or minimized if (1) missions are tailored to their capabilities; (2) membership is kept as small as possible; (3) institutionalization of staff and procedures is held to a minimum; and (4) the end product is advice to someone who has authority to decide and who wants the advice. Committees perform poorly when compelled to act as collective decision makers, either as program administrators or as policy coordinators.

Standing interagency committees with responsibility to coordinate in general are to be distinguished from ad hoc interagency groups organized by the president or agency heads to study and report on *specific problems*, such as delays in the processing of federal grants, management of automatic data processing equipment, and contracting for research and development. These committees operate with a high degree of informality and are staffed by agency personnel with the requisite professional skills rather than by professional coordinators. The committees go out of business once their assigned task is accomplished. Problem-oriented working committees have been extremely useful.

Interagency committees and lead agencies are basically organized ways of promoting voluntary cooperation. Many believe that they are fatally flawed because there is no provision for a central directive authority. The Area Redevelopment Act of 1961 attempted to overcome this deficiency by centralizing authority and funding in a small coordinating agency—the Area Redevelopment Administration (ARN)—and requiring decentralized operations through delegate agencies. The ARA was thought of as the "prime contractor" for federal depressed-area assistance, with the delegate agencies performing in the role of subcontractors.[17] The administration's primary focus was expected to be on the development and approval of overall economic development plans for each depressed area and coordination of proposed projects with the approved plans. Much the same concept was incorporated, to a major or minor degree, in the foreign assistance, civil defense, and poverty programs.

The delegate agency approach appeared to have considerable promise and offered an opportunity to move toward "systems managers" for designated program areas. This promise was not realized, however, because of the inability to resolve the novel problems of relationships among federal agencies that are introduced by the delegation process. These relate to selection and direction of personnel, communications, and final project approval.

ARA was unable to exercise effective control over the selection of personnel to administer delegated programs. When responsibility for ARA programs was merely added to an employee's normal duties, first priority was inevitably given to the work for his or her own agency. A study by Sar Levitan indicated that "communications between the ARA and its cooperating agencies were so poor that in some cases field offices were issued conflicting instructions from their parent agencies. Suspicions and resentments were widespread among officials both in Washington and in the field."[18] Delegate agencies were inordinately slow in processing applications for ARA financial assistance, but it was the ARA officials who were blamed for the delays. Convinced that the system was inherently defective, the ARA urged in 1963 that it be modified drastically or abandoned.

If left to its own devices, ARA in time could probably have established a mutually acceptable and workable modus vivendi with delegate agencies. The insuperable obstacle was the pressures from the White House and the Congress, These pressures meant that ARA could not divorce itself wholly from decisions on individual applications. Political realities compelled ARA to divert its major efforts from overall economic development plans to projects of interest to the White House and influential members of Congress. Consequently, ARA tended to duplicate the reviews conducted by delegate agencies, thus contributing to the excessive delays in processing applications. Some believe that the delegate agency system was never given a fair test in ARA.

Evaluations of Office of Economic Opportunity (OEO) experience with delegate agencies are conflicting. OEO contended that it "was the first agency at the federal level to develop, set up and live by a system of interagency delegation agreements."[19] Delegate agencies included the Departments of Labor (Neighborhood Youth Corps); Agriculture (rural loan program); Health, Education, and Welfare (work experience and adult basic education); and Small Business Administration (economic loans). Although the system had not "worked perfectly," in OEO's judgment "a significant start" had been made.

The comptroller general did not share OEO's optimism and recommended that the Congress permanently transfer those programs that were administered under delegation from OEO or recommended for delegation by the president. In five instances—work study, lending and loan guarantees, adult basic education, upward bound, and work experience—the Congress had directed transfer of the programs to delegate agencies. The comptroller general held that OEO had "not been in an effective position to exercise oversight and direction for programs which have been delegated to other agencies."[20] He asserted that the appearance of central direction and coordination had been obtained at the expense of further dividing responsibility for closely related programs and blunting OEO's innovative capacity by weighing it down with administrative burdens.

Much the same line of reasoning is to be found in President Nixon's 1969 message outlining a proposed reorganization of the Office of Economic Opportunity.[21] To maintain strict accountability for the way in which work was performed, President Nixon recommended that functions should be assigned to specific agencies whenever possible, thus avoiding the blurring of lines of responsibility resulting from OEO delegations. The reorganized OEO's mission would be concerned principally with innovating new domestic programs. When an experiment proved successful, the program would be transferred "to other agencies or other levels of government or even the private sector if that seems desirable." OEO would retain certain proven programs, however, which were national in scope, particularly in those cases in which OEO's "special identification with the problems of the poor" made this desirable.[22]

The Congress has been willing to experiment with almost every conceivable type of coordinating formula, but it has drawn the line at proposals for "supercoordinators" or "supercabinet" officers. Except in wartime, the Congress objects to changes that transfer power from the heads of the established agencies to "czars" who are answerable to the president only.

In 1955 Herbert Hoover had suggested creating two appointive vice presidents, one responsible for foreign and the other for domestic affairs. President Eisenhower had recommended the establishment of a "first secretary" of the government who would function, in effect, as prime minister with respect to national security and international affairs. From time to time it has been suggested seriously that the vice president be made "coordinator-in-chief," although it is doubtful that any president would be willing to delegate this kind of power to a person whom he did not appoint and cannot remove. Paul David has observed, "The functions, duties and prerogatives of the vice president, as a member of the executive branch, are not likely to be expanded except with the formal or informal concurrence of the president; but once such functions, duties and prerogatives are in place, withdrawal through action by the president becomes more difficult than their initial establishment."[23]

The problems of the modern presidency clearly cannot be resolved by converting the White House into a corporate headquarters with several appointed subexecutives authorized to speak for the corporation. Within the executive branch the president alone has the constitutional duty to exercise leadership in establishing national goals and priorities. The setting of these goals and priorities in terms that can be understood and communicated in actionable form to the operating agencies is the first prerequisite for coordination.

Under existing law the president can delegate coordinating responsibilities to officers appointed by and with the advice and consent of the Senate and agency heads (White House staff are excluded), but he cannot delegate those powers necessary to carry out the responsibility.[24] The president's political powers as our one nationally elected official other than the vice president, and as the leader of his political party, and his constitutional powers to approve legislation and to hire and fire the heads of executive agencies are nondelegable. An assistant president or supercabinet officer without political influence or statutory powers would have nothing going for him but the majesty of his title, unless he were accepted as the president's alter ego. It is doubtful that our constitutional system can accommodate both an elected president and appointed presidential alter egos without impairing the unity of executive power.

If statutory functions were transferred from the departments to a counselor or supercabinet officer, or if the performance of functions were made subject to his control, he would cease to be a coordinator and become a superdepartment head. Arguments can be made for superdepartments, but no one contends that superdepartments will improve the coordination of programs that cut across superdepartmental jurisdictions.

The Jackson Subcommittee was of the view that super Cabinet officers would not ease the president's problems but "would make his burdens heavier." The committee concluded that reforms, to be effective, must be made in terms of the real requirements and possibilities of the American governmental system. That system provides no alternative to relying upon the president as the judge and arbiter of the forward course of policy for his administration. It provides no good alternative to reliance upon the great departments for the conduct of executive operations and for the initiation of most policy proposals relating to those operations.[25]

By holding out the promise of a perfect coordinating formula, we have provided a plausible excuse for not facing up to the hard political choices that now confront us. Layers of coordinating machinery can conceal but not cure the defects and contradictions in our governmental system.

If we want coordination, we must first be able to identify and agree on our national goals and priorities and to design programs to accomplish them. Our present mechanisms for national planning and goal-setting work very imperfectly and are in a highly rudimentary stage of development. Solution of the urgent problems confronting America in the 1990s and twenty-first century demands something more than skills in political tactics and public relations. We no longer can afford indiscriminately to fritter away our human and material resources on poorly conceived and often contradictory programs whose major purpose is to pacify competing and conflicting group interests.

The Government and Performance Results Act of 1993 directs agencies to develop strategic plans and performance measurement systems and to "manage for results." The development of individual agency strategic plans cannot provide an effective substitute for a more coherent approach to establishing national goals and priorities.

II

THE POLITICS OF
INSTITUTIONAL TYPE

10

Administrative Agencies

The interplay of competing and often contradictory political, economic, social, and regional forces within our constitutional system and pluralistic society has produced a smorgasbord of institutional types. There is something to suit almost every taste, no matter how exotic. Choices from among this rich assortment are seldom determined by strict application of established organizational "principles." Choices are influenced by a complex of tangible and intangible factors reflecting divergent views about the proper sphere of government activity, politics, institutional folklore, program importance and status, visibility, political and administrative autonomy, and, most important, who should exercise control. The theoretical arguments frequently have little relevance to the real issues. The president, the Congress, the bureaucracy, and the constituencies each judge institutional types from a somewhat different perspective and favor those arrangements they believe will best serve their interests.

The Constitution itself provides few guides for institutional development. Numerous proposals in the Constitutional Convention of 1787 to spell out the details of executive branch structure were rejected. The intent of the Constitution makers can be inferred only from the provisions vesting executive power in the president, including the power to appoint, by and with the advice and consent of the Senate, all officers of the United States, whose appointments are not otherwise provided for in the Constitution, and authorizing the president to "require the opinion in writing, of the principal officer in each of the executive departments, upon any subject relating to the duties of their respective offices." Under the Constitution the Congress may by law vest the appointment of inferior officers, as they think proper, in the courts of law, or in the heads of departments.

The references to the "principal officer in each of the executive departments" and the "heads of departments" are significant. There appears to have been a clear intention that the departments of administration be headed by a single officer. George Washington was expressing a view widely held at the time when he stated that, "Wherever, and whenever one person is found adequate to the discharge of a duty by close application thereto it is worse executed by two persons, and scarcely done at all if three or more are employed therein. . . ."[1] Federalists generally joined with Washington and Hamilton in considering multiheaded administrative agencies to be weak and irresponsible.

In the successive enactments of the Congress establishing executive agencies, there was no departure from the principle of single-headed administration. Some argued that the Treasury Department ought to be administered by a board of commissioners because "the duties of the office of financier were too arduous and too important to be entrusted to one man," but the proposal was rejected.[2]

Although the Constitution is almost wholly silent on the subject of executive branch organization, there seems to be little doubt that the framers intended that all executive functions be grouped under a limited number of single-headed executive departments. James Monroe, as secretary of state, reflected the prevailing concept of executive branch organization when he said:

> I have always thought that every institution, of whatever nature soever it might be, ought to be comprised within some one of the Departments of Government, the chief of which only should be responsible to the Chief Executive Magistrate of the Nation. The establishment of inferior independent departments, the heads of which are not, and ought not to be mem-

bers of the administration, appears to me to be liable to many serious objections. . . . I will mention only, first that the concerns of such inferior departments cannot be investigated and discussed with the same advantage in the meetings and deliberations of the administration, as they might be if the person charged with them was present. The second is that, to remedy this inconvenience, the President would, necessarily, become the head of that department himself. . . .[3]

Until 1913, it was most unusual for agencies to be created outside of the principal departments. A considerable number of commissions were established from time to time to perform special tasks, but these were always a temporary nature. The one notable exception is the incorporation of the Smithsonian Institution provided in the 1846 act, but the Smithsonian was funded initially by the Smithson bequest and, consequently, was looked on as a quasipublic institution rather than as a government agency. The first major departures from the accepted pattern of organization came with the establishment of the Civil Service Commission in 1883 and the Interstate Commerce Commission in 1887. In the case of the ICC the Congress did not break completely with tradition. The secretary of the interior was given authority to approve the number and compensation of all commission personnel, except the secretary to the commission. A link between the ICC and the executive department was maintained by requiring that the commission's annual reports be submitted to the secretary. Independent status was not accorded to the ICC until 1889, when the Congress granted the secretary of the interior's request to be relieved of his supervisory responsibilities. Although the concept of an integrated executive branch structure is accepted in principle, it has encountered strong opposition from those seeking independence and autonomy for programs benefitting their interests. Ronald C. Moe has observed that "the opposition to an integrated executive branch tends to be pluralistic in approach, narrow in its interests, and generally seeks an exception to a general rule instead of promoting its own rule."[4]

Hubert Humphrey described our constitutional system as "a Government of pressures, outside pressures, working on inside people."[5] Outside pressures began to mold and shape executive branch structure as early as the 1860s. The U. S. Agricultural Society sought the establishment of a Department of Agriculture to place "agriculture upon a plane of equality with the other executive departments."[6] The National Association of School Superintendents lobbied for a Department of Education, and the Knights of Labor lobbied for a Department of Labor. In response to these constituency pressures, the Congress created three departments of less than cabinet rank headed by commissioners: Agriculture (1862), Education (1867), and Labor (1888). The Department of Agriculture was given cabinet rank in 1889 and the Department of Labor was made a constituent of the Department of Commerce and Labor in 1903. The Department of Commerce and Labor was divided into two separate executive departments in 1913.

Restraints on the organization of agencies independent of the executive departments began to crumble with the establishment of the Federal Reserve Board and Board of Mediation and Conciliation in 1913 and practically disappeared during World War I. World War I also witnessed the first significant use of the corporate form of organization. Except for the War Finance Corporation, which was created by the Congress, World War I corporations such as the Shipping Board, Food Administration, and War Trade Board were chartered under the general incorporation laws of either the states or the District of Columbia. Federal control was maintained over the corporations mainly through the power to appoint directors and such supervision as might be exercised by the Cabinet officer who organized the corporation. The corporate form of organization did not achieve legitimacy until the 1940s, although it was widely employed during the Depression of the 1930s, when such alphabet agencies as the RFC, HOLC, TVA, CCC, FDIC, USHA, and RACC achieved considerable notoriety.[7] Many believed that only war or depression could justify resort to the corporate device.

By 1937 the President's Committee on Administrative Management was able to identify more than a hundred separately organized establishments and agencies presumably reporting to the president. President Franklin Roosevelt endorsed the committee's recommendation that the country return to first principles and organize the government's activities within twelve major executive departments. Roosevelt contended that this reorganization was necessary to "bring many little bureaucracies under broad coordinated democratic authority."[8]

We have made some progress since 1937 in reducing the number of independent agencies, but the *1995–1996 Government Manual* shows that there are still at least sixty-one agencies organized outside the fourteen executive departments. If there were added to the fifty-eight mixed-ownership government corporations, government-sponsored enterprises, private corporations organized and financed by the government to furnish contractual services to federal agencies, and intergovernmental bodies, the decrease in the number of independent agencies since 1937 would be even smaller.

The number and variety of institutional arrangements presently used by the federal government almost defies classification. Each major grouping contains important subcategories, and significant differences may be identified within any of the subcategories. The following classification makes no claim to scientific exactness; it is intended merely to identify significant organizational types. The word *independent* means only independence from an executive department, and does not imply independence from the president or the executive branch. In popular usage the word has come to have the latter meaning, particularly when applied to the independent regulatory commissions. The listings under each of the headings are not necessarily complete.

EXECUTIVE DEPARTMENTS

State, Treasury, Defense, Justice, Interior, Agriculture, Commerce, Labor, Health and Human Services, Housing and Urban Development, Transportation, Energy, Education, Veterans.

EXECUTIVE OFFICE OF THE PRESIDENT

White House Office, Council of Economic Advisers, Council on Environmental Quality, Office of Policy Development, National Security Council, Office of Science and Technology Policy, Office of Administration, Office of Management and Budget, Special Representative for Trade Negotiations, Office of National Drug Control Policy.

INDEPENDENT AGENCIES

Single-headed: ACTION, Central Intelligence Agency, Environmental Protection Agency, Federal Emergency Management Agency, General Services Administration, National Aeronautics and Space Administration, National Credit Union Administration, Office of Personnel Management, Peace Corps, Selective Service System, Small Business Administration, U.S. Arms Control and Disarmament Agency, U.S. Information Agency, Veterans Administration, Social Security Administration.

Multiheaded: American Battle Monuments Commission, Appalachian Regional Commission, Board for International Broadcasting, Commission on Civil Rights, Commission on Fine Arts, Farm Credit Administration, Federal Labor Relations Authority, Federal Maritime Commission, Federal Mediation and Conciliation Service, Merit Systems Protection Board, National Capital Planning Commission, National Mediation Board, National Transportation Safety Board, Panama Canal Commission, Postal Rate Commission, U.S. International Trade Commission, U.S. Postal Service, Federal Housing Finance Board.

FOUNDATIONS

National Science Foundation, National Foundation on Arts and Humanities, African Development Foundation, Inter-American Foundation.

INSTITUTIONS AND INSTITUTES

Smithsonian Institution.

HHS: National Institutes of Health, National Cancer Institute, National Heart Institute, National Institute of Allergy and Infectious Diseases, National Institute of Arthritis and Metabolic Diseases, National Institute of Dental Research, National Institute of Neurological Diseases, National Institute of General Medical Sciences, National Institute of Child Health and Human Development, National Eye Institute, National Institute on Aging.

Commerce: Institutes for Environmental Research, Institute for Basic Standards, Institute for Materials Research, Institute for Applied Technology.

State: Foreign Service Institute.

Justice: National Institute for Law Enforcement and Criminal Justice.

REGULATORY COMMISSIONS

Federal Communications Commission, Federal Home Loan Bank Board, Federal Maritime Commission, Federal Reserve Board, Federal Trade Commission, National Labor Relations Board, Securities and Exchange Commission, Consumer Product Safety Commission, Commodity Futures Trading Commission, Nuclear Regulatory Commission, Federal Energy Regulatory Commission, Federal Election Commission, Equal Opportunity Commission, Occupational Health and Safety Review Commission.

GOVERNMENT CORPORATIONS

Wholly Owned Corporations Under Executive Department Single-headed: St. Lawrence Seaway Development Corporation, Government National Mortgage Association.

Multiheaded: Commodity Credit Corporation, Federal Crop Insurance Corporation, Federal Financing Bank, Federal Prison Industries, Inc., Federal Savings and Loan Insurance Corporation,

Pension Benefit Guaranty Corporation, Neighborhood Reinvestment Corporation, Pennsylvania Avenue Development Corporation, Solar Energy and Energy Conservation Bank, U. S. Enrichment Corporation, National Corporation for Community and Public Service.

Wholly Owned Independent Corporations Multiheaded: Federal Deposit Insurance Corporation,[9] Export-Import Bank of Washington, Tennessee Valley Authority, Inter-American Foundation, Overseas Private Investment Corporation, Panama Canal Commissions.

Mixed-Ownership Government Corporations Multiheaded: Rural Telephone Bank, Agricultural Credit Banks, Resolution Trust Corporation.

INTERGOVERNMENTAL ORGANIZATIONS

Regional: Appalachian Regional Commission, Delaware River Basin Commission, Pacific Northwest Council.

TWILIGHT ZONE

Federal Reserve Banks, Farm Credit Banks, Federal Home Loan Banks, Federal National Mortgage Association, National Home Ownership Foundation, Corporation for Public Broadcasting, National Parks Foundation, National Railroad Passenger Corporation, Securities Investor Protection Corporation, Student Loan Marketing Association, U.S. Railway Association, Legal Services Corporation, National Consumer Cooperative Bank, Resolution Funding Corporation, Financing Corporation.

PRIVATE INSTITUTIONS ORGANIZED AND FINANCED BY THE FEDERAL GOVERNMENT TO PROVIDE CONTRACTUAL SERVICES

Independent Nonprofit Corporations: Aerospace Corporation, Institute for Defense Analyses, Logistics Management Institute, Rand Corporation.

University-Affiliated Research Centers: Applied Physics Laboratory, Brookhaven Laboratory, MITRE, Lincoln Laboratory, Los Alamos National Laboratory, etc.

Research Center Operated by Private Industry: Oak Ridge National Laboratory.

No general federal laws define the form of organization, powers, and immunities of the various institutional types. Each possesses only those power enumerated in its enabling act or, in the case of organizations created by executive action, set forth by executive order or in a contract. Whatever special attributes may have been acquired by the various organizational classes are entirely a product of precedent, as reflected in successive enactments by the Congress, judicial interpretations, and public, agency, and congressional attitudes. For some of the organizations, public attitudes tend to be based more on folklore than on fact.

Few of these institutional types emerged full-blown in their present form. There is very little evidence of conscious thought and planning in the development of new institutions. The approach generally has been highly pragmatic and eclectic. The process has been more derivative than creative. The Interstate Commerce Commission was established in the image of the regulatory organizations then existing in a number of states. The search for an agency with sufficient operating and financial flexibility to conduct the business enterprises undertaken in World War I was ended by borrowing the corporate form of organization from private enterprise. As we have indicated previously, most of the World War I corporations were chartered under the general incorporation laws of states or the District of Columbia. These laws often prescribed forms of organization and financing not particularly well adapted to a public body, and subterfuges were sometimes required to provide pro forma compliance. Until the Panama Railroad Company was reincorporated under federal charter in 1948, it was necessary to issue each director one share of stock to comply with the provisions of the corporation's New York charter. The foundation represents the culmination of efforts by scientists to duplicate within the federal government an organization structure devised for institutions of higher learning. The "captive" corporation was born of improvisations by the Office of Scientific Research and Development

(OSRD) in World War II to meet its unique requirements. The Defense Department and the National Institutes of Health inherited certain contractual arrangements when the OSRD was liquidated after the war. Inherited factors have been of considerable significance in influencing relationships within the executive branch, internal organization, mode of operations, method of financing, and public and congressional responses.

Some institutional types are more acceptable than others because they have been borrowed from and are identified in the public mind with nongovernment institutions. This has proved to be of critical importance when the federal government has entered into new and controversial areas of activity. Harold Laski has noted that "most Americans have a sense of deep discomfort when they are asked to support the positive state. . . . They tend to feel that what is done by a government institution is bound to be less well done than if it were undertaken by individuals, whether alone or in the form of private corporations."[10] If a service cannot be performed by private enterprise, then obviously the next best thing is an organization that appears to be insulated against "politics" and that looks as nearly as possible like a private institution. This feeling is evident in the argument raised by the chair of the Federal Deposit Insurance Corporation against legislation proposed in 1960 to subject the corporation to budget control. Chair Wolcott contended that "an agency having responsibility for protection of the Nation's money supply should be independent while remaining in the framework of Government. It must be part of the Government in order to escape private pressures; yet, within the Government it must be free of political pressures."[11] Public distrust of government is somewhat alleviated when programs are administered by corporations or foundations and these agencies are organized in such a way that they are of, but not in, the government. The same distrust underlies arguments for the use of nonprofit intermediaries and reprivatization.

Analysis of statutory provisions reveals that the Congress has followed a reasonably consistent pattern with respect to the organization structure, powers, and immunities of each of the major institutional types. Critical differences among the types are to be found in the provisions of law relating to composition of the directing authority (single-headed or multiheaded), qualifications for appointment, procedures for the appointment and removal of principal officers, method of financing, budget and audit controls, personnel regulations, and advisory councils and committees. These provisions determine the degree of organizational and operating autonomy and in large measure control an agency's relationship to the president, the Congress, and its clientele.

The one official guide to the relative status and protocol ranking of executive agencies is to be found in the Executive Schedule Pay Rates. Agencies are by no means equal in terms of their prestige within the executive establishment or standing in the Congress and the community. The significance of their heads being included in Level II rather than in Level III goes beyond the mere $10,500 difference in salary. The infighting can be bitter when amendments to the Executive Schedule are being considered, and some congressional favorites, such as the director of the Federal Bureau of Investigation, have been rewarded with higher rankings than their position would seem to warrant.

The following pecking order is established by the Executive Schedule:

Level I: Executive departments.

Level II: Major agencies of the Executive Office of the President, such as the Office of Management and Budget; major independent agencies, such as the National Aeronautics and Space Administration, Central Intelligence Agency, Federal Reserve; Military departments, Agency for International Development.

Level III: Independent agencies, such as the General Services Administration, Small Business Administration; major regulatory agencies, such as the Interstate Commerce Commission and Federal Communication Commission; government corporations, such as the Federal Deposit Insurance Corporation, Export-Import Bank, Tennessee Valley Authority; foundations; major administrations or bureaus within executive departments, such as the Federal Bureau of Investigation, Comptroller of the Currency, and Highway Administration.

Level IV: Independent agencies, such as the Selective Service System, Equal Employment Opportunity Commission, National Transportation Safety Board, St. Lawrence Seaway Development Corporation; bureau heads within executive departments.

Level V: Minor agencies, such as Foreign Claims Settlement Commission; heads and deputy heads of principal constituent units within executive departments and agencies.

Next to the top pay levels, heavy sedans are the most eagerly sought-after status symbols. Under Office of Management and Budget regulations, heavy sedans are reserved for heads of executive departments, the ambassador to the United Nations, and chiefs of Class I diplomatic missions. All others must ride in medium or light sedans.

Executive Departments. The executive departments' position at the apex of the organizational hierarchy remains unchallenged, although the principal assistants to the president now rank above cabinet officers in public prestige and influence. Major independent agencies such as the Social Security Administration and the General Services Administration may employ more people and spend more money than some of the executive departments, but both the White House and the Congress make subtle distinctions between the heads of these agencies and cabinet secretaries. Although there is no statutory basis for the distinctions, other than the Executive Schedule Pay Rates, those who have served in both capacities can testify that the distinctions are real and important.

No exact criteria have ever been prescribed for establishing executive departments. A National Academy of Public Administration panel recommended guidelines which should be considered by Congress in evaluating legislation to establish an executive department. The panel proposed that the following basic questions be asked:

• Does the agency or set of programs serve a broad national goal or purpose not exclusively identified with a single class, occupation, discipline, region or sector of society?

- Would a cabinet department increase the "visibility" and thereby substantially strengthen political and public support for programs?
- Is there evidence that becoming a cabinet department would provide better analysis, expression, and advocacy of the needs and programs that constitute the agency's responsibilities?
- Is there evidence that elevation to a cabinet department would improve service?
- Is a cabinet department required better to coordinate or consolidate programs scattered throughout the executive branch?
- Is there evidence that the increase of political authority in a secretary's office would improve internal administration?
- Would elevation to a cabinet department help to recruit and maintain better qualified leadership?
- Is there evidence that a cabinet department would facilitate more uniform achievement of broad, cross-cutting policy goals?
- Would a cabinet department provide a better policy and management guide to the president?
- Would a cabinet department improve accountability to the president and Congress.[12]

The House Committee on Government Reform and Oversight urged that executive departments should be limited to those entities "with programs high in policy content and decisive issues" which require coordination by the president and his staff.[13]

Executive departments do symbolize basic national commitments and values, and for this reason the Congress has responded slowly to demands for new departments. Creation of a new department is always regarded as an historic occasion. The reorganization establishing the Department of Defense in 1949 marked the first change in the top executive branch structure since 1913, although this represented more of a merger of the previously existing War and Navy departments than the birth of a new department. The first genuinely new executive department was Health, Education, and Welfare, established in 1953. This was followed by the Department of Housing and Urban Development in 1965, the Department of Transportation in 1966, the Department of Energy in 1977, and the Department of Education in 1979, and the Department of Veterans Affairs in 1988.

Each of the executive departments created since the Civil War, except Energy, Commerce, and Transportation, was required to serve an apprenticeship as a noncabinet department or agency before being elevated to executive department status. Proposals to convert the Federal Security Agency, the predecessor of HEW, and the Housing and Home Finance Agency, the predecessor of HUD, to executive departments were flatly turned down by the Congress on more than one occasion before they were adopted. The first bill to establish a Department of Transportation was introduced in the Congress in 1890.[14] Seventy-six years were to go by before the department became a reality.

Except for such aberrations as the Tenure of Office Act, the Congress has observed faithfully the organizational precepts laid down by the framers of the Constitution in creating executive departments. Congress has not felt bound by these precepts in dealing with agencies below the executive department level.

Each executive department has a single head. No restrictions are placed on the president's authority to appoint or remove department heads. The statutes differ in specifying presidential authority to direct and supervise a cabinet officer. The secretary of defense is "subject to direction by the president," and the secretary of state "shall conduct the business of the Department in such manner as the president shall direct." Other acts are silent on the subject of presidential direction. Regardless of the statutory language, Congress recognizes that the heads of executive departments are the "president's men and women."

Except for a few prerogatives, such as the right to request a formal opinion of the attorney general, there is little that a cabinet officer can do as a matter of law that cannot also be done by an independent agency head. Budget Bureau witnesses were hard pressed to explain the legal differences between a Housing and Home Finance Agency and a Department of Housing and Urban Development. The differences have their roots in custom and tradition and cannot be discovered in law books.

The cabinet itself is a creature of custom and tradition without a constitutional or statutory basis. The cabinet has always functioned at the pleasure of the president and in the manner of his choosing. Whatever the role assigned to the cabinet as a collective entity— and this has varied greatly from one president to another—membership in the cabinet is of tremendous importance as a symbol of status and rank. Appointment as head of an executive department has always been assumed to confer cabinet membership without further presidential designation. Of the original cabinet, all except the attorney general were department heads. The attorney general was included as the government's legal adviser. The Department of Justice became an executive department in 1870.

Others may be invited by the president to attend cabinet meetings or accorded cabinet rank. These have included the vice president, the ambassador to the United Nations, the director of OMB, as well as from time to time various special assistants to the president. There are shades of difference between those who are invited to attend cabinet meetings and those who are present because of the office they hold. Under Eisenhower, only the vice president and the heads of executive departments had high-backed chairs, with their names on engraved plaques, at the cabinet table.

Invitees are reluctant to volunteer opinions unless the president specifically calls on them. In 1956 the Housing and Home Finance administrator was invited to discuss a subject of vital concern to his agency. But he was seated in the back row against the wall, and President Eisenhower appeared to be wholly unaware of his presence.

Except for those in the inner circle, cabinet status does not necessarily translate into easier access to the president. It does generally enhance an agency's bargaining position in inter agency disputes and result in more media coverage for the secretary.

The gradations that exist within the executive hierarchy also may be found among the executive departments. Executive departments are by no means equal in power, prestige, or closeness to the president. The presidential inner circle is generally composed of cabinet members without strong constituency ties, the secretaries of state, defense, and treasury, and the attorney general, to whom the president looks for expert advice, rather than for political support. President Nixon formalized the "inner cabinet" by his designation of the secretaries of state and treasury and the director of OMB as assistants to the president, and the secretaries of agriculture, HEW, and HUD as presidential counselors. As we have seen, departments differ significantly in personality and outlook, administrative habits, and relationships to the president, the Congress, and the outside community.

Executive Office of the President. Relatively youthful upstarts in the Executive Office of the President have stolen some of the glamour from the cabinet secretaries. Such Level II luminaries as the director of the Office of Management and Budget (OMB) wield more power and receive a greater press coverage than the heads of most executive departments. In arguing for Senate confirmation of the director of OMB, the House Committee on Government Operations emphasized "the reality" that the director "with his vast power and importance, holds and office of superior rank."[15] As these executive office institutions have approached middle age, their "passion for anonymity" has waned noticeably. But, contrary to popular belief, there is no special magic associated with location in the Executive Office of the President. Heads of executive departments are vested with a certain status by reason of the office they hold; this is not true of those in the Executive Office. The directors of some Executive Office units would like to give the impression that they are the powers behind the throne, but they are often so far behind the throne as to be almost invisible.

Classic concepts of organization have not been observed as rigorously by the Congress in establishing the constituent elements of the Executive Office of the President as they have been in the case of executive departments. When the Executive Office of the President was created in 1939, it contained one multiheaded unit, the National Resources Planning Board. Today the Executive Office includes one agency headed by an interagency committee: the National Security Council. The Council of Economic Advisers (CEA) and the Council on Environmental Quality are also collegiate bodies, but Reorganization Plan No. 9 of 1953 transferred to the CEA chairman the function of reporting to the president with respect to the Council's work.

The Budget and Accounting Act of 1921 recognized that the relationship between a president and his budget director must necessarily be one of intimacy and trust. Consequently, the president was given the power to appoint the director and assistant director without Senate confirmation. Congressman Good pointed out during the floor debate on the act that "these offices would be so peculiarly the president's staff, the president's force, the president, without being questioned with his regard to his appointment, should appoint the men whom he could trust to do his will in the preparation of the budget. . . ."[16] This special status was revoked in 1974, a casualty of Watergate and resentment toward President Nixon's use of impoundment to curtail or discontinue programs authorized by the Congress. Except for White House staff, the heads of the principal Executive Office agencies are now all subject to Senate confirmation. The Congress has refrained from establishing terms of office, or, except for members of the Council of Economic Advisers and the Council on Environmental Quality, specifying qualifications for appointment.

Congress has been unwilling to give the president a free hand with respect to the organization of the Executive Office of the President. Most department heads now have authority to organize and reorganize their agencies without formal congressional approval, but the president lacks comparable power. President Eisenhower recommended in his 1961 Budget Message that the president be authorized to reorganize the Executive Office so as to "ensure that future presidents will possess the latitude to design the working structure of the Presidential Office as they deem necessary for the effective conduct of their duties under the Constitution and the laws." A bill was introduced for this purpose, but no further action was taken, partly because of a conspicuous absence of enthusiasm on the part of some of the more important people in the Bureau of the Budget who wanted to preserve the bureau's unique position as primus inter pares.

The structure of the Executive Office of the President has not always reflected the Committee on Administrative Management's intention that no institutional resources be provided within the office other than those the president found essential to advise and assist him in carrying out functions that he could not delegate. Congressional pressure to provide visibility and enhanced status for favored programs diverted the Executive Office of the President from its exclusive concern with presidential business by establishing within it the Office of Economic Opportunity, the National Council on Marine Resources and Engineering Development, and the Council on Environmental Quality. The president was similarly motivated in recommending the establishment of the Special Office for Drug Abuse. As a consequence, recent presidents have tended to look to the White House office, not to the institutional agencies within the Executive Office of the President, for necessary staff support.[17]

The implications of Executive Office organization for the effective functioning of our constitutional system and the distribution of power among the three coequal branches of government are as yet insufficiently recognized. Given the present involvement of White House staff in functions formerly performed by career personnel within the Executive Office, the exodus of senior staff upon the inauguration of a new president could threaten the continuity of government. The president ought to have the capability to adapt the Executive Office to his perceived needs, but he should not be permitted, in the process, to ignore the needs of future presidents, the Congress, and the people.

Independent Agencies. Columnist David Lawrence was reflecting a common misconception when he wrote, "Basically the RFC is supposed to be an 'independent agency' and not part of the executive department or the White House, but a creature of Congress, *as are all other independent Boards and Agencies*" (italics supplied).[18] The Constitution makes no provision for a fourth branch of government, independent of the president, or for limitations on the president's exercise of executive powers. Whether or not the president can exercise his powers effectively is another matter. Some of the independent agencies have been so structured as to blunt the president's powers and provide de facto independence.

Independent agencies come in all shapes, sizes, and forms. Both the Small Business Administration and the Federal Aviation Agency, before its incorporation in the Department of Transportation, were spun off from the Department of Commerce in an effort to escape an unsympathetic operating environment. Except for the Environmental Protection Agency, none of the independent agencies at present are embryo executive departments comparable to the Housing and Home Finance Agency. As we have indicated, the General Services Administration and the Social Security Administration do exceed smaller executive departments in size, measured in personnel and budget. Some, such as the General Services Administration, are expressly subject to presidential direction.

As far as independent agencies are concerned, the Congress does not believe that the injunctions against multiheaded agencies and limitations on the president's powers of appointment and removal apply. Several have been given all the trappings of a regulatory commission, including multimember boards selected on a bipartisan basis with fixed, overlapping terms of office. Qualifications for appointment may be spelled out in detail, as for the Small Business Administrator and members of the Farm Credit Board.

The U.S. Postal Service is the most independent of the independent agencies and is practically a law unto itself. The Postal Service is defined by law as "an independent establishment of the executive branch of the United States," but in all other respects it is endowed with the powers and characteristics of a wholly owned government corporation. The service is headed by an eleven-member part-time board of governors, appointed by the president with Senate confirmation. Governors serve for nine-year overlapping terms. The service's chief executive officer, the postmaster general, is appointed by and serves at the pleasure of the board.

The U.S. Postal Service is not subject to the Government Corporation Control Act or the controls normally applied to wholly owned government corporations. The Postal Service Act (Public Law 91–375) includes language comparable to that in Section 102 of the Government Corporation Control Act requiring annual submission of a business-type budget to the Office of Management and Budget but does not authorize OMB to amend or modify the budget. There is no requirement that the budget be transmitted to the Congress. As it is now written, the act creates the impression of control where in fact none exists. Indeed, elsewhere the Postal Service Act provides specifically that "no federal law dealing with public or federal contracts, property, works, employees, budgets, or funds . . . shall apply to the exercise of the powers of the Postal Service."

The Postal Service is intended to be self-financing, except for reimbursement of any "public service costs" incurred in providing "a maximum degree of effective and regular postal service nationwide." The service is authorized to borrow money and to issue and sell such obligations as it determines necessary in amounts not to exceed $10 billion outstanding at any one time. Avoidance of the "annual battle between the Post Office Department and the Bureau of the Budget, which notoriously results in limitations upon funds available to be appropriated" was cited by the Senate Post Office and Civil Service Committee as "the basic purpose in authorizing the sale of bonds by the Postal Service and exempting it from budget control."[19]

When he proposed that the Post Office Department be reorganized as an autonomous and independent noncabinet Postal Service, President Nixon contended that an efficient postal service could not be obtained without insulating the Postal Service "from direct control by the president, the Bureau of the Budget and the Congress" and "partisan political pressure."[20] This argument reflects distrust of our governmental institutions and loss of faith in the democratic process.

Institutions, Foundations, and Institutes. It seems somehow fitting that the Smithsonian Institution should have an organization charter worthy of display with other museum pieces. The Smithsonian Institution remains *sui generis*, and does so for reasons that shall become evident. Purists would find it difficult to reconcile the organizational arrangements established for the Smithsonian with the constitutional doctrine of separation of powers. Appointing authority is vested in the speaker of the House of Representatives and the president of the Senate, seemingly in direct violation of Article 2, Section 2 of the Constitution.

The Smithsonian has an "establishment" composed of the president, the vice president, the chief justice, and the heads of executive departments, but with no known functions, other than as the institution's "incorporators." The business of the institution is conducted by a board of regents consisting of the vice president, the chief justice, three members of the Senate appointed by the president of the Senate, three members of the House of Representatives appointed by the speaker, and six other persons appointed by joint resolution of the Senate and the House. Presumably the president could veto the joint resolution, but this is the extent of his powers over appointments to the board of regents. The institution's principal executive officer, the secretary, is selected by the board.

Congress has appropriated to the institution the annual interest on the $541,379.63 Smithson bequest, but this income constitutes an infinitesimal part of the institution's budget. Today, approximately 90 percent of the Smithsonian's funds come from either direct appropriations by the Congress or grants by federal agencies. Private financing has a symbolic value, and civil service restrictions applicable to most Smithsonian employees do not apply to the secretary and others who are paid from private funds.

In holding that the Smithsonian Institution was not subject to the Freedom of Information Act and the Privacy Act, the Department of Justice concluded that while not "free of doubt," the Smithsonian was not an agency of the United States of the type the Congress intended to be covered. The Department of Justice found that the Smithsonian was "so uniquely distinctive a fusion of public and private cooperation and of joint action by all three traditional branches of government that it seems fairly evident that the Congress could not have meant it to be treated as a traditional agency covered by the three statutes."[21]

Although problems of relationships within the executive branch have been minimal, the Smithsonian's ambiguous status has stood in the way of its being assigned responsibility for the National Archives and other federal programs related to the arts and humanities. The mixing of private and federal funds has led to practices that have been criticized by the General Accounting Office and the Congress.[22] The Smithsonian has used its private funds to launch programs without congressional approval.

Foundations and institutes have become the preferred form of organization for institutions making grants to local governments, universities, nonprofit organizations, and individuals for research in the natural and social sciences, or artistic endeavors. The unique characteristic of these organizations is an elaborate superstructure of advisory arrangements designed to give representatives of grantee groups maximum influence over the allocation of funds. In Chapter 1 we described the structure of the National Science Foundation. The National Foundation on the Arts and Humanities creates the appearance of a single organization, although, in fact, it consists of two independent entities: the National Endowment for the Arts and the National Endowment for the Humanities. Each endowment is headed by a chairperson appointed by the president, subject to Senate confirmation, for a four-year term. The chairmen, however, cannot approve or disapprove grant applications without first obtaining the recommendations of a council. The National Council on the Arts is composed of the secretary of the Smithsonian Institution and twenty-four members appointed by the president for six-year terms. In making appointments, the president is requested to give consideration to the recommendations of leading national organizations in each branch of the arts. The National Council on the Humanities has twenty-six members, also appointed for six-year terms. Recommendations for appointments are to be submitted by the leading national organizations concerned with the humanities.

A National Advisory Council is attached to each of the institutes under the National Institutes of Health. The councils consist of twelve members, appointed for four-year terms by the surgeon general, with the approval of the secretary of health and human services. Members must be leaders in fundamental sciences, medical sciences, and public affairs, and six must be specialists in the field covered by the institute. No grants may be made without council approval.

The title "institute" has been used for agencies engaged in research and training, but the name has had no significance except to provide a better academic standing.

Regulatory and Claims Commissions, Administrative Conference. The independent regulatory commissions and claims commissions have evolved into what the President's Committee on Administrative Management termed "a headless 'fourth branch' of the Government." From what were intended originally to be somewhat differently structured executive agencies, these commissions have been transformed into "arms of the Congress" by constituency pressures, custom, and Supreme Court decisions.

When the Interstate Commerce Commission (ICC) was established in 1887, the Congress did not believe it was violating sacred writ by giving the secretary of the interior powers over the commission's personnel. In 1902 there was strong sentiment in the Congress for transferring the ICC to the new Department of Commerce and Labor.[23] No conflict was seen in designating the secretary of the treasury as chairman of the Federal Reserve Board in 1913. The secretaries of agriculture, interior, and war constituted the Federal Power Commission when it was established in 1920. By deliberate congressional choice, regulatory functions under the Packers and Stockyards Act of 1921 were assigned to the secretary of agriculture rather than to the Federal Trade Commission. Concepts drawing sharp distinctions between regulatory and executive functions are of relatively recent origin and, to some extent, are an historical accident.

Marver Bernstein has defined *independence*, as the term is applied to the regulatory commissions, as relating to one or more of the following conditions: "location outside an executive department; some measure of independence from supervision by the president or a cabinet secretary; immunity from the president's discretionary power to remove members of independent commissions from office."[24] The last condition listed by Bernstein has been of key importance.

The ICC Act authorized the president to remove any commissioner "for inefficiency, neglect of duty, or malfeasance in office." Similar language is found in almost all of the statutes creating regulatory commissions, although it has been omitted for some performing exclusively judicial functions. There is indisputable evidence, however, that the language that the Supreme Court has construed to be a limitation on the president's powers was intended by the Congress to be just the opposite. The Tenure of Office Act of 1867 was still in effect when Congress enacted the ICC Act. By including a provision authorizing the president to remove commissioners, even though only for specified causes, the Congress conferred on the president considerably more latitude than he had with respect to other executive officers appointed with the consent of the Senate.

The Supreme Court decisions in the case of *Humphrey's Executor v United States*, 295 US 602 (1935), and *Wiener v United States*, 357 US 349 (1958), have provided the legal foundation for the theory of commission independence. In the *Humphrey* case, the Court drew a distinction between an agency that performs quasi-legislative and quasi-judicial functions, such as the Federal Trade Commission, and an agency primarily concerned with administrative or executive duties. Justice Sutherland held that the Federal Trade Commission "to the extent that it exercises any executive function, as distinguished from executive power in the constitutional sense, it does so in the discharge of its quasi-judicial and quasi-legislative powers, or as an agency of the legislative or judicial branches of government." It was the Court's unanimous view that the president could remove an FTC commissioner for the causes enumerated in the statute and for no other reasons. The Court went beyond the *Humphrey* case when it ruled in the *Wiener* case that President Eisenhower could not remove a member of a claims commission, even though the Congress had not specifically limited the president's removal powers.

Regardless of the Supreme Court decisions, until 1973 the regulatory commissions in some areas enjoyed less independence than some executive agencies. The president, through OMB review of budgets, legislation, and data questionnaires, and Department of Justice control of litigation, was able significantly to influence commission policies, administration, and operations. The Congress in 1973 overrode White House objections and amended the Alaska pipeline bill (1) to authorize the Federal Trade Commission to represent itself in civil court proceedings, and (2) to transfer authority for review of independent regulatory commission data requests under the Federal Reporting Services Act from OMB to the General Accounting Office.

Congressional emphasis on independence was reflected in the exclusion of regulatory commissions from the president's reorganization authority. Until 1977 such a limitation was not contained in the Reorganization Statute. To protect further the independence of regulatory programs, the Senate Committee on Governmental Affairs recommended the following: (1) independent regulatory commissions should conduct and control their own substantive litigation, except for litigation taking place in the Supreme Court; (2) independent regulatory commissions should transmit any budget request to the Congress at the same time such messages are submitted to the Office of Management and Budget, as now provided for the Commodity Futures Trading Commission, Consumer Product Safety Commission, and the Interstate Commerce Commission; (3) legislative communications from an independent commission to the Congress should not be subject to prior clearance by the Office of Management and Budget; and (4) top staff officials at the independent regulatory commissions should be selected wholly on the basis of merit, and the selection decision by the agency should not be subject to clearance by officials outside the agency.

To increase political accountability, the Senate committee proposed that the heads of other executive departments be accorded powers comparable to those now vested in the secretary of energy. The secretary of energy is authorized to intervene in proceedings before the Federal Energy Regulatory Commission that have a significant policy impact and to initiate proposed rulemaking.[25]

Presidents are willing to concede a degree of, but not total, independence to the regulatory commissions. President Kennedy stressed the continuing responsibilities of the president with respect to the operations of these agencies in his message on "Regulatory Agencies of Our Government."[26] He asserted that, "the president's responsibilities require him to know and evaluate how efficiently these agencies dispatch their business, including any lack of prompt decision of the thousands of cases which they are called upon to decide, any failure to evolve policy in areas where they have been charged by the Congress to do so, or any other difficulties that militate against the performance of their statutory duties."

President Kennedy did agree that intervention in individual cases would be improper, unless the executive departments appeared formally as an intervenor in a particular proceeding.

Indirect means may be employed, however, to convey the president's views to the commission on an individual case. President Eisenhower sent a letter to the chairman of the Senate Foreign Relations Committee urging that "the United States should promptly take whatever action might be necessary to clear the way for commencement of the project [St. Lawrence Seaway]," and forwarded a copy of his letter to the chairman of the Federal Power Commission.[27] The project could not proceed until the commission approved a pending New York–Ontario power application. The commission got the message and acted favorably.

Evidence has yet to be produced that demonstrates that an autonomous commission most effectively ensures protection of the public interest. On the contrary, the evidence would indicate that "independence" makes the commissions more susceptible to industry influence and congressional intervention. Roger Noll concludes that "independence serves primarily to insulate the agency from the general public."[28]

Many researchers have isolated and confirmed the regulatory commission syndrome. The symptoms of this geriatric malady are disorientation and growing inability to distinguish between the public interest and the interests of those subject to regulation. Noll brands the agencies "as a form of legal cartel for regulated firms."[29]

Similar problems arise from a commission's intimate involvement with the legal profession and the practitioners appearing before it. The domination of the commissions by lawyers can be seen in the case-by-case approach to regulation, emphasis on adversary proceedings, and complex judicialized processes and procedures.

Government Corporations. Institutional types are seldom loved or hated for themselves alone. Partisan heat may be aroused by the substance of a program or the personality of the administrator, but rarely by the institutional type. The one notable exception is the government corporation. Although emotions are not as strong as they once were, there are still those who regard the corporate device as good or evil, regardless of how it is used or the purpose it serves.[30]

No responsible person or organization has ever demanded that all departments, bureaus, boards, or commissions be abolished. But the Congress from time to time has been flooded with mail demanding that all government corporations be abolished, and bills have been introduced with this objective. At the other extreme are a number of businesspersons and scholars who attribute almost mystic qualities to the corporation and find in it a panacea for most of the ills that beset the government.

The government corporation has become a symbol, and symbols stir strong, and often ambivalent, emotions. At one and the same time the corporation represents the evils of government in business and the virtues of business efficiency and organization in government. The latter view was embraced by the president's Commission on Postal Organization, chaired by Frederick R. Kappel, retired chairman of the board of directors of American Telephone and Telegraph Company, which advocated conversion of the post office from an executive department to a government corporation as a means of solving the postal "crisis" and ensuring that the postal service would be run as a "business."[31] Differences of opinion about the value and uses of government corporations are not necessarily a reflection of differences in economic and political ideologies.

Preconceptions have so colored most discussions of government corporations that folklore is often mistaken for fact. Among the most commonly accepted myths are the following: (1) incorporation by itself gives a government corporation certain basic authorities not possessed by other government agencies; (2) a government corporation is not a part of the executive branch but an agency of the Congress; (3) a government corporation is by definition autonomous; and (4) a board of directors is an indispensable attribute of a government corporation. None of these is true.

States have enacted general incorporation laws, but the federal government has not. The distinguishing attributes of a U.S. government corporation are not inherent in the corporate form but stem solely from specific grants of power that have been customarily included in corporate charters enacted by the Congress. The Government Corporation Control Act is, as its name implies, a control act and confers no authority on a corporation.

The government corporation is essentially an empirical response to problems posed by increasing reliance on government-created business enterprises and business-type operations to accomplish public purposes. The United States acquired the Panama Railroad Company when it purchased the assets of the French Canal Company in 1904, but it was not until World War I that the U.S. government became a business entrepreneur on a large scale and established the first wholly owned government corporations.

To accomplish its wartime objectives, the government found it necessary to construct and operate a merchant fleet, to build, rent, and sell houses, to buy and sell sugar and grain, to lend money, and to engage in other commercial enterprises. All these activities had certain unique characteristics that clearly set them apart from what up to then had been construed as "normal" and acceptable government functions: (1) the government was dealing with the public as a businessperson rather than a sovereign; (2) users, rather than the general taxpayer, were expected to bear a major share of the cost for goods and services; (3) expenditures necessarily fluctuated with consumer demand and could not be predicted accurately or realistically financed by annual appropriations; (4) additional expenditures to meet increased demand did not necessarily increase the net outlay from the Treasury Department in the long run; and (5) operations were being conducted within areas in which there were well-established commercial trade practices. Experience demonstrated that enterprises with such characteristics could not be managed effectively under an administrative and financial system designed to control totally different types of government activities.

The keystone of financial control was then, and to a large extent still is, the requirement that Congress provide funds through annual appropriation acts. For this reason, most agencies are not permitted to retain and use incidental revenues or to carry over unexpended balances at the end of the fiscal year. Governmental accounting and auditing had the limited purposes of preventing the overobligation of appropriated funds and unlawful expenditures. Furthermore, the Congress was unwilling to permit administrative discretion in those areas of most vital concern to a business—procurement, contracts, sales of goods and property, and personnel. Administrators often found the myriad regulatory and prohibitory statutes a serious inconvenience, however, loss of flexibility was considered a small sacrifice to place on the altar of public honesty and accountability. But it became evident that any attempt to operate a business enterprise within such a framework would entail not mere inconvenience but certain failure.

The first solution was to charter government corporations under the general incorporation laws of the states and the District of Columbia. Although this device provided necessary flexibility, it created new and equally difficult problems. Considerable doubt existed concerning the propriety of subjecting a federal instrumentality to the provisions of state law. Furthermore, most existing controls to ensure public accountability were abandoned without satisfactory substitutes being provided. Sporadic attempt were made by the Congress and the comptroller general to apply traditional budget and audit controls to government corporations, but the results were such as to discourage further efforts along these lines.

The Government Corporation Control Act of 1945, represents the first official recognition by the Congress of the need for a new type of government institution tailored to the requirements of business programs and for new types of controls over such institutions that would ensure accountability without impairing essential flexibility. The Congress expressly recognized that "the corporate form loses much of its peculiar value without reasonable autonomy and flexibility in its day-to-day decisions and operations. The budget and financial controls imposed upon Government corporations should not deprive them of this freedom and flexibility in carrying out authorized programs. . . ."[32]

As a body corporate, a government corporation has a separate legal personality distinct from that of the United States. A corporation, therefore, does not enjoy the traditional immunity of the United States from being sued without its consent. A corporation can also be authorized to borrow money in its own name without directly pledging the credit of the United States, although the financial community recognizes that the government would be most unlikely to refuse to make good in the event of default. The principal advantage is that such unguaranteed corporate obligations are not included under the public debt ceiling.

A corporation is usually given power "to determine the character and the necessity for its expenditures, and the manner in which they shall be incurred, allowed and paid." A corporation is thus exempted from most of the regulatory and prohibitory statutes applicable to the expenditure of public funds, except those specifically applicable to government corporations. Although subject to audit, their expenditures cannot be "disallowed" by the General Accounting Office, which is limited to reporting questionable transactions to the Congress.

A very great part of the difference between a corporation and an agency arises from the method of financing its operations. A corporation's funds are generally derived from such sources as capital appropriations, which are not subject to fiscal year limitations, revenues, and borrowing from the Treasury Department or public. With a few exceptions, such as the Federal Crop Insurance Corporation (administrative expenses) and the TVA (nonrevenue programs), corporations rarely depend on annual appropriations for their funds.

The Congress and the public now generally accept the principle that a government corporation should endeavor to operate, as far as practicable, on a self-sustaining basis and recover through user charges all costs of its operations, including interest, depreciation, and the cost of services furnished by other government agencies. Some fall short of this goal, notably the Commodity Credit Corporation's price support program, which incurs substantial annual losses; but, for most, a break-even operation remains the ultimate objective. Attempts to recover the costs of noncorporate programs from user charges have met with considerable resistance on the grounds that these are no different from traditional government services properly chargeable, in whole or in part, to the general taxpayer.

Mixed-ownership government corporations and government sponsored enterprises are not subject to any form of budget review and control, although the budgets of the Student Loan Marketing Association, Federal Home Loan Mortgage Corporation, Bank for Cooperatives, Agricultural Credit Banks, Resolution Funding Corporation, Federal Agricultural Mortgage Corporation, and Federal Loan Banks are included in the budget appendix.

Wholly owned government corporations are generally required by law to present "business-type" budgets, which the Corporation Control Act provides shall be plans of operations "with due allowance for flexibility." Unlike an agency, which requests specific appropriations, a corporation seeks congressional approval of its budget program as a whole. Congress is authorized to limit the use of corporate funds for any purpose, but it has seldom chosen to do so, except for administrative expenses. In essence, the business-type budget provides for a qualitative rather than a quantitative review of proposed corporate expenditures.

The Chief Financial Officer Act of 1990 provides that the financial statements of government corporations be audited annually by the Inspector general of the corporation or an external auditor is determined by the inspector general. Corporations are also required to submit an annual management report to the Congress including statements of financial position, operations, cash flows and such other information as may be necessary to inform the Congress about the corporation's financial condition and operations.

Employees of government corporations are considered to be employees of the United States,[33] subject to the general laws and regulations applicable to government employees. Exceptions have been granted when a need has been established for special flexibility in hiring and dismissing employees and establishing wage scales, as in the case of the Panama Canal Company, Tennessee Valley Authority and Federal Deposit Insurance Corporation.

A board of directors was once considered to be the hallmark of a government corporation, largely because state incorporation laws generally require the establishment of boards of directors elected by the stockholders. Boards of directors persist in many varieties and forms, even though the need for and usefulness of most boards are highly debatable. David Lilienthal began to entertain serious reservations about the usefulness of the Tennessee Valley Authority board when he served as its chairman. He wrote in his diary that "the board has come to mean me."[34] The Congress replaced the board of directors of the Reconstruction Finance Corporation with a single administrator because the board arrangement had resulted in "diffusion of responsibility." It was noted that existence of a five-man board of directors had made it possible "for individual members to avoid, obscure, or dilute their responsibilities by passing the buck from one to another."[35] Existing corporations or quasi-corporations with single heads are the St. Lawrence Seaway Development Corporation, the Federal Housing Administration, and the Government National Mortgage Association.

The secretary of housing and urban development, in effect, has been constituted as a "corporation sole" for the purpose of administering the college housing, urban renewal, and other public enterprise funds. These funds have not been organized as corporations, but, nonetheless, the secretary in carrying out his duties under the laws creating the funds may sue and be sued, borrow money, and exercise comparable powers and is subject to the budget and audit provisions of the Government Corporation Control Act applicable to wholly owned government corporations. This approach was developed initially to shore up the position of a weak Housing and Home Finance administrator by vesting powers in him rather than in one of the highly autonomous agency constituents subject only to his "coordination." Other agencies, such as the Bonneville Power Administration, have gradually over the years acquired some but not all of the attributes of a government corporation.

Government corporations are organized to achieve a public purpose authorized by law. As far as purpose is concerned, a wholly owned government corporation cannot be distinguished from any other government agency.[36] This view was vigorously stated by the U.S. Supreme Court in the case of *Cherry Cotton Mills v U.S.*, 327 US 536 (1945), when it held that the fact "that the Congress chose to call it a corporation [Reconstruction Finance Corporation] does not alter its characteristics so as to make it something other than what it actually is, an agency selected by the government to accomplish purely governmental purposes." The functions of a corporation are the same as those of any administrative agency; the differences between the two are to be found in the *methods* employed to perform the functions and in the techniques used by the president and the Congress to fulfill their constitutional responsibilities.

Not since Arthur E. Morgan, the first chairman of the Tennessee Valley Authority, has a director of a wholly owned corporation attempted to challenge the president's overriding authority. Morgan insisted that he was responsible solely to the Congress, not the president, and refused to answer questions asked by President Franklin D. Roosevelt.[37] When President Roosevelt removed Morgan for "contumacy," his action was sustained by the courts.[38]

As a general rule, the president looks to the heads of executive departments and agencies for immediate direction and supervision of government corporations. Corporations are generally made subject to supervision by the department head responsible for the functional area in which the corporation is operating. Only three wholly owned corporations—the Tennessee Valley Authority, Export-Import Bank, and Federal Deposit Insurance Corporation[39]—report directly to the president. In some instances, independence has been the equivalent of "isolation" from those with ultimate authority for making national policy. As a regional agency without a national constituency, the Tennessee Valley Authority is especially vulnerable if it does not have strong presidential backing, because no cabinet officer is responsible for defending its interests and some have looked on it as a competitor. Not until the Congress authorized the TVA to market its own revenue bonds was the authority able to obtain funds necessary to finance major expansion of its power-producing facilities.

Mixed-ownership corporations and government sponsored enterprises present a distinct class of supervisory problems. These corporations have at times demanded all of the privileges of a public agency without being willing to accept the responsibilities. Mixed-ownership corporations have been successful in maintaining at least a degree of independence from both the president and the Congress, particularly those that are self-financing and have a majority of directors nominated or elected by private stockholders. Wholly owned corporations such as the Federal Deposit Insurance Corporation and the Resolution Trust Corporation have been classified as "mixed-ownership" solely for the purpose of keeping them "off-budget."

The very fact that government corporations are "different" causes them to be viewed with some suspicion. Bureaucracies, whether in the legislative or executive branches, have an innate distaste for institutions that do not fit neatly into the existing system and upset established routines. Nonetheless, the legitimacy of the government corporation as a member of the federal institutional family is no longer open to question. The corporation gained full respectability when President Truman laid down criteria for the use of government corporations in his budget Message.[40] President Truman stated the following:

> Experience indicates that the corporate form of organization is peculiarly adapted to the Administration of governmental programs which are predominantly of a commercial character-those which are revenue producing, are at least potentially self-sustaining, and involve a large number of business-type transactions with the public. In their business operations such programs require greater flexibility than the customary type of appropriation budget ordinarily permits. As a rule the usefulness of a corporation lies in its ability to deal with the public in the manner employed by private enterprise for similar work.

Due to problems of definition, there is no accurate listing of the number of government corporations. Estimates have been as high as forty-five, including such organizations as Howard and Gallaudet universities. There are at present twenty four active wholly owned government corporations subject to the Government Corporation Control Act. The Bonneville Power Administration, Patent and Trademark Office, and Federal Housing Administration have been proposed for incorporation.[41]

Congressional failure scrupulously to observe established criteria and the letter and spirit of the Government Corporation Control Act has created a false image of government corporations as uncontrolled and uncontrollable organizations. The ill-fated Synthetic Fuels Corporation is a prime example. The law in one place defines the corporation as "an independent federal entity" and in another states that it is "not an agency and instrumentality of the United States." No law applied to the corporation "as if it were a federal agency" except when the law provided that it should be treated as a federal agency.

To cite other relevant examples:

- Government corporations have been created that are not revenue producing and potentially self-sustaining. National Corporation for Community and Public Service, Oversight Board of the Resolution Trust Corporation (RTC) and U.S. Railway Association.
- Government corporations have not been made subject to the Government Corporation Control Act. Oversight Board of RTC, Securities Investor Production Corporation, Legal Services Corporation and Corporation for Public Broadcasting.
- Wholly owned corporations have been improperly classified as mixed-ownership. U.S. Railway Association, Resolution Trust Corporation, Federal Deposit Insurance Corporation and National Railroad Passenger Corporation (AMTRAK).
- In direct violation of a provision of the Government Corporation Control Act, corporations have been made subject to the laws of a state or the District of Columbia. AMTRAK, U.S. Enrichment Corporation, and U.S. Railway Association.

The House Committee on Government Reform and Oversight found that "government corporations and other government-sponsored enterprises have assumed roles and responsibilities very different from those for which the Government Corporation Control Act of 1945 was intended. Today a conceptual framework is needed for setting up these kinds of enterprises and centralized oversight of their management operations.[42] Legislation to provide such a conceptual framework (S.R.2095) was introduced by Senators Simon and Pryor in waning days of the 104th Congress but was not acted upon.

I I

Advisory and Intergovernmental Bodies: Twilight Zone

Advisory Bodies. Alexander Hamilton in Federalist Paper No. 70 argued that the unity of executive power could be destroyed "either by vesting the power in two or more magistrates of equal dignity and authority, or by vesting it ostensibly in one man, subject in whole or in part to the control and cooperation of others, in the capacity of counselors to him."[1] No executive can disregard with impunity "advice" by his counselors, particularly when they represent powerful elements in the community and their advice is not offered privately. Advice becomes limiting when an executive's discretion in the choice of his advisers is restricted by law or executive order and advisory bodies assume an independent status.

As with interagency committees, a distinction needs to be maintained between ad hoc, task-oriented advisory groups and continuing advisory bodies with a right to review, question, and be consulted about program policies and execution. It is the latter category that is of concern to us here.

For several so-called advisory bodies the title "advisory" is a misnomer. Advice ceases to be advice when a grant cannot be made without first obtaining the approval or recommendations of an advisory council. In the previous chapter, we cited the powers vested in advisory councils to the National Foundation on Arts and Humanities and the various institutes under the National Institutes of Health. Other advisory committees have coveted such authorities and some have succeeded in obtaining them.

Congress customarily has established fixed, overlapping terms of office for committee members. Qualification for committee membership are normally couched in quite broad language. For example, the seventeen members of the National Council on Vocational Education shall be selected from owners, chief executives or chief operating officers of non-profit or small businesses, health and education institutions, and organized labor. Exceptions are statutory provisions, such as those authorizing the Council of the American Historical Association to appoint two members of the National Historical Publications Commission or permitting designated organizations or groups to nominate or recommend committee members.

While the statutes may appear to allow considerable executive latitude in selecting "advisers," the president or other appointing officer is seldom in a position to ignore suggestions from the constituencies they represent. Self-designated elites in some professional groups have monopolized appointments to advisory committees. The House Committee on Government Operations noted with concern that a majority of the advisers to the National Institutes of Health (NIH) were drawn from the relatively small number of institutions that receive the bulk of NIH grant funds.[2] Few nonmembers of the National Academy of Sciences were named to serve on the prestigious and influential President's Science Advisory Committee.[3] The peer review system of the National Endowment for the Arts was criticized in a report initiated by the House Appropriations Committee for relying "too heavily on a 'closed circle' of advisors" from the arts community.[4] If members of advisory committees are supposed to reflect the views of broad sectional, professional, economic, or social interests, obviously they must have a standing with and be acceptable to the organizations that represent those interests.

Advisory committees are by no means essential to ensure that affected individuals or groups have a voice with respect to federal programs or policies. Consultation is considered to be a prerequisite for democratic administration. Indeed, Section 4 of the Administrative Procedures Act requires, with some exceptions, public notice of proposed agency rulemaking and an opportunity for interested persons to express their views before a final decision is taken. In some instances, advisory committees merely formalize and legitimatize consultative arrangements established by custom and practice.

David Truman correctly points out that for groups with effective access to the president, department heads, and congressional committees, "the advisory committee and similar devices of consultation may be more a handicap than an advantage."[5] It is no accident that the veterans organizations have made no efforts to institutionalize their role as advisers to the Veterans Department. Whatever the intentions of the government or interest group, formalization of consultative arrangements is likely to result in mutual "co-optation,"—to borrow a word from the social psychologists. Each may find its freedom of action significantly reduced. The outside organization may be identified with government policies that are unpopular among some elements of its constituency, but that for one reason or another it is unable or unwilling to oppose publicly. An organization quickly loses influence when it becomes known that its advice on major issues has been rejected. Consequently, it must be highly selective in choosing the issues on which it is willing to risk a public rebuke. Furthermore, once arrangements are formalized, privileged access may be jeopardized by the admission into the club of others with competing or contrary interests.

What the government basically wants from advisory committees is not "expert" advice, although occasionally this is a factor, but support. Advisory boards may be used to lend respectability to new or controversial programs such as poverty and foreign assistance. It is hoped that board members will act as program missionaries and assist in mobilizing support for the program both in their home communities and in the Congress. Many have been extremely effective in this role, although their zeal does not always reflect selfless dedication to the public interest. The House Committee on Government Operations observed that "when some of the same individuals who have served on advisory councils for many years receive substantial NIH grants, and also testify before the Congress in support of the agency's appropriations, the appearance of favoritism is unavoidable."[6] Testimony by these expert witnesses, coupled with skillful behind-the-scenes lobbying, certainly played a part in persuading the Appropriations Committees to recommend more money for NIH programs than was requested in the president's budget.

Missionary ardor can boomerang and be turned against the president or department head. Zealots are predisposed to be willing accomplices of agency dissidents in covert and overt campaigns not only to overcome budgetary limits but also to thwart proposed policies and reorganizations that are not to their liking. Advisers are not subject to the restraints applicable to public employees and cannot be disciplined for insubordination. The Advisory Council to the National Institute of Mental Health worked closely with the institute director in organizing opposition to a 1960 proposal to reorganize the Public Health Service. The plan called for transfer of important elements of the NIMH to a new Division of Mental Health. The surgeon general was reluctant to alienate the council by going forward with the plan and it was abandoned.[7]

Attempts to use advisory bodies as "window-dressing" can also boomerang. President Kennedy created a Consumer Advisory Council under the aegis of the Council of Economic Advisers (CEA) as what he hoped would be an innocuous alternative to a White House Office of Consumer Counsel promised during the campaign. Unfortunately, council activists took the executive order rhetoric seriously and were very aggressive in pressing demands for an elaborate program and budgetary resources. Wearied from his efforts to control this fractious group, a CEA staff member wrote a plaintive memorandum titled "Who left this bastard on our doorstep?" recommending that the Council of Economic Advisers be relieved of its onerous responsibilities. No agency was willing to volunteer for the assignment, so the council was reorganized and given independent status.

Individuals are attracted to service on advisory groups for a variety of reasons—honor, prestige, influence, curiosity, and opportunity for public service. The last is by no means the least important. Many people do accept a moral obligation to serve their country, but would prefer to do so in a way that does not compel them to give up their private interests.

Individuals may be motivated by dedication to the public interest, but this is seldom true of organizations concerned with promoting the economic interests of their members. Like the government, these organizations may try to utilize advisory groups for their own benefit. This poses a threat when advisory committees are allowed to develop into an invisible government responsible neither to the president, the Congress, nor the people. The danger is very real when public officials confuse advice with direction.

The Federal Advisory Committee Act of 1972 (Public Law 92–463) declares that "new advisory committees should be established only when they are determined to be essential and their number should be kept to the minimum necessary." Committee meetings shall be open to the public and "fairly balanced in terms of points of view represented and the functions to be performed." The act directs that a Committee Management Secretariat be established within the Office of Management and Budget with responsibility for reviewing committee performance, recommending the abolition of unnecessary or obsolete committees, and prescribing administrative guidelines and management controls.

When President Clinton took office there were 801 advisory committees created by federal agencies and 410 established by law. Cost to the government was estimated at $144 million. Executive order 12838, February 10,1993, directed agencies to reduce non-statutory committees by one-third, eliminating those that had become obsolete. OMB Circular No. A-135 indicated that the Clinton administration would not support establishment of new statutory committees or legislation exempting them from the Federal Advisory Committee Act.

JOINT CONGRESSIONAL-EXECUTIVE AGENCIES

Federal courts have held consistently that members of Congress or congressional agencies may not sit on or appoint members of boards or commissions performing executive functions,[8] but this prohibition has not been construed to apply to joint executive-legislative study commissions. Joint executive legislative study commissions have been common since the first Hoover Commission. Membership on these commissions generally is weighted in favor of the congressional representatives. Congressional appointees outnumbered executive appointees on the Hoover Commission two to one. Furthermore, executive and legislative representatives do not serve in comparable capacities. Members appointed by the president, particularly from the executive branch, are construed to be administration spokespersons and can make commitments on the president's behalf. Congressional members obviously cannot commit the Congress and speak only for themselves. Any compromises are likely to be entirely one-sided.

While congressional membership on ad hoc study commissions can be defended as not constituting an overt violation of the separation-of-powers doctrine, congressional membership on permanent executive bodies does raise serious constitutional questions. Six of the fifteen members of the Smithsonian Institution's governing body, the Board of Regents, come from the Senate and House (three each). The Migratory Bird Conservation Commission consists of the secretary of the interior as chairman, the secretary of agriculture, two members of the House of Representatives selected by the speaker, and two senators selected by the president of the Senate. The commission has various administrative duties, including approval of land purchases or rentals and the fixing of prices at which bird sanctuaries may be purchased or rented.

Intergovernmental Organizations. Our Constitution makers anticipated that the several states might be confronted by problems that
cut across state boundaries and would have to devise suitable arrangements to facilitate interstate cooperation in dealing with
them. Article I, Section 10 of the Constitution permits states, with
the consent of the Congress, to enter into compacts and agreements with each other, although the authority is stated negatively.
There is no evidence that the Constitution drafters envisaged circumstances that would warrant comparable agreements or compacts between the federal government and one or more sovereign
states.

Until recently the constitutional, legal, financial, and organizational obstacles to the development of workable intergovernmental institutions were considered to be nearly insuperable. When
the Tennessee Valley Authority (TVA) was created, it was assumed
generally that there was no feasible alternative to a strictly federal
approach to regional development. But the TVA proved not to be
the answer. Moves to duplicate the successful TVA experiment in
the Columbia and Missouri river basins failed to generate enthusiasm either in the regions or within the federal establishment. The
TVA seems destined to be the first and the last wholly federal regional development agency.

Halting steps were taken in the 1950s to provide for state participation in river basin planning. States were invited to propose individuals for appointment to the Arkansas-White-Red and New Eng-
land–New York River Basin Committees chaired by the Army Corps
of Engineers. In 1958, the Congress established a U.S. Study Commission for the Southeast River Basins and a similar study commission for Texas. These commissions consisted of federal and state
representatives, with an unaffiliated chairman appointed by the
president. There was no departure, however, from the concept
that these commissions were federal agencies, and to conform with
constitutional provisions it was believed necessary to give the state
representatives federal appointments.

The same pattern was adopted when the Advisory Commission on Intergovernmental Relations was created in 1959. Panels of names were submitted by the Governors' Conference, Council of State Governments, American Municipal Association and U.S. Conference of Mayors, and the National Association of County Officials, but appointments to the Commission were made by the president. The president has some leeway, since a panel had to include two names for each vacancy. For example, the president selected four governors from a panel of eight proposed by the Governors' Conference.

The 1961 Governors' Conference urged federal-state collaboration to devise "a more comprehensive approach to joint federal-state planning, and to closer federal-state coordination in the development of plans and programs."[9] The emphasis was on *joint* federal-state planning within an appropriate institutional framework.

The proposed Water Resources Planning Act of 1961 became a target for those demanding a new approach. States objected strongly to presidential appointment of the states' representatives on the river basin commissions because this would make them mere instruments of the federal government. The bill was not enacted.

Different but no less vexing constitutional doubts had to be satisfied before the Congress approved the Delaware River Compact in 1961. The Delaware River Basin Advisory Committee—consisting of representatives of the governors of Delaware, Pennsylvania, New Jersey, and New York and the mayors of New York and Philadelphia—developed a legislative proposal for creation by interstate-federal compact of a unified water resources agency for the Delaware River Basin. Inclusion of the federal government as a party to an interstate compact was without precedent. Even though the plan called for the federal government to become a signatory, a federal representative was not invited to participate in negotiating the compact.

Apart from the general question of whether a federal-state compact was permissible under the Constitution or desirable as a mat-

ter of public policy, specific objections were registered against provisions that had the effect of limiting federal power in such critical
areas as control of navigable waters, interstate and foreign commerce, and project authorizations. The Congress approved the
compact with reservations protecting federal powers in these areas,
authorizing the president to modify any provision of the comprehensive plan adopted by the Delaware River Basin Commission in-
sofar as it affects the powers and functions of federal agencies, and
preserving the president's freedom to act in national emergencies.

Although fears that a federal-state compact would make it possible for the signatory states to exert undue political pressure on
federal agencies have not materialized, many remain uneasy
about the compact approach. The Delaware River Commission's
accomplishments to date are modest. Potential controversy was
avoided when the commission accepted as its own the comprehensive plan for the Delaware River Basin developed by the Army
Corps of Engineers.

Some have questioned the constitutionality of the Pacific Northwest Electric Power and Planning Council established by the 1980
Pacific Northwest Electric Planning and Conservation Act. The
council is declared not to be an agency or instrumentality of the
United States. The council is composed of two persons from the
states of Montana, Oregon, and Washington, appointed by state
governors or as otherwise provided by state law. Council members
and employees "shall not be deemed to be officers and employees
of the United States for any purpose." Although defined as a nonfederal agency, the council is fully funded by a federal agency, the
Bonneville Power Administration. The council's powers go beyond
advice, and actions taken by the Bonneville Power Administrator
"shall be consistent" with the regional conservation and electric
power plan adopted by the council. The vesting of such powers
over a federal agency in a nonfederal body is without precedent.

The Appalachian Regional Development Act spelled out the
terms of the new partnership between the states and the federal
government. Federal membership of the Appalachian Regional
Commission is limited to the "Federal co-chair" appointed by the

president. Each participating state in the Appalachian region is also entitled to one member, who shall be the governor or his designee. Decisions by the commission require the affirmative vote of the federal co-chairman and of a majority of state members. The federal government agreed to pay administrative expenses for the first two years, but after that each state is to pay its pro rata share of the costs, as determined by the commission. No one employed by the commission "shall be deemed a federal employee for any purpose."

The Appalachian Regional Commission has not fulfilled its promise of creating "a new and unique federal-state partnership" and fostering a coordinated regional approach to economic development. The commission was able to develop sufficient local and congressional support to forestall its demise under President Reagan. The commission has proved to be a useful vehicle for obtaining federal project funds and promoted a sense of shared mission and friendly working relationships among federal, state and local officials.[10]

TWILIGHT ZONE

The period since World War II is notable for the proliferation of quasi-government and quasi-nongovernment institutions that exist in a twilight zone between public and private. It may be said that the United States government has gone quasi. These quasis include agencies and corporations established by Congress for a public purpose and funded directly or indirectly by the U.S. Treasury, but defined by law as "private," federally funded research and development centers, and government-sponsored enterprises. Creation of these institutions outside the formal government structure has been motivated by a number of factors including off-budget financing and avoidance of government personnel and procurement regulations.

Profound constitutional questions are raised by the vesting of government functions and authorities in institutions that are incorrectly classified by law as private. Both Ronald C. Moe and Harold J. Sullivan have pointed out that private individuals and agencies are not subject to the same body of laws as federal agencies, their officers and employees.[11] Except for prohibition of slavery, the U.S. Constitution limits the government, not the private sector. Maintenance of a distinction between government and nongovernment is considered essential to protect private rights from government's intrusion and to prevent private usurpation of public power.

Serious questions are raised by Congress mislabeling of such institutions as the Legal Services Corporation, National Passenger Railroad Corporation, Corporation for Public Broadcasting, Securities Investor Protection Corporation, U.S. Institute for Peace, National Endowment for Democracy, and the Corporation for the Promotion of Rifle Practice and Fire Arms Safety.

The Corporation for the Promotion of Rifle Practice and Fire Arms Safety created by 1996 Defense Authorization Act is a prime example of a corporation defined as a "private nonprofit" even though its initial board of directors is appointed by the secretary of the army and its revenues are to be derived from the sale of firearms and ammunition transferred from the army and Defense Reutilization Marketing Service. No provision is made for an annual audit or reports to Congress. Upon dissolution, assets of the corporation revert to the army or, if sold, proceeds from sales are to be deposited in the treasury.

Mislabeling of public entities as private for political or public relations purposes contributes to public mistrust of government. The nongovernment private status of these corporations and institutes is susceptible to legal challenge. The U.S. Supreme Court ruled that the National Passenger Railroad Corporation (AMTRAK) was a government entity and that the provisions of its congressional charter defining it as a private corporation could not exempt it from constitutional provisions applicable to government agencies.[12] For the court, status was determined by purpose, degree of government control and funding, not by language in the law. It held that there was no valid basis for distinguishing between AM-TRAK and other types of government activities except that is designated by law as "not an agency and instrumentality of the Unites States government."

FFRDCs

Federally Funded Research and Development Centers (FFRDCs) have been a topic of recurrent executive branch and congressional concern. A 1995 report of the Office of Technology Assessment lists thirty-nine active FFRDCs that perform various function for their agency sponsors including analytical studies, systems engineering and technical direction and laboratory research. FFRDCs are private nonprofit corporations organized at government initiative for the purpose entering into contracts to furnish services to the government.

In some instances, the government selected the "incorporators" of the nonuniversity-affiliated institutions. Charters were obtained under the laws of the state where the institution was incorporated. Individuals invited to serve as trustees were either picked by the contracting agency or chosen with its approval. Except for grants made by the Ford Foundation to provide initial working capital to Rand and the Institute for Defense Analyses, financing came entirely from the federal government.

In many respects the nonprofit corporations are indistinguishable from early government corporations chartered under state law. Seemingly, the Government Corporation Control Act provision that "no corporation shall be created, organized, or acquired by any officer or agency of the Federal Government. . . for the purpose of acting as an agency or instrumentality of the United States, except by or pursuant to an act of Congress specifically authorizing such action" would apply to nonprofit corporations. Committee counsel raised this point during hearings on the Bell report but did not press his question. The comptroller general has been discreetly silent on the subject.

General H. H. Arnold certainly did not intend to "create, organize, or acquire a corporation" when in 1945 he entered into a contract with the Douglas Aircraft Company for Project RAND. His objective was not to innovate, but to preserve the close association between the scientific community and the military that had been nurtured under Office of Scientific Research and Development auspices during World War II. The working partnership of the military and the scientists had produced significant advances in weaponry and in the deployment and use of weapons systems. This kind of capability could not be built into the formal air force organization structure without either bypassing the established chain of command or sacrificing direct access to the chief of staff. The first alternative was wholly unacceptable to the military and the second to the scientists.

By 1948 RAND had proved itself and there was every indication that the program would be continued and expanded. But the association with the Douglas Aircraft Company was a source of increasing uneasiness because of the potential for conflicts of interest. University affiliation was considered and rejected. With the concurrence of the air force and the Douglas Company, Rand was organized as an independent nonprofit corporation under the laws of the state of California.

Few realized at the time that Rand was the precursor of a new generation of federal instrumentalities. Rand itself fathered the System Development Corporation and Analytic Services, Inc. The Operations Research Organization established by the army in 1947 as a Johns Hopkins University affiliate was converted in 1961 to the independent Research Analysis Corporation. In 1956 the Department of Defense asked a number of leading universities to sponsor the Institute for Defense Analyses. The Department of Defense organized the Logistics Management Institute in 1961. Use was confined to the military until 1968, when the Urban Institute was created.

Until 1948 there were no comprehensive government policies and regulations with respect to the establishment and operation of FFRDCs. Relationships to agency sponsors were formalized in 1984 by Office of Federal Procurement Policy guidelines which were subsequently codified in the Federal Acquisition Regulations.

Regulations require that an FFRDC:

- Meet some special long-term research or development effort that cannot be met effectively by in-house or contractor resources.
- Conducts business in a manner befitting the special relationship with government, to operate in the public interest with objectivity and independence, to be free from organizational conflicts of interest, and to have full disclosure of its affairs to the sponsoring agency.

Sponsoring agencies are required to:

- Establish that existing alternative sources cannot meet agency needs.
- Assure that the basic purpose and mission and work to be performed are clearly stated.
- Maintain reasonable continuity in the level of support.
- Approve work performed for agencies other than the sponsor.

The Department of Defense 1995 Appropriation Act prohibits the creation of new FFRDCs in Defense.

The General Accounting Office identified four major issues concerned with the management and operation of FFRDCs: (1) appropriateness of work assignments; (2) safeguard of objectivity; (3) effectiveness of sponsor oversight; and (4) consideration of cost-effective alternatives to FFRDCs.[13]

The Professional Services Council has protested that FFRDCs unfairly compete with the private sector which now has the capability of providing many of the services furnished by FFRDCs. Particularly troublesome is the creation of non-FFRDC affiliates to perform non FFRDC work both for government and commercial customers. The Aerospace Corporation has signed a letter of intent to renounce the FFRDC status and become a profit making subsidiary of the Science Applications International Corporation.[14] The question is whether the access and expertise obtained by an FFRDC through its "special relationship" would give it an unfair competitive advantage if it were allowed to move into the private sector.

The 1962 report chaired by Budget Director David E. Bell concluded that "many kinds of arrangements—both federal operations and various patterns of contracting now in use—can and should be used to mobilize the talent and facilities needed to carry out the Federal research and development effort." The report suggested that consideration be given to the establishment of research institutes within the government with many of the attributes of an FFRDC including exemptions from personnel and other regulations ill-suited for a research organization.[15]

Whatever may have been the original reason for creating FFRDCs, the survival of some is the result of downsizing the federal work force. According to the General Accounting Office, several sponsors cited personnel ceilings as the obstacle to transferring FFRDC functions in-house. Sponsors seeking to replace FFRDC capabilities would have to compete for a shrinking pool of civil service positions.[16]

GOVERNMENT SPONSORED ENTERPRISES

Government sponsored enterprises (GSEs) are a unique class of institutions. Thomas H. Stanton, the foremost authority on GSEs, has defined them as "a privately owned, federally chartered financial institution with nationwide scope and specialized lending powers that benefits from an implicit federal guarantee to enhance its ability to borrow money."[17] The Federal National Mortgage Association (Fannie Mae), Federal Home Loan Mortgage Corporation (Freddie Mac), Student Loan Marketing Association (Sallie Mae), Federal Agriculture Credit Corporation (Farmer Mac), and Farm Credit banks have private stockholders and directors elected by stockholders. The Financing Corporation and Resolution Funding

Corporation are classified as GSEs but merely are funding vehicles for the bailout of savings and loan institutions.

GSEs are among the largest financial institution in the United States. Fannie Mae and Freddie Mac are today the primary source of home mortgage financing. As Thomas H. Stanton has noted, GSEs have "immense political resources" and have been able to minimize efforts by the Congress or executive branch to regulate their activities.[18] In 1986 Fannie Mae established a political action committee to funnel donations to members of Congress, particularly those on its oversight committees. No government agency may legally make such contributions.

These hybrid organizations are private for profit institutions but retain many of the privileges of government status including exemption in whole, or in part, from federal, state or local taxes and Securities and Exchange Commission regulation. The rights of shareholders are not the same as those of investors in private companies subject to state corporation laws.

GSEs usually have a direct or indirect line of credit with the U.S. Treasury. GSE securities are accorded the preferred investment status of U.S. Treasury obligations.

Government appointed directors tend to reinforce the public perception that government stands behind GSEs. Five of Fannie Mae's and Freddie Mac's eighteen member boards of directors are appointed by the president of the United States. The president appoints seven of Sallie Mae's twenty-one-member board.

Of all of the means available to exert government influence and safeguard the public interest, presidential appointment of directors is probably the least effective and may have undesirable side effects. The two government directors of the Union Pacific Railroad were treated as spies and antagonists and in 1887 recommended that the appointment of public directors be discontinued.[19] Such directors owe their fiduciary obligation to the corporation, not the government. According to Herman Schwartz, "their presence may reinforce the belief that the government assures the profitability of the corporation" and "may dampen the zeal of regulatory agencies."[20]

Although the obligations of most GSEs are not guaranteed by the government or backed by the full faith and credit of the United States, they are regarded, nonetheless, as government obligations by the financial community and are assumed to have the implicit support of the U. S. government. It is believed that, if necessary, the government would bail out these institutions as it did when Congress enacted legislation to cover Farm Credit's $4 billion losses.

The ambiguous status of GSEs inevitably generates a conflict between their public and private roles. What does the government receive in return for the substantial benefits they confer on GSEs? It is argued that GSEs reduce interest rate to home buyers, stabilize mortgage markets and increase home ownership. The Congressional Budget Office questions whether these benefits are worth the cost. The Congressional Budget Office concluded: "Government sponsored enterprises are costly to the tax payers in that they receive a benefit for which others would pay a substantial sum. In addition, the GSEs are retaining a substantial share of that benefit for management and shareholders rather then passing it through to home buyers."[21]

The Congress in 1992 created the Office of Federal Housing Enterprise in the Department of Housing and Urban Development to protect the Treasury from a loss resulting from a GSE insolvency. The office's mandate is to safeguard the tax payers' interest, not to assure that GSEs act with due regard for the public interest.

Advocates of public-private ventures would do well to evaluate lessons learned from experience with GSEs. Intermingling of public and private purposes in a profit making corporation almost inevitably means subordination of public responsibilities to corporate goals. We run the danger of creating a system in which we privatize profits and socialize losses.

III

CONCLUDING OBSERVATIONS

12

Concluding Observations

If any thesis emerges from the previous chapters, it is that in the choice of institutional types and structural and procedural arrangements, we are making decisions with significant political implications. This is not to imply that the administrative consequences of those decisions can be safely ignored. By allowing political expediency to dictate the design of administrative systems, a president can create major obstacles to the accomplishment of his basic political goals and the effective functioning of the democratic process.

If we are to redesign our institutional structure and body of laws and regulations to meet the challenges of the twenty-first century, the president and the Congress must first identify goals and devise soundly based strategies for accomplishing them. Solutions will not be found by demonizing the federal government, describing it as "broken" and playing the numbers game with executive departments, the budget, and federal employment. This approach confirms public distrust of politicians while providing at best short term political benefits.

We will not make progress unless we acknowledge the vital role that the federal government must play, whether it be small, big, or something in between. Other countries recognize the essentiality of public institutions in promoting economic efficiency and policy effectiveness.[1]

By atomizing political power and balkanizing the United States government we are going in the wrong direction. In an age of global economies, technological revolution, and mobile populations and industries, the boundaries between states and even nations have ceased to have the importance they once had. Fifty independent states cannot be expected to develop and enforce coherent national policies with respect to such things as the economy, environment, trade, immigration, and transportation safety. In seeking a smaller government we should take care not to diminish the federal government's capability to perform its constitutionally defined role in dealing with matters affecting the whole country. Historian Alan Brinkley has cautioned, "Far from restoring power to individuals disempowering the federal government will do precisely the opposite. It will weaken the only national institution capable of checking some of the other large organizations that dominate modern life. It will leave individuals with even less control over their own fates. It is not the route to more democracy. It is the route to less."[2]

Public confidence in government is undermined by using agencies that are not fully accountable to the president, Congress, and the people to perform public functions. By blurring the distinction between public and private we have permitted the creation of maverick institutions which are able to play both sides, thus making it possible for them to reduce accountability to the government, their shareholders, if any, and the public.[3] It may be difficult to define functions that are inherently governmental, but vesting conduct of security investigations in a profit-making ESOP (employee stock ownership plan), for example, would certainly appear to cross the line. Authority of law-enforcement agencies to divulge information to a private corporation is questionable.

The U.S. Constitution provides in article 2 that "the executive power shall be vested in a president and that "he shall take care that the laws be faithfully executed. . . ." As reported by the House

Committee on Government Reform and Oversight, "the capacity of the president as chief executive officer of the federal government and the principal manager has been diminished over several administrations. The Executive Office of the President has abrogated its responsibility to oversee and improve the government's management structure."[4]

The president's primary task is leadership: setting national goals and priorities and mobilizing public support for his programs. Once he has established his goals, then he needs to consider carefully the means to be employed in reaching them. His decisions on program design, institutional type, organizational jurisdiction, and management system may well determine who will control and benefit from a program and, ultimately, whether national objectives are achieved. These decisions should not be governed solely by application of traditional organization doctrines. In evaluating the design and organization of new programs or proposed reorganizations of existing programs, the basic questions to be asked are the following:

1. What is the nature of the constituency that is being created, or acquired, and to what extent will it be able to influence policies and program administration?
2. Is the constituency broadly based or does it represent narrow interests antithetical to some of the public purposes to be accomplished by the program?
3. What committees of the Congress will exercise jurisdiction and to what extent do they reflect the interests of the constituencies to be served by the program or those of groups hostile to program objectives?
4. What is the culture and tradition of the administering department or agency? Will it provide an environment favorable to program growth, stunt development, or produce a hybrid?
5. What are the constituencies to whom the administering agency responds? Would there be any obvious conflicts of interest?

6. Where are the loci of power with respect to program administration: the president, the agency head, the bureaus, congressional committees, professional guilds, interest groups, and so on? Are provisions made to ensure an appropriate balance of power and to prevent domination by any single group? Are the ultimate powers of the president protected and supported?

7. To what extent and in what way is access to those with decision-making power limited?

8. Does the program design foster dominance by a particular professional perspective and will this result in distortion of program goals?

9. Is provision made for an "open" system engineered in such a way that there are no built-in obstacles to joint administration with related government programs and cooperative efforts?

10. What safeguards are provided to ensure that no group or class of people is excluded from participation in the program and an equitable share in program benefits?

11. Do the type of institution and proposed organization provide the status, visibility, public support, and administrative system appropriate to the function to be performed?

12. Do the organizational and procedural arrangements simplify or complicate the problems of defining responsibility and maintaining accountability for program results? To what extent do they encourage "buck passing"?

Whether or not meaningful improvements in executive branch organization and in the management of the federal system can be obtained will depend in part on reorganization of the congressional committee structure. The particularistic elements in our society will always triumph over the general interest as long as they are nourished and supported by committees and subcommittees that share their limited concerns. At a minimum, committee and subcommittee jurisdictions should be compatible with current assignments of responsibilities within the executive branch and take into account interrelationships among programs so as to permit unified consideration of closely related and interdependent programs and evaluation of program objectives. Even modest reforms are unlikely, however, unless an informed and aroused electorate demands that the Congress modernize its organization and procedures. The assumption that only members of Congress are affected by congressional organization is no longer tenable.

Improved organizational effectiveness will also depend on the treatment of regulatory and management issues by the Judiciary. The much enlarged role of the courts as administrative overseers and a parallel increase in demands for more formalized procedures at all levels not only have increased organizational rigidity and complexity, they have further blurred the lines of responsibility and accountability. Because judicial toleration of administrative discretion is now far less than in the past, the procedural demands of statutory mandates to administrators must be determined in advance by Congress and the president. Otherwise they will be discovered by the courts.

We will compound the problems if we demand simple answers. The growing interdependence of the federal government, state and local governments, and many private institutions; increasing reliance on administration by grant, contract, and regulation; and the greater utilization of multijurisdictional programs have added new dimensions to public administration. Whatever strategy is devised must be as sophisticated as the problems it seeks to solve and retain sufficient flexibility to permit rapid adjustments to changing circumstances. It cannot deal with the executive branch as if it existed in isolation and must take into account the linkages between congressional and executive organization, and the judiciary. If we persist in thinking of organization in terms of lines and boxes on an organization chart, our efforts to discover viable approaches to our current dilemma will certainly fail.

Notes

CHAPTER 1

1. Herbert C. Hoover, *The Memoirs of Herbert Hoover: The Cabinet and the Presidency*, 1920–1933, The Macmillan Co., 1952, pp. 282–283.

2. James G. March and Johan P. Olson, "Organizing Political Life: What Administrative Reorganization Tells Us About Government," *American Political Science Review*, No. 77, 1983. Also see Ronald C. Moe, *The Hoover Commissions Revisited*, Westview Press, 1982.

3. *Press Release*, October 12, 1995.

4. The Commission on Organization of the Executive Branch of the Government, *General Management of the Executive Branch*, a report to the Congress, February 1949.

5. Luther Gulick, "Notes on the Theory of Organization" in *Papers on the Science of Administration*, Luther Gulick and L. Urwick, eds., Institute of Public Administration, 1937, p. 3.

6. Ibid.

7. Ibid., pp. 6–7.

8. Ibid., pp. 6, 31, 37.

9. Library of Congress, *A Compilation of Basic Information on the Reorganization of the Executive Branch of the Government of the United States*, 1912–1947, Washington, D.C., 1947, pp. 1,214–23.

10. Luther Gulick, "Science, Values and Public Administration," in *Papers on the Science of Administration*, Luther Gulick and L. Urwick, eds., Institute of Public Administration, 1937, p. 191.

11. Luther Gulick, "Notes on the Theory of Organization," p. 10.

12. Luther Gulick, "Science, Values and Public Administration," p. 192.

13. Paul H. Appleby, *Policy and Administration*, University of Alabama Press, 1949.

14. Dwight Waldo, *The Administrative State*, The Ronald Press Co., 1948, Chapter 10.

15. William G. Scott, *Organization Theory: A Behavioral Analysis for Management*, Richard D. Irwin, Inc., 1967, p. 109.

16. For critiques of orthodox organization theory, see Warren G. Bennis, *Changing Organizations: Essays on the Development and Evolution of Human Organization*, McGraw-Hill Book Co., 1966; Bertram M. Gross, *The Managing of Organizations: The Administrative Struggle*, Vol. I, The Free Press of Glencoe, 1964; Daniel Katz and Robert L. Kahn, *The Social Psychology of Organization*, John Wiley & Sons, Inc., 1966; Douglas McGregor, *The Human Side of Enterprise*, McGraw-Hill Book Co., 1960; John D. Millett, *Organization for the Public Service*, D. Van Nostrand Co., Inc., 1966; William G. Scott, *Organization Theory: A Behavioral Analysis for Management*, Richard D. Irwin, Inc., 1967; Herbert A. Simon, *Administrative Behavior*, 2nd ed., The MacMillan Co., 1957; Herbert A. Simon, Donald W. Smithburg, and Victor A. Thompson, *Public Administration*, Alfred A. Knopf, 1950; Dwight Waldo, *The Administrative State*, The Ronald Press Co., 1948; Stephen J. Wayne, *The Reflections on Administrative Reorganization in setting National Priorities: The 1978 Budget*, The Brookings Institution, 1977.

17. Stuart M. Butler, Michael Senera, and W. Bruce Weinrod, *Mandate for Leadership II, Continuing the Conservative Revolution*, The Heritage Foundation, 1984, p. 531.

18. U. S. Government Printing Office, September 7, 1993.

19. James Q. Wilson, "Reinventing Public Administration," *PS: Political Science and Politics*, December 1994.

20. Ronald C. Moe and Robert S. Gilmour, "Rediscovering Principles of Public Administration. The Neglected Foundation of Public Law," *Public Administration Review*, March/April, 1995. Vol. 55, No. 2.

21. For critiques of National Performance Review, see Donald F. Kettl and John J. Dilulio, Jr. editors, *Inside the Reinvention Machine*, Brookings, 1995; Peri E Arnold, "Reform's Changing Role," *Public Administration Review*, September/October 1995, Vol. 55, No. 3; Dwight Ink, "Does Reinventing Government Have an Achilles Heel?" *The Public Manager*, Winter 1995–1996; Herbert N. Jasper and Anita F. Alpern, "National Performance Review: The Good, the Bad, the Indifferent," *The Public Manager*, Spring 1994.

22. Donald F. Kettl, Patricia W. Ingraham, Ronald R. Sanders, and Constance Horner, *Civil Service Reform: Building a Government That Works*, Brookings, 1996, pp. 38–39.

23. House Report 104–435, December 21, 1995, p. 11.

24. House Report 104–434, December 21, 1995, p. 3.

25. National Academy of Public Administration, Standing Panel on Executive Organization and Management, *Principles of Organization*, January, 1997.

26. National Academy of Public Administration, Standing Panel on Executive Organization and Management, ibid, 1997.

27. Italics Supplied, Dwight Waldo, "Organization Theory: An Elephantine Problem," *Public Administration Review*, Vol. 21, No. 4, 1961.

28. Wallace S. Sayre, "Premises of Public Administration: Past and Emerging," *Public Administration Review*, Vol. 18, No. 2, 1958.

29. Statement of William F. Clinger, *Press Release*, October 12, 1995.

30. Richard Polenberg, *Reorganizing Roosevelt's Government*, Harvard University Press, 1966, p. 81.

31. Comptroller General of the United States, *Implementation: The Missing Link in Planning Reorganizations*, March 20, 1981.

32. *Meyers v the United States*, 272 US 52, 293.

33. Richard E. Neustadt, *Presidential Power—The Politics of Leadership*, John Wiley & Sons, Inc., 1960, p. 47.

34. Lloyd M. Short, *The Development of National Administrative Organization in the United States*, The Johns Hopkins Press, 1923, p. 89.

35. Stephen Skowronek, *Building a New American State*, Cambridge University Press, 1982, Chapter 4.

36. For excellent analyses of the role played by the American Farm Bureau Federations in organizational politics, see Sidney Baldwin, *Poverty and Politics*, University of North Carolina Press, 1968; Philip Selznick, *TVA and the Grass Roots*, University of California Press, 1949.

37. The Commission on Organization of the Executive Branch of the Government, *Federal Business Enterprises, A Report to the Congress*, March 1949, p. 102.

38. Marriner S. Eccles, *Beckoning Frontiers*, Alfred A. Knopf, 1951, p. 268.

39. Committee on Governmental Affairs, U.S. Senate, *Principal Recommendations and Findings of the Study on Federal Regulation*, Committee Print, 96th Congress, 1st Session, September 1979, p. 50.

40. National Academy of Science, *Federal Support of Basic Research in Institutions of Higher Learning*, Washington, D.C., 1964.

41. Alan Dean, Dwight Ink and Harold Seidman,"OMB's M Fading Away," *Government Executive*, June 1994.

42. House Committee on Government Reform and Oversight, *Making Government Work: Fulfilling the Mandate for Change*, House Report No. 104–435, 104th Congress, First Session.

43. National Academy of Public Administration, *A Performance Based Organization for Nautical Charting and Geodesy*, June 1996, p. 7.

44. *Papers Relating to the President's Departmental Reorganization Program*, pp. 14–15.

45. Attributed to Rufus Miles, formerly assistant secretary for administration, Department of Health, Education and Welfare.

46. House Select Committee on Foreign Aid, *Preliminary Report Eleven—Comparative Analysis of Suggested Plans of Foreign Aid*, November 22, 1947.

47. Daniel S. Greenberg, *The Politics of Pure Science*, The New American Library, Inc., 1967, p. 107.

48. Harry S. Truman, Memorandum of Disapproval of the National Foundation Bill (S.R. 526), August 6, 1947.

49. Herbert Hoover, *The Memoirs of Herbert Hoover*, p. 281.

50. Geodfrey Parsons, "Royal Commission," *Punch*, August 24, 1955. © *Punch*, London.

51. Senate Committee on Government Operations, hearings on "Federal Role in Urban Affairs," 1967, p. 40.

52. *Government Executive*, "The Top 200 Federal Contractors," 1996.

53. *New York Times*, December 14, 1969.

54. Herbert Emmerich, *Essays on Federal Reorganization*, University of Alabama Press, 1950, p. 7.

55. According to Peri Arnold, "it was the supreme political accomplishment of the first Hoover Commission that it masked the managerial presidency with the older value of administrative orthodoxy." Peri Arnold, "The First Hoover Commission and the Managerial Presidency," *Journal of Politics*, Vol. 38, February 1976.

56. Emmet J. Hughes, *The Living Presidency*, Coward, McCann & Geoghegan, Inc., 1973, p. 344.

57. Senate Report No. 97–179, 97th Congress, 1st Session, August 13, 1981, p. 16.

CHAPTER 2

1. National Academy of Public Administration, *Beyond Distrust: Building Bridges Between Congress and the Executive*, 1992, p. 21.

2. *Congressional Quarterly*, July 27, 1996, p. 2093.

3. David Maraniss and Michael Weisskopf, *Tell Newt to Shut Up!*, a Touchstone Book, 1996.

4. *Congressional Record*, February 18, 1909, p. 2654.

5. Joseph A. Califano, Jr., *Governing America*, a Touchstone Book, 1981, p. 451.

6. Warren L Nelson, "The Powerhouse," *Government Executive*, May 1996.

7. Richard F. Fenno Jr., *Congressmen in Committees*, Little Brown and Co., 1973.

8. Neil MacNeil, *Forge of Democracy: The House of Representatives*, David McKay Co., Inc., 1963, p. 130.

9. *Washington Post*, September 28, 1994, p. A23.

10. Samuel G. Patterson, "Staffing House Committees," in working papers, House Select Committee on Committees, June 1973.

11. Roger H. Davidson and Walter J. Oleszek, *Congress Against Itself*, Indiana University Press, 1977, p. 263.

12. James L. Sundquist, *The Decline and Resurgence of Congress*, The Brookings Institution, 1981, p. 411.

13. Steven S. Smith and Christopher J. Deering, *Committees in Congress*, Congressional Quarterly Press, 1984, p. 106

14. Monroney-Madden, Joint Committee on Organization of the Congress (1965); Bolling, House Select Committee on Committees (1973); Stevenson, Select Committee to Study the Senate Committee Systems (1976); Quayle, Select Committee to Study the Senate Committee System (1984).

15. *Congressional Record*, April 7, 1992, p. S 4932.

16. Comptroller General of the United States, *Increasing the Department of Housing and Urban Development's Effectiveness through Improved Management*, January 10, 1984, p. 3.

17. *New York Times*, May 7, 1984. A rider to a continuing resolution in Public Law 98–473 prohibited reduction of the regions, districts, or entry processing locations by the U.S. Customs Service.

18. Michael S. Gordon, "Reflections on Selected Issues of Private Pension Regulation," *National Journal*, August 11, 1984.

19. Richard Corrigan, "Heading Back into the Future," *National Journal*, November 5, 1983.

20. *Washington Post*, May 30, 1996.

21. *Congressional Quarterly*, June 22, 1996, p. 1758.

22. National Academy of Public Administration, *Renewing HUD: A Long-Term Agenda for Effective Performance*, July 1994, p. IX.

23. *Washington Post*, September 4, 1996, p. A13.

24. *National Journal*, January 28, 1984, P. 167.

25. See Arthur Maass, *Muddy Waters—The Army Engineers and the Nation's Rivers*, Harvard University Press, 1951.

26. Frank E. Smith, *The Politics of Conservation*, Pantheon Books, 1966, p. 306.

27. Senate Committee on Government Operations, Subcommittee on Executive Reorganizations, hearing on S.R. 886 to establish a Department of Natural Resources, October 17, 19, and 20, 1967, p. 36.

28. Herbert Kaufman, *The Administrative Behavior of Federal Bureau Chiefs*, The Brookings Institution, 1981, p. 170.

29. Ibid., p. 169.

30. Randall Ripley, House Select Committee on Committees, Panel Discussions, Vol. 2 of 3, Part 1 of 3, June 1973, p. 52.

31. Incident recounted in Katherine Crane, *Mr. Carr of State—Forty-seven Years in the Department of State*, St. Martin's Press, 1960, pp. 328–29.

32. For discussion of congressional influence on appointments and removals see Louis Fisher, "Congress and Removal Power," *Congress and the Presidency*, Vol. 10, No. 1, Spring 1983.

33. U.S. General Accounting Office, "Observations on Oversight Reform," PAD 81–17, 1981, p. 5.

34. Michael W. Kirst, *Government Without Passing Laws*, The University of North Carolina Press, 1969.

35. James L. Sundquist, *The Decline and Resurgence of Congress*, pp. 358–59.

36. *Congressional Record*, November 8, 1967, p. S16080.

37. Senate Committee on Government Operations, Report No. 1828 on S.R. 2771 to establish a Commission on Science and Technology, 87th Congress, 2nd Session, p. 9.

38. Morgan Thomas and Robert M. Northrop, *Atomic Energy and Congress*, University of Michigan Press, 1956, p. 174.

39. Senate Committee on Expenditures in Executive Departments, hearing on Reorganization Plan no. 24 of 1950, June 14 and 15, 1950, p. 8.

40. Ibid., p. 39.

41. Ibid., p. 15.

42. Senate Committee on Expenditures in Executive Departments, Senate Report No. 1868, 81st Congress, 2nd Session, June 26, 1950, p. 10.

43. Herbert C. Hoover, *The Memoirs of Herbert C. Hoover, The Cabinet and the Presidency, 1920–1933*, The Macmillan Co., 1952, p. 43.

44. Commission on Organization of the Executive Branch of the Government, *General Management of the Executive Branch, a Report to the Congress*, February 1949, p. 4.

45. Judith H. Parris, *The Office of Management and Budget: Background Responsibilities, recent Issues*, Congressional Research Service, July 27, 1978.

46. *Meyers v United States*, 272 US 52 (1926).

47. 42 USC 2996c (E).

48. *Buckley v Valeo*, 424 US 1 (1976).

47. 501 US 252 (1991).

49. Social Security Administration Independence Act of 1993

51. *Congressional Research Service Review*, Fall 1983, p. 5.

52. For pros and cons of legislative veto and discussion of post-Chadha alternatives, see Robert S. Gilmour and Barbara H. Craig, "After the Congressional Veto: Assessing Alternatives," *Journal of Policy Analysis and Management*, Vol. 3, 1984; Frederick M. Kaiser, "Congressional Control of Executive Actions in the Aftermath of the Chadha Decision," *Administrative Law Review*, Vol. 36, Summer 1984; Louis Fisher, *The Politics of Shared Power*, Congressional Quarterly Press, 1981, pp. 92–103; James L. Sundquist, *The Decline and Resurgence of Congress*, Chapter XII; Barbara H. Craig, *The Legislative Veto: Congressional Control of Regulation*, Westview Press, 1983.

53. James Rowe, Jr., "Cooperation or Conflict: The President's Relation with an Opposition Congress," *Georgetown Law Journal*, Vol. 36, 1947.

54. General Accounting Office, Report GAO-HRO 87–47, April 1987, p. 6.

55. Hearing on H.R. 3343 and H.R. 3443, October 27, 1987, p. 309.

56. Senate Report 103–221, 103d Congress, 2nd Session, p. 3.

57. *Congressional Quarterly*, August 3, 1996, pp. 2169–2173.

58. Frances Perkins, *The Roosevelt I Knew*, The Viking Press, 1946, p. 172.

59. Senate Report 97–179, 97th Congress, 1st Session, p. 8.

60. Roger H. Davidson and Walter J. Oleszek, *Congress Against Itself*, p. 9.

61. House Select Committee on Committees, Vol. 1 of 3. Part 1 of 2, May 1973, p. 15.

62. National Academy of Public Administration, *Beyond Distrust: Building Bridges Between Congress and the Executive*, 1992, p. 3.

CHAPTER 3

1. Quoted in Clinton Rossiter, *The American Presidency*, The New American Library, Inc., 1956 p. 92.

2. John W. Gardner, *No Easy Victories*, Harper & Row, 1968, p. 28.

3. Senate Committee on Government Operations, Subcommittee on Executive Reorganization, hearings on Modernizing the Federal Government, January-May 1968, p. 2.

4. Quoted in Douglas Cater, *Power in Washington*, Vintage Books, 1964, p. 253.

5. Louis Brownlow, *The President and the Presidency*, Public Administration Service, 1949, p. 91.

6. Martha Derthick, *Agency Under Stress*, Brookings Institution, 1990, pp. 3–4.

7. Message of the President of the United States transmitting Reorganization Plan No. 2 of 1970, House Document No. 91–275, 91st Congress, 2nd Session.

8. For analysis of the change in the Bureau of the Budget's role, see Allen Schick, "The Budget Bureau That Was: Thoughts on the Rise, Decline and Future of a Presidential Agency," *Law and Contemporary Problems,* School of Law, Duke University, Vol. 35, Summer 1970.

9. Ronald C. Moe, "The HUD Scandal and the Case for an Office of Federal Management," *Public Administration Review,* July/August 1991.

10. Alan Dean, Dwight Ink and Harold Seidman, "OMB's M: Fading Away," *Government Executive,* June 1994.

11. Office of Management and Budget, office memorandum No. 94–16, March 1, 1994.

12. House Report 104–435, 104th Congress, 1st Session, December 21, 1995, p. 8.

13. National Academy of Public Administration, *Revitalizing Federal Management: Managers and their Overburdened Systems,* November 1983, p. 12.

14. Stephen J. Wayne, *The Legislative Presidency,* Harper & Row, 1978, pp. 54–55.

15. Letter to the author from James H. Rowe, Jr., February 17, 1969.

16. Ibid.

17. Report of the President's Committee on Administrative Management, U.S. Government Printing Office, 1939, p. 5.

18. See column of Rowland Evans and Robert Novak, *Washington Post,* January 16, 1969.

19. Senate Select Committee on Presidential Campaign Activities, hearings May-August 1973, pp. 1682, 2514–17, 2599.

20. Thomas E. Cronin, "The Swelling of the Presidency," *Saturday Review,* February 1973.

21. Elizabeth Drew, *On the Edge: The Clinton Presidency*, a Touchstone Book, 1995, p. 98.

22. Elizabeth Drew, ibid., p. 426. Jeffrey H. Birnbaum, *Madhouse: The Private Turmoil of Working for the President*, Times Books, 1996, pp. 245–246.

23. Kermit Gordon, *Reflections on Spending*, The Brookings Institution, 1967, p. 15.

24. Committee on Energy and Commerce, *Presidential Control of Agency Rulemaking*, Committee Print 97, 97th Congress, 1st Session.

25. Jesse H. Jones, *Fifty Billion Dollars: My Thirteen Years with the RFC* (1932–1945), The Macmillan Co., 1951, p. 262.

26. Rossiter, *The American Presidency*, p. 149.

27. Louis Brownlow, *The President and the Presidency*, p. 64.

28. Senate Committee on Government Operations, op. cit. p. 282.

29. Ibid., p. 281.

30. U.S. Office of Personnel Management, Federal Executive Institute, *Management Improvement Agenda for the Eighties*, June 30–July 2, 1980, p. 2.

31. *Washington Post*, August 24, 1972.

32. Don Bonafede, "Carter Sounds Retreat form Cabinet Government," *National Journal*, July 17, 1976.

33. Joseph W. Bartlett and Douglas N. Jones, "Managing a Cabinet Agency: Problems of Performance at Commerce," *Public Administration Review*, Vol. 34, No. 1 January-February 1974.

34. Bernard J. Frieden and Marshall Kaplan, *The Politics of Neglect*, The MIT Press, 1975, p. 112.

35. *Washington Post*, February 1969.

36. See for example, Richard N. Haass, "Bill Clinton's Ad Hocracy," *New York Times Magazine*, May 29, 1995.

37. Sidney W. Souers, "Policy Formulation for National Security," *The American Political Science Review*, June 1949.

38. Morton H. Halperin, "Why Bureaucrats Play Games," *Foreign Policy*, No. 2, Spring 1971.

39. *Diplomacy for the 70's: A Program of Management Reform for the Department of State*, U.S. Government Printing Office, 1970, p. 306.

40. Hugh Heclo, *A Government of Strangers: Executive Politics in Washington*, The Brookings Institution, 1977, p. 220.

41. *Foreword to Preliminary History of the National Aeronautic and Space Administration During the Administration of Lyndon B. Johnson*, National Aeronautics and Space Administration, January 15, 1969.

42. Meg Greenfield, Joe Califano: "Lessons of Experience on Decentralization," *Washington Post*, December 16, 1968.

43. Memorandum for the Director of the Bureau of the Budget, July 20, 1939.

44. Louis W. Koenig, *The Chief Executive*, Harcourt Brace and World, Inc., 1964, pp. 166–68.

45. Quoted in A. J. Wann, "Franklin D. Roosevelt and the Bureau of the Budget," *Business and Government Review*, University of Missouri, March-April 1968.

46. Richard Polenberg, *Reorganizing Roosevelt's Government*, Harvard University Press, 1966, p. 17.

47. Senate Committee on Government Operations, Subcommittee on National Policy Machinery, *Organizing for National Security, Vol. 2 Studies and Background Materials,* p. 421, and footnote, p. 422.

48. See, for example, the signing statements of the 1956 Defense Appropriation Act and the Small Reclamation Act of 1966.

49. Statement of President Eisenhower on signature of H.R. 4353, August 6, 1953.

50. Statement of President on H.R. 10258, July 26, 1956.

51. Theodore C. Sorensen, *Decision-Making in the White House: The Olive Branch and the Arrows*, Columbia University Press, 1963, p. 3.

52. Memorandum from Joseph A. Califano, Jr., to the heads of executive departments on reorganization proposals, January 15, 1966.

53. Emmette S. Redford and Marlin Blissett, *Organizing the Executive Branch: The Johnson Presidency,* The University of Chicago Press, 1981, p. 220.

54. *Washington Monthly,* February 1969.

CHAPTER 4

1. President's Message on Reorganization, March 25, 1971.

2. President's Message on Administrative Organization, January 12, 1937.

3. President's Message on Reorganization, March 29,1972.

4. Nicos P. Mouzelis, *Organization and Bureaucracy,* Aldine Publishing Co. 1968, pp. 15–16.

5. Report of the President's Committee on Administrative Management, 1937.

6. Rowland Evans, Jr., and Robert D. Novak, *Nixon in the White House,* Random House, 1971, p. 12.

7. Senate Select Committee on Presidential Campaign Activities, June-July 1973, Book 4, p. 1683.

8. Douglas M. Fox, "The President's Proposals for Executive Reorganization: A Critique," *Public Administration Review,* Vol. 33, No. 5, September-October 1973.

9. Senate Select Committee on Presidential Campaign Activities, Book 6, p. 2518.

10. Evans and Novak, *Nixon in the White House,* pp. 238–240.

11. Ibid., p. 11.

12. *Washington Post,* January 20, 1969.

13. Evans and Novak, *Nixon in the White House,* p. 240.

14. House Committee on Government Operations, Subcommittee on Legislation and Military Operations, *Reorganization of Executive Departments (Overview),* June-July 1971, p. 226.

15. House Report No. 91–1066.

16. Herbert Roback, "Problems and Prospects in Government Reorganization," *Selected Papers of the National Academy of Public Administration*, No. I, January 1973.

17. Herbert Roback, "The Congress and Super Departments," *The Bureaucrat*, Spring 1972.

18. Papers Relating to the President's Departmental Reorganization, March 1971, pp. 160–61.

19. Ibid., p. 168.

20. Ibid., p. 162.

21. House Committee on Government Operations, *Executive Reorganization: A Summary Analysis*, House Report No. 92–922, March 1972, p. 26.

22. Ibid., p. 25.

23. *House Committee on Government Operations (Overview)*, p. 154.

24. Frederick C. Mosher et al., *Watergate: Its Implications for Responsible Government*, Basic Books, 1974, p.11.

25. *Washington Post*, August 24, 1972.

26. *Washington Post*, July 19, 1973.

27. *New York Times*, December 23, 1972.

28. *Washington Post*, August 23, 1974.

29. *Weekly Compilation of Presidential Documents*, May 11, 1973, pp. 662–63.

30. Aaron Wildavsky, "Government and the People," *Commentary*, August 1973.

31. Mosher et al., *Watergate*, pp. 8–9.

32. Emmet J. Hughes, *The Living Presidency*, Coward, McCann & Geoghegan, 1973, p. 186.

CHAPTER 5

1. *Congressional Quarterly*, October 16, 1976, p. 3009.

2. Quoted in John R. Dempsey "Carter Reorganization: A Midterm Appraisal" *Public Administration Review,* Vol. 39, No. 1, January-February 1979

3. Jules Witcover, *Marathon,* The New American Library, Inc., 1978, p. 221.

4. Rochelle Stanfield, "The Reorganization Staff Is Big Loser in Latest Shuffle," *National Journal,* March 10, 1979.

5. Jimmy Carter, *Why Not the Best?,* Bantam Books, 1976, p. 172.

6. Statement by Richard A. Pettigrew, assistant to the president for reorganization, at meeting of the American Society for Public Administration on "Reorganizing the Federal Establishment," Washington, D.C., December 1–2, 1977.

7. Richard A. Pettigrew, "Improving Government Competence," *Publius,* Vol. 8, No. 2, Spring 1978.

8. Thomas E. Cronin, "The Carter Presidency," *National Journal,* Reprint Series, "The Carter Presidency: The White House at Mid-Term," 1978–79.

9. Jean Conley and Joel Havemann, "Reorganization—Two Plans, One Department Down, Much More to Come," *National Journal,* December 3, 1977.

10. Senate Committee on Governmental Affairs, hearing on nomination of James T. McIntyre, Jr., to be director of the Office of Management and Budget, March 16, 1978, p. 39.

11. House Report No. 95–661, 95th Congress, 1st Session, p. 60.

12. Peter S. Szanton, ed., *Federal Reorganization: What Have We Learned?* Chatham House Publishers, 1981, p. 5.

13. Stanfield, "The Best Laid Reorganization Plans," *National Journal,* January 20, 1979.

14. Timothy B. Clark, "The Power Vacuum Outside the Oval Office," *National Journal,* February 24, 1979.

15. U.S. Senate Committee on Governmental Affairs, *The Federal Executive Establishment: Evolution and Trends,* Committee Print, 96th Congress, 2nd Session, May 1980, p. 20.

16. Jimmy Carter, *Keeping Faith,* Bantam Books, 1982, pp. 69–71.

CHAPTER 6

1. See *Report of the President's Private Sector Survey on Cost Control* (Grace Commission), Vol. II of II, VIII, 1984, p. 92.

2. Lester M. Salamon, "Rethinking Public Management: Third-Party Government and the Changing Forms of Government Action," *Public Policy*, Vol. 29, No. 3, Summer 1981.

3. General Accounting Office, *Government Management Issues*, December 1992, p. 13.

4. Statement of Senator David Pryor on the Department of the Environment Act of 1990, February 6, 1996.

5. *Washington Post*, July 11, 1995.

6. Edward L. Koch, *Mayor*, Warner Books, 1985, p. 58.

7. Bruce L.R. Smith, "Changing Public-Private Sector Relations: A Look at the United States," *Annals, AAPSS*, Vol. 466, March 1983.

8. Peter F. Drucker, *The Age of Discontinuity*, Harper & Row, 1969, p. 233.

9. Comptroller General of the United States, report to Congress on "Civil Servants and Contract Employees: Who Should Do What for the Federal Government?" June 19, 1981.

10. *Washington Post*, March 2, 1985.

11. Report of the National Performance Review, September 7, 1993, p. 2.

12. Ibid., p. 6.

13. Frederick C. Mosher, "The Changing Responsibilities and Tactics of the Federal Government," *Public Administration Review*, November-December 1980.

14. Lester M. Salamon, *Rethinking Public Management.*

15. National Academy of Public Administration, *Privatization: The Challenge to Public Management*, March, 1989.

16. See testimony of OMB Deputy Director Edwin L. Harper before the Committee on Governmental Affairs, U.S. Senate, on S.893, May 6, 1981.

17. Office of Management and Budget, *Management of the United States Government,* p. 1.

18. Comptroller General of the United States, *Analysis of Energy Reorganization, Estimates and Plans,* August 2, 1982.

19. *Washington Post,* January 1, 1985.

20. Allen Schick, "The Budget as an Instrument of Presidential Policy," in *The Reagan Presidency and the Governing of America;* Lester M. Salamon and Michael S. Lund, eds., Urban Institute, 1985, p. 95.

21. Ibid., p. 113.

22. Lou Cannon, "Appointments by the White House Take Right Turn," *Washington Post,* June 18, 1981.

23. Calvin Mackenzie, *Cabinet and Subcabinet Personnel Selection in Reagan's First Year,* paper presented to the American Political Science Association convention, 1981.

24. Lester M. Salamon and Michael S. Lund, "Governance in the Reagan Era: an Overview," in *The Reagan Presidency and the Governing of America,* Salamon and Lund, eds., p. 9. For analysis and evaluation of the Cabinet Councils, see Chester A. Newland, "Executive Office Policy Apparatus: Enforcing the Reagan Agenda," in the same volume.

25. Dick Kirschten, "Decision Making in the White House: How Well Does It Serve the President?" *National Journal,* April 3, 1982.

26. Martha Derthick, *The Influence of Federal Grants,* Harvard University Press, 1970, p. 198.

27. *Immigration and Naturalization Service v Chadha,* 103 S.Ct. 2764 (1983). For an analysis of congressional control of regulation, see Barbara H. Craig, *The Legislative Veto: Congressional Control of Regulation,* Westview Press, 1983.

28. Robert S. Gilmour, *Presidential Clearance of Regulations,* paper presented to the National Conference of the American Society for Public Administration, April 17, 1983.

29. Ronald W. Reagan, "The Presidency: Roles and Responsibilities," *National Forum,* Fall 1984.

30. *Presidential Control of Agency Rulemaking*, Committee Print 97–0, 97th Congress, 1st Session, June 15, 1981, p. 80.

31. Ibid., pp. 46–73.

32. Memorandum to Agency Heads from Douglas H. Ginsburg, administrator for Information and Regulatory Affairs, January 14, 1985.

33. Executive Order 12866, September 30, 1993.

34. Lester Salamon, "The Invisible Partnership: Government and the Nonprofit Sector," *Bell Atlantic Quarterly*, Vol. 1, No. 1, Autumn 1984.

35. Advisory Commission on Intergovernmental Relations, *The Federal Role in the Federal System: Dynamics of Growth (A-86)*, June 1981.

36. David B. Walker, *Toward a Functioning Federalism*, Winthrop Publishers, 1981, p. 146.

37. Senate Document No. 94, 87th Congress, 2nd Session, May 17, 1962, pp. 21–22.

38. Donald F. Kettl, Patricia W. Ingraham, Ronald P. Sanders, and Constance Horner, op. cit. p. 50.

39. Ibid., p. 16.

40. David E. Lilienthal, "Skeptical Look at Scientific Experts," *New York Times Magazine*, September 29, 1963.

41. See Chester A. Newland, "A Mid-Term Appraisal—The Reagan Presidency: Limited Government and Political Administration," *Public Administration Review*, January-February 1983, pp. I-21.

CHAPTER 7

1. Peter F. Drucker, "Really Reinventing Government," *Atlantic Monthly*, February 1995.

2. Adam Smith, *The Wealth of Nations*, Vol. II, The Modern Library, Random House, 1937, p. 384.

3. Vice President Al Gore, a report to President Bill Clinton, *The Best Kept Secrets In Government*, U.S. Government Printing Office, September 1996, p. 1.

4. Ibid, p. 1.

5. Office of Management and Budget, Table 17.5 Government Employment and Population 1962–1995.

6. Paul C. Light, *Thickening Government: Federal Hierarchy and Diffusion of Accountability*, Brookings, 1995.

7. Ibid, pp. 7–12.

8. House Report 104–435, December 21, 1995, p. 5.

9. Donald F. Kettl, *Reinventing Government? Appraising the National Performance Review*, Brookings, August, 1994, p. 3.

10. *Congressional Record*, October 5, 1991, p. 2,846.

11. *Press Release*, September 14, 1995. "Reinvention's Next Steps," speech by Vice President Gore, March 4, 1996.

12. Ronald C. Moe and Robert Gilmour, "Rediscovering Principles of Public Administration: The Neglected Foundation of Public Law," *Public Administration Review*, March/April 1995.

CHAPTER 8

1. H. G. Jones, *The Records of a Nation*, Athenaeum, 1969, p. 160.

2. Quoted in Richard E. Neustadt, *Presidential Power*, John Wiley & Sons Inc., 1966.

3. A. J. Wann, *The President as Chief Administrator—A Study of Franklin D. Roosevelt*, Public Affairs Press, 1968, pp. 103–4.

4. Francis Biddle, *In Brief Authority*, Doubleday & Co., Inc., 1962, p. 257.

5. James E. Webb, *Space-Age Management*, McGraw-Hill Book Co., 1969, p. 128.

6. Ibid.

7. Speech Before National Housing Policy Forum, February 14, 1967.

8. David C. Jones, "What's Wrong with Our Defense Establishment," *New York Times Magazine*, November 7, 1982.

9. James Q. Wilson, *Bureaucracy: What Government Agencies Do and Why They Do It*, Basic Books, 1989, p. 91.

10. Victor S. Navasky, *Kennedy Justice*, Athenaeum, 1971. For a discussion of bureaucratic culture, see Morton H. Halperin, *Bureaucratic Politics and Foreign Policy*, The Brookings Institution, 1974.

11. Daniel Katz and Robert L. Kahn, *The Social Psychology of Organization*, John Wiley & Sons, Inc., 1966, p. 33.

12. Chester I. Barnard, *The Functions of the Executive*, Harvard University Press, 1942, p. 146

13. A typical example is Admiral King's reaction to Secretary Forrestal's tampering with the established promotion processes in the U.S. Navy. See Ernest J. King and Walter M. Whitehill, *Fleet Admiral King—A Naval Record*, W. W. Norton & Co., Inc., 1952, p. 635.

14. For a description of the Forest Service technique, see Herbert Kaufman, *The Forest Ranger—A Study in Administrative Behavior*, The Johns Hopkins Press, 1960.

15. See Ninth Semiannual Report of the Atomic Energy Commission, January 31, 1951.

16. Subcommittee of the House Committee on Government Operations, hearings on Reorganization Plan No. 2 of 1977, October 18 and 21, 1977, p. 99.

17. Lester M. Salamon, "Rethinking Public Management: Third Party Government and the Changing Forms of Government Action," *Public Policy*, Vol. 29, No. 3, Summer 1981.

18. Lester M. Salamon, ed., *Beyond Prevalization: The Tools of Government Action*, Urban Institute Press, 1989, p. 8.

19. *Kent Farm Co. v Hills*, 413 F. Supp. 297 (1976).

20. Harold Orlans, "The Political Uses of Social Research," *Annals of the American Academy of Political and Social Science*, Vol. 384, March 1971.

21. National Academy of Public Administration, *The Roles, Mission and Operation of the U.S. General Accounting Office*, October 1994, p. 27.

22. Paul C. Light, *Monitoring Government: Inspectors General and the Search for Accountability*, Brookings, 1993, pp. 160–61.

23. Report of National Performance Review, September 1993, p. 31–32.

24. Robert A. Katzmann, *Regulatory Bureaucracy*, The MIT Press, 1980, p. 51.

25. Harold Orlans, *The Political Uses of Social Research*.

26. Commission on Organization of the Executive Branch of Government, report on "Legal Service and Procedures," March 1955, p. 17.

27. W. Henry Lambright, *Governing Science and Technology*, Oxford University Press, 1976, p. 146.

28. Commission on Organization of the Executive Branch of the Government, task force report on "Public Welfare," January 1949, p. 11.

29. Ibid., p. 6.

30. Senate Committee on Government Operations, hearings on S. 561, Intergovernmental Cooperation Act, March 31, 1965, pp. 196, 197, 199.

31. *Congressional Quarterly*, January 24, 1969, p. 170.

32. Statement by William H. Charterner, assistant secretary of commerce for economic affairs, *Washington Post*, September 27, 1968.

33. Frederick C. Mosher, *Democracy and the Public Service*, 2nd ed., Oxford University Press, 1982, p. 113. For a discussion of the role of lawyers, economists, engineers, accountants, and scientists, see "Symposium on Professions in Government," *Public Administration Review*, Vol. 38, No. 2, March-April 1978.

34. Malcolm Moos and Francis E. Rourke, *The Campus and the State*, Johns Hopkins Press, 1958, p. 6.

35. H. G. Jones, *The Records of a Nation*, p.21.

36. Mosher, *Democracy and the Public Service*, p. 230.

37. *United States Investor*, February 23, 1946.

38. Comptroller of the Currency, *Annual Report*, 1923, p. 18.

39. Harry S. Truman, *Memoirs of Harry S. Truman*, Vol. 1, Doubleday Co., Inc., 1955, p. 110.

40. *New York Times*, November 12, 1971.

41. John Gardner, *No Easy Victories*, Harper & Row, 1968, p. 44.

42. For origins of the farmer committee system and soil conservation districts, see John M. Gaus, "The Citizen as Administrator," in *Public Administration and Democracy*, Roscoe Martin, ed., Syracuse University Press, 1965, pp. 175–76; Robert J. Morgan, *Governing Soil Conservation*, The Johns Hopkins Press, 1965, pp. 317, 318, 353, 354; Morton Grodzins, *The American System*, Rand McNally & Co., 1966, pp. 351, 352, 356.

43. *Washington Post*, June 23, 1994.

44. House Report No. 1215, 83rd Congress, 2nd Session.

45. See E. Pendleton Herring, *Public Administration and the Public Interest*, McGraw-Hill Book Co., 1936; David Truman, *The Governmental Process*, Alfred A. Knopf, 1964; Harmon Zeigler, *Interest Groups in American Society*, Prentice-Hall, Inc., 1964; Grant McConnell, *Private Power and American Democracy*, Alfred A. Knopf, 1976; Theodore J. Lowi, *The End of Liberalism*, W.W. Norton Co., 1969.

46. Donald V. Allison, *The Development and Use of Political Power by Federal Agencies: A Case Study of the U.S. Forest Service*, May 1965 (unpublished thesis, University of Virginia).

47. Harold Seidman, Dominic Del Guidice, and Charles Warren, *Reorganization by Presidential Plan: Three Case Studies*, National Academy of Public Administration, 1971.

48. William Macleish, "The United States Coast Guard: Poor, But Proud and Looking Ahead," *Smithsonian*, Vol. 13, No. 4, 1982.

49. Lieutenant Commander Lawrence I. Kiern, "Changing the Guard," *Naval Institute Proceedings*, February 1985.

50. Luther Gulick, "Notes on the Theory of Organization," in *Papers on the Science of Administration*, Luther Gulick and L. Urwick, eds., Institute of Public Administration, 1937.

51. Michael J. Malbin, "You Can Please Some of the Senators Some of the Time," *National Journal*, January 15, 1977.

52. Quoted in the *Washington Post*, June 8, 1969, p. B1.

53. Hugh Heclo, "Political Executives and the Washington Bureaucracy," *Political Science Quarterly*, Vol. 92, Fall 1977.

54. Independent Industry Panel, report to Congress on Naval Petroleum Reserve No. 1, October, 1993.

55. Memorandum to staff of Division of Administrative Management from Donald C. Stone, assistant director for administrative management, April 5, 1948.

CHAPTER 9

1. Comptroller General of the United States, *Review of Economic Opportunity Programs,* March 18, 1969, pp. 163–65.

2. See, for example, Section 4 of Executive Order No. 11452, January 23, 1969, establishing the Council for Urban Affairs.

3. Senate Committee on Government Operations, hearings on S.R. 886 to redesignate the Department of the Interior as a Department of Natural Resources, October 17, 1967, p. 16.

4. James D. Mooney, "The Principles of Organization," in *Papers on the Science of Administration,* Luther Gulick and L. Urwick, eds., Institute of Public Administration, 1937, p. 93.

5. Ibid.

6. Stuart M. Butler, Michael Sanera, and W. Bruce Weinrod, *Mandate for Leadership II,* The Heritage Foundation, 1984, p. 484.

7. Senate Committee on Government Operations, Subcommittee on National Policy Machinery, *Organizing for National Security, Hearing,* Vol. 1, p. 15.

8. Ibid., p. 30.

9. Ibid., p. 17.

10. Ibid., p. 945.

11. Ibid., p. 635.

12. Lyndon B. Johnson, Memorandum for Heads of Departments and Agencies, February 25, 1965.

13. Executive Order, Federal Information Technology, July 17, 1996.

14. Senate Committee on Government Operations, Subcommittee on National Policy Machinery, Vol. 3, p. 50.

15. Bureau of the Budget and U.S. Civil Service Commission, Memorandum for the President, "Evaluation of Federal Executive Boards," July 22, 1969.

16. Robert W. Gage, "Federal Regional Councils: Networking Organizations for Policy Management," *Public Administration Review*, Vol. 44, No. 2, March/April 1984.

17. Sar A. Levitan, *Federal Aid to Depressed Areas*, The Johns Hopkins Press, 1964, p. 4227.

18. Ibid., p. 45.

19. Comptroller General, *Review of Economic Opportunity Programs*, p. 22.

20. Ibid., p. 168.

21. *Weekly Compilation of Presidential Documents*, August 18, 1969, pp. 1,132–36.

22. President Nixon recommended in his 1975 Budget Message that OEO be abolished.

23. Paul T. David, "The Vice-Presidency: Its Institutional Evolution and Contemporary Status," *The Journal of Politics*, November 1969.

24. McCormack Act, 3 U.S.C. 302.

25. Senate Committee on Government Operations, Subcommittee on National Policy Machinery, Vol. 3, pp. 21–22.

CHAPTER 10

1. Quoted in Leonard White, *The Federalists*, The Macmillan Co., 1948, p. 91.

2. Lloyd M. Short, *The Development of National Administrative Organization in the United States*, The Johns Hopkins Press, 1923, p. 92.

3. Ibid., footnote, pp. 417–18.

4. Ronald C. Moe, *The Federal Executive Establishment Evaluation and Trends*, prepared for the Senate Committee on Governmental Affairs by the Congressional Research Service, Committee Print, 96th Congress, 2nd Session, May 1980, p. 11. An excellent study of U.S. administrative development and the typology of federal organizations.

5. Senate Committee on Government Operations, hearings on S.R. 1571 to establish a Department of Consumers, June 23 and 24, 1960, p. 34.

6. Lloyd M. Short, *The Development of National Administrative Organization*, p. 383.

7. Reconstruction Finance Corporation, Home Owners Loan Corporation, Tennessee Valley Authority, Commodity Credit Corporation, Federal Deposit Insurance Corporation, U.S. Housing Authority, Regional Agricultural Credit Corporation.

8. Franklin D. Roosevelt, *Message to the Congress on Administrative Reorganization*, January 12, 1937.

9. Classified as mixed-ownership in Government Corporation Control Act, but in fact wholly owned since the retirement of capital stock in 1948.

10. Harold J. Laski, *The American Democracy*, The Viking Press, 1948, p. 167.

11. Committee on Government Operations, hearings on H.R. 12092 to make the FDIC subject to budget review, June 21, 1960, p. 34.

12. National Academy of Public Administration, *Evaluation of Proposals to Establish a Department of Veterans Affairs*, March 1988, pp. 7–22.

13. House Report 104–435, December 21, 1995, p. 25.

14. S.R. 4106 introduced by Congressman John J. Ingalls (Kansas) in the 51st Congress, 1st Session.

15. House Report No. 93–109.

16. Bureau of the Budget, *Staff Orientation Manual*, April 1958, p. 7.

17. The Office of Economic Opportunity and National Council on Marine Resources and Engineering Development have been abolished.

18. *Washington Star*, February 27, 1951.

19. Senate Report No. 91–912, p. 9.

20. House Document No. 91–313.

21. Ronald C. Moe, *The Federal Executive Establishment Evaluation and Trends*, p. 64.

22. Ibid., p. 65.

23. Lloyd M. Short, *The Development of National Administrative Organization*, p. 422.

24. Marver H. Bernstein, *Regulating Business by Independent Commission*, Princeton University Press, 1955, p. 130.

25. Senate Document No. 95–91, 95th Congress, 2nd Session, December 1977, p. xiii.

26. Message to the Congress, April 13, 1961.

27. *Congressional Record*, April 25, 1953, p. 40009.

28. Roger G. Noll, *Reforming Regulation: An Evaluation of the Ash Council Proposals*, The Brookings Institution, 1971, p. 35.

29. Ibid., p. 38.

30. For history, see Harold Seidman, "Public Enterprise in the United States," *Annals of Public Cooperative Economy*, January-March 1983. Ronald C. Moe, "Managing the Government's Business," *Federal Government Corporations*, Senate PRT, 104–18, April 1995.

31. President's Commission on Postal Organization, *Towards Postal Excellence*, a report to the President, June 1968.

32. Senate Report No. 694, 79th Congress.

33. Sidney D. Goldberg and Harold Seidman, *The Government Corporation: Elements of a Model Charter*, Public Administration Service, 1953, pp. 23–29.

34. David E. Lilienthal, *The Journals of David E. Lilienthal; The TVA Years 1939–1945*, Vol. 1, Harper & Row, 1964, pp. 280–81.

35. Senate Report No. 76, 82nd Congress.

36. Harold Seidman, "The Theory of the Autonomous Government Corporation: A Critical Appraisal," *Public Administration Review*, Vol. 12, No. 2, 1952. Harold Seidman, "Public Enterprise Autonomy: Need for a New Theory," *International Review of Administrative Sciences*, Vol. XLIX, No. 1, 1983.

37. Senate Document No. 155, 75th Congress, 3rd Session, p. 105.

38. *Morgan v Tennessee Valley Authority*, 115 F 2d. 900, certiorari denied, 312 US 701.

39. The Federal Deposit Insurance Corporation is classified in the Government Corporation Control Act as a "mixed-ownership" corporation, but the stock held by the Federal Reserve Banks has been retired. FDIC is presently a "no-stock" corporation, as are most wholly owned government corporations.

40. House Document No.19, 80th Congress, pp. M57—M62.

41. National Academy of Public Administration, *Incorporating the Patent and Trademark Office*, August 1991; National Academy of Public Administration, *Reinventing the Bonneville Power Administration*, December 1993.

42. House Report 104–435, December 21, 1995, pp. 7–8.

CHAPTER 11

1. Clinton Rossiter, ed., *The Federalist Papers*, The New American Library, Inc., 1961, p. 424.

2. House Committee on Government Operations, *The Administration of Research Grants in the Public Health Service*, House Report No. 800, 90th Congress, 1st Session, p. 61.

3. Daniel S. Greenberg, *The Politics of Pure Science*, The New American Library, Inc., 1967, p. 15.

4. *Washington Post*, May 4, 1979.

5. David B. Truman, *The Governmental Process*, Alfred A. Knopf, 1964.

6. House Committee on Government Operations, p. 62.

7. Edith T. Carper, "The Reorganization of the Public Health Service," in *Governmental Reorganization: Cases and Commentary*, Frederick C. Mosher, ed., The Bobbs-Merrill Co., Inc., 1967.

8. *Citizens for the Abatement of Aircraft Noise Inc. v Metropolitan Washington Airport Authority*, 501 US 252 (1990); *Bowsher v Synor*, 478 US 714, 726–27 (1906); *Buckley v Valeo*, 424 US 1 (1976) and *Federal Election Commission v NRA Political Victory Fund*, 6F 3D.821 (D.C. Co. 1993); *Springer v Philippine Islands*, 273 US 189 (1928).

9. Resolution adopted by the Governors' Conference, June 28, 1961.

10. National Academy of Public Administration, *The Resilient Partnership: An Assessment of the Intergovernmental Model of the Appalachian Regional Commission,* May, 1996.

11. Ronald C. Moe , "Exploring the Limits of Privatization," and Harold J. Sullivan, "Privatization of Public Service: A Growing Threat to Constitutional Rights," *Public Administration Review,* November/December 1987.

12. *Lebron v National Passenger Railroad Corporation,* February 21, 1995.

13. General Accounting Office, *Federally Funded R&D Centers,* August 6, 1996, GAO/NSIAD-96–112.

14. *Washington Post,* August 28, 1996.

15. Bureau of the Budget, report to the President on Contracting for Research and Development, Senate Doc. 94, 87th Congress, 2nd Session, May 17, 1962.

16. General Accounting Office, op. cit.

17. Thomas H. Stanton, *A State of Risk,* Harper Business, 1991, p. 17.

18. Thomas H. Stanton, ibid., p. 12.

19. Lloyd D. Musolf, *Mixed Enterprise,* Lexington Books, 1972, p. 55.

20. Lloyd D. Musolf, *Communications Satellites in Political Orbit,* Chandler Publishing Company, 1968, p. 136–37.

21. Congressional Budget Office, *Assessing the Public Costs and Benefits of Fannie Mae and Freddie Mac,* May 1996, p. 24.

CHAPTER 12

1. *Public Management Focus,* Public Management Service of OECD, June, 1996, p. 1.

2. Alan Brinkley, "Big Government is a Check," *New York Times Magazine,* August 18, 1996.

3. Harold Seidman, "The Quasi World of the Federal Government," *Brookings Review,* Summer, 1988.

4. House Report 104–435, December 21, 1995, p. 5.

Select Bibliography

GENERAL

Arnold, Peri, Making *The Managerial Presidency: Comprehensive Reorganization Planning, 1905–1980.* Princeton University Press, 1986.

Comptroller General of the United States, *Implementation: The Missing Link in Planning Reorganization.* March 20, 1981.

Derthick, Martha, *Agency Under Stress.* The Brookings Institution, 1990

Gore, Al, Vice President, "Creating a Government That Works Better and Costs Less." Report of *National Performance Review,* September 7, 1993.

Kettl, Donald F. and Dilulio, John J., eds., *Inside the Reinvention Machine.* The Brookings Institution, 1995.

March, James G. and Olson, Johan P., "Organizing Political Life: What Administrative Reorganization Tells Us About Government." *American Political Science Review,* No. 77, 1983.

Moe, Ronald C., *The Hoover Commissions Revisited.* Westview Press, 1982.

Moe, Ronald C. and Gilmour, Robert S., "Rediscovering Principles of Public Administration, the Neglected Foundation of Public Law." *Public Administration Review,* March/April 1995.

Polenberg, Richard, *Reorganizing Roosevelt's Government: The Controversy Over Executive Reorganization 1936–1939.* Harvard University Press, 1966.

Short, Lloyd Milton, *The Development of National Administrative Organization in the United States.* The Johns Hopkins Press, 1923.

Szanton, Peter, ed., *Federal Reorganization: What Have We Learned?* Chatham House, 1981.

Waldo, Dwight, *The Administrative State.* 2nd ed,. Holmes and Meier, 1984.

CONGRESS

Craig, Barbara H., *The Legislative Veto: Congressional Control of Regulation.* Westview Press, 1983.

Davidson, Roger H. and Oleszek, Walter J., *Congress Against Itself.* Indiana University Press, 1977.

Fenno, Richard F., Jr., *Congressmen in Committee.* Little, Brown and Co., 1973.

Fisher, Louis, *The Politics of Shared Power.* Congressional Quarterly Press, 1981.

Gilmour, Robert S. and Craig, Barbara H., "After the Legislative Veto: Assessing Alternatives." *Journal of Policy Analysis and Management,* Vol. 3, No. 3, 1984.

Kirst, Michael W., *Government Without Passing Laws.* University of North Carolina Press, 1969.

Maraniss, David and Weisskopf, Michael, *Tell Newt To Shut Up!* A Touchstone Book, 1996.

Sundquist, James L. *The Decline and Resurgence of the Congress.* The Brookings Institution, 1981.

Wilson, Woodrow, *Congressional Government.* Meridian Books, 1956.

THE PRESIDENCY

Califano, Joseph A., Jr., *Governing America.* A Touchstone Book, 1981.

Drew, Elizabeth, *On the Edge: The Clinton Presidency.* A Touchstone Book, 1994.

Heclo, Hugh A., *A Government of Strangers: Executive Politics in Washington.* The Brookings Institution, 1977.

Mosher, Frederick C., et al., *Watergate: Implications for Responsible Government.* Basic Books, 1974.

Nathan, Richard P., *The Administrative Presidency.* John Wiley & Sons, Inc., 1983.

Redford, Emmette S. and Blissett, Marlin, *Organizing the Executive Branch: The Johnson Presidency.* The University of Chicago Press, 1981.

Salamon, Lester M., "Rethinking Public Management: Third Party Government and the Changing Forms of Government Action." *Public Policy,* Vol. 29, No. 3, Summer 1981.

Szanton, Peter, ed., *Federal Reorganization: What Have We Learned?* Chatham House, 1981.

Wayne, Stephen, *The Legislative Presidency.* Harper & Row, 1978.

THE EXECUTIVE ESTABLISHMENT

Crozier, Michael, *The Bureaucratic Phenomenon.* University of Chicago Press, 1963.

Halperin, Morton H., *Bureaucratic Politics and Foreign Policy.* The Brookings Institution, 1974.

Heclo, Hugh A., *A Government of Strangers: Executive Politics in Washington.* The Brookings Institution, 1977.

Katzman, Robert A., *Regulatory Bureaucracy.* The MIT Press, 1980.

Kaufman, Herbert, *The Administrative Behavior of Federal Bureau Chiefs.* The Brookings Institution, 1981.

Lambright, W. Henry, *Governing Science and Technology.* Oxford University Press, 1982.

Light, Paul C., *Thickening Government.* The Brookings Institution, 1995.

Mosher, Frederick C., *Democracy and the Public Service.* 2nd ed. Oxford University Press, 1982.

Navasky, Victor S., *Kennedy Justice.* Atheneum, 1971.

Walker, Wallace Earl, *Changing Organizational Culture*. University of Tennessee Press, 1986.

Wilson, James Q., *Bureaucracy: What Government Agencies Do and Why They Do It*. Basic Books, 1989.

TYPOLOGY

Goldberg, Sidney D. and Seidman, Harold, *The Government Corporation: Elements of a Model Charter*. Public Administration Service, 1983.

Moe, Ronald C., *Managing The Public's Business: Federal Government Corporations*. Senate Print 104–18, April 1995.

———, *The Federal Executive Establishment: Evolution and Trends*. Prepared for the Senate Committee on Governmental Affairs by the Congressional Research Service, Committee Print, May 1980.

Musolf, Lloyd, *Uncle Sam's Private Profit Seeking Corporations*. Lexington Books, 1983.

National Academy of Public Administration, *Privatization, The Challenge to Public Management*. March 1989.

Orlans, Harold, ed., *Nonprofit Organization: A Government Management Tool*. Praeger, 1980.

Salamon, Lester, ed., *Beyond Privatization: The Tools of Government Action*. Urban Institute Press, 1989.

Seidman, Harold, *Government Sponsored Enterprise in the United States*. In *The New Political Economy*, Bruce L.R. Smith, ed., Macmillan & Co., London, 1975.

———, "Public Enterprise Autonomy: Need for a New Theory." *International Review of Administrative Sciences*, Vol. XLIX, No. 1, 1983.

———, "Public Enterprise in the United States." *Annals of Public and Cooperative Economy*, No. 1, March 1983.

———, *A Typology of Government*. In *Federal Reorganization: What Have We Learned?* Peter Szanton, ed., Chatham House, 1981.

———, "The Quasi World of the Federal Government." *Brookings Review*, Summer, 1989.

Stanton, Thomas H., *A State of Risk*. Harper Business, 1991.

Index

Acheson, 14
Adams, Sherman, 81
Administration for Business Development, 84
Administrative agencies, 161–196; *see also* specific agencies
Administrative Procedures Act, 199
Advisory bodies, 197–202
Advisory Commission on Intergovernmental Relations, 107, 204
Advisory Council on Executive Organization, 80
Aerospace Corporation, 22, 97, 210
Agencies of the Congress, 40–41
Agency for International Communications, 127
Agency heads, 60, 65
Agricultural Credit Banks, 191
Agricultural Extension Service, 14
Agricultural Society, U.S., 164
Agriculture Committee, 35
Alaska pipeline bill, 185
Alaska Reconstruction Commission, 150
Albert, Carl, 49
Alliance for Redesigning Government, 3

American Association of State Highway Officials, 132
American Farm Bureau Federation, 14
American Federation of Labor, 134
American Foreign Service Association, 127
American Municipal Association, 204
AMTRAK (National Railroad Passenger Corporation), 196, 207–208
Analytic Services, Inc., 209
Annual authorizing bill, 38–39
Antitrust policy, 130
Appalachian Regional Commission, 205–206
Appalachian Regional Development Act, 205
Appleby, Paul, 6
Appropriation Act, 210
Appropriation bills, 47
Appropriations Committee, 38, 47
Appropriations rider, 39–40
Area Redevelopment Act of 1961, 152
Area Redevelopment Administration (ARN), 152–153
Arkansas-White-Red River Basin Committee, 203
Army, 13

Army Corps of Engineers, U.S., 38, 40, 119, 137, 203
    Delaware River Basin and, 205
    Eisenhower and, 72
    Everglades National Park and, 144
    Manhattan Project and, 125
    Nixon and, 83–84
    water resource programs and, 34–36
Arnold, H.H., 209
Ash, Roy L., 80, 86
Ash Council, 81, 82
Associational attractiveness, 124
Association of American Colleges, 18
Association of Land Grant Colleges and Universities, 18
Atomic Energy Commission (AEC), 41, 73, 125, 136
Attorney general, 119, 175
Audit culture, 129–130

Baker, Howard, 106
Baker, James, 103, 106
Ballinger, 126
Bankers, 128
Bank for Cooperatives, 191
Banking industry, 14, 134
Barnard, Chester, 124
Bartlett, Joseph W., 64
Bell, David E., 211
Bernstein, Marver, 183
Blissett, Marlin, 75
Block grants, 107
Board of Mediation and Conciliation, 164
Board of Review, 45
Boeing Co., 22
Bonneville Power Administration, 114, 193, 195, 205
Bottom-up reorganization, 90–95
Branders, Louis D., 12
Brinkley, Alan, 218
Brookings Institution, 108, 131
Brownlow, Louis, 54, 70
Brownlow Committee, 7, 9, 25, 78, 118–119

Budget, 113–114
    centralization of process, 102
Budget and Accounting Act of 1921, 177
Budget and Impoundment Control Act of 1974, 32
Budget Enforcement Act of 1990, 113
Bundy, McGeorge, 62
Bureaucracy, 13
    Carter and, 90–91, 92
    Congress and, 30
    contest between executive branch and, 62–63, 67–68
    Nixon and, 79–80, 84, 85–86, 89
    Reagan and, 109
    White House staff in, 59
Bureau of Indian Affairs, 126
Bureau of Mint, 39
Bureau of Prisons, 33
Bureau of Reclamation, 35, 36
Bureau of the Budget, 15–16, 54–55, 81, 107, 123, 140, 151
    Executive Office of the President and, 177–178
    Johnson and, 76
    Kennedy and, 73
    Postal Service and, 180
Burford, Anne Gorsuch, 121
Bush, George, 55, 113–114
Byrd, Robert C., 40

Cabinet councils, 102–103
Cabinet officers, 60, 62–64, 66, 118, 121–123
    Carter and, 63–64
    Clinton and, 121
    Nixon and, 80–81, 83, 86
    super, 154–155, 156
    tenuous position of, 119
Califano, Joseph A., Jr., 29, 65, 69, 81, 94
Campbell, J. Phil, 85
Cannon, Joseph C., 28
Cardozo, Benjamin, 107
Carr, Wilbur K., 38

Carter, James, 3, 101, 102, 104, 105
bottom-up reorganization of, 90–95
cabinet officers and, 63–64
interagency committees and, 147
Chadha decision, 45–46
Challenger disaster, 20
Cherry Cotton Mills v. U.S., 193
Chief Financial Officer Act of 1990,
191
Chief Information Officers Council,
149
Chiles, Lawton, 44
Citibank, 134
Civil service, 79, 92, 94, 109, 124
Civil Service Commission, 31, 151, 163
Claims commissions, 183–187
Clinger, William F., Jr., 4, 33
Clinton, William, 66, 98, 106, 110
advisory bodies and, 201
cabinet officers and, 121
expenditure reduction and, 11–12
interagency committees and, 147,
149, 150
Office of Management and Budget
and, 55, 115
plans to reduce government size,
111–112
reinvention and, 3, 12, 27
White House staff and, 59, 64
Coast Guard, 38, 138
Cohen, Wilbur J., 131–132
Commerce and Trade Council, 103
Commerce institutes, 167
Commercial banks, 14
Commission on More Effective Government, 48
Commission on Project Government
Reform, 31–32
Committee on Science and Public Policy, 15
Committee to Re-elect the President, 87
Commodity Credit Corporation, 191
Commodity Futures Trading Commission, 45, 185
Community Relations Service, 127
Conference of Mayors, U.S., 204

Congress, 13, 27–50, 51–54, 217, 218,
219, 221
accessibility of institutional types to,
40–41
administrative agencies and, 162,
163, 164, 170–171
advisory bodies and, 198, 199
annual authorizing bill and, 38–39
coordination and, 154–155
decentralization and, 47–48
division of power in, 28–29
executive departments and, 172,
173–175
Executive Office of the President
and, 43–44, 176, 177–178
government corporations and, 187,
188, 189–191, 191–192, 193, 195
government sponsored enterprises
and, 212
independent agencies and, 179
intergovernmental organizations and,
203, 205
Interstate Commerce Commission
and, 163
Johnson and, 74
Nixon and, 81–82, 83
presidential history of service in,
51–52
Reagan and, 101–102, 103–104, 105,
107
regulatory and claims commissions
and, 185–186
role of committees and subcommittees in, 29–31
Smithsonian Institution and, 182
staffing in, 30–31, 37–38
Tennessee Valley Authority and, 194
turf problems in, 32–33
twilight zone agencies and, 207
water resource programs and, 34–37
weakness on follow-through, 53
Congressional Budget Office, 213
Congressional Research Service, 94
Congress of Industrial Organizations,
134
Connally, John B., 80

Connor, 75, 127
Constitution, U.S.
  on executive branch power, 9, 218
  on executive branch structure,
    161–162
  on intergovernmental organizations,
    203
  twilight zone agencies and, 206–207
Constitutional Convention, 161
Consumer Advisory Council, 200
Consumer Product Safety Commission,
    45, 46, 185
Continuing the Conservative Revolu-
    tion (Mandate for Leadership II),
    6–7
Co-optation, 199
Coordination, 142–157
  community of interests in, 144
  defined, 145
  formula for, 143
  informal (lateral), 145–146
  interagency committees in, 147–152
Corporation for Public Broadcasting,
    97, 196, 207
Corporation for the Promotion of Rifle
    Practice and Fire Arms Safety, 207
Council of Economic Advisers (CEA),
    132, 177, 200–201
Council of State Governments, 204
Council of the American Historical As-
    sociation, 198
Council on Environmental Quality,
    177, 178
Council on Wage and Price Stability,
    104, 105
Craig, Larry E., 47
Credit unions, 14
Cronin, Thomas E., 58
Customs service, 47, 127
Czars, 155

David, Paul, 155
Davidson, Roger H., 30, 48
Dawes, Charles G., 60
Dean, John, 57
Deaver, Michael, 106

Decentralization, 47–48
Decision-making, centralization of,
    102–103
Decision-Making in the White House
    (Sorensen), 73
Defense Authorization Act, 207
Defense industry, 22
Defense Reutilization Marketing Serv-
    ice, 207
de Gaulle, Charles, 88–89
Delaware River Basin Advisory Commit-
    tee, 204–205
Delaware River Basin Commission, 205
Delaware River Compact, 204
Delegate agencies, 152–153
Democrats
  National Security Council and, 19
  Nixon and, 79
Department heads, 117–123, 139–141
  conflicting responsibilities of, 120
  importance of maintaining prestige
    of, 67
  individual agendas of, 121–122
  managerial role of, 139–140
Department of Agriculture, 123, 125,
    126, 135
  coordination and, 153
  lobbyists for, 164
  Nixon and, 82, 83–84, 85, 134
  water resource programs and, 34–36
Department of Commerce, 24, 42, 126,
    179
  Johnson and, 75–76
  Nixon and, 82
  plans to abolish, 12, 33, 110–111
  Truman and, 134
Department of Commerce and Labor,
    164, 183
Department of Community Develop-
    ment, 82, 84, 85, 134
Department of Defense, 34, 72, 99,
    170, 173, 209, 210
Department of Defense Commissaries,
    115
Department of Development Assis-
    tance, 93

Department of Economic Affairs, 82, 84, 85, 134
Department of Economic Development, 75, 76
Department of Education, 13, 21
  Carter and, 92
  establishment of, 174
  lobbyists for, 164
  plans to abolish, 110–111
  Reagan and, 101–102
Department of Energy, 38, 126, 136, 140
  Carter and, 92
  establishment of, 20, 174
  plans to abolish, 110–111
  Reagan and, 97, 99, 101–102
Department of Energy and Natural Resources, 83–84
Department of Health, Education, and Welfare (HEW)
  coordination and, 153–154
  Eisenhower and, 72
  establishment of, 173
  Johnson and, 75
  lack of representation and, 150
  Nixon and, 86, 87–88
  professionalization in, 131–132
Department of Health and Human Services, 132, 135
Department of Housing and Urban Development (HUD), 32, 34, 128, 135
  establishment of, 174
  Johnson and, 74
  lack of representation and, 150
  Nixon and, 86
  Office of Federal Housing Enterprise in, 213
  plans to abolish, 110–111
Department of Human Resources, 82, 84, 134
Department of Justice, 16, 32, 33, 38, 127, 175, 181
Department of Labor, 32
  coordination and, 153
  Johnson and, 75–76

  lack of representation and, 150
  lobbyists for, 164
  Nixon and, 82
  Truman and, 134
Department of Natural Resources, 37, 82, 83, 93, 134
Department of the Interior, 126
  Eisenhower and, 72
  Johnson and, 75
  Nixon and, 87
  opposition to, 13
  water resource programs and, 34–36
Department of the Treasury, 32, 47, 162
  Coast Guard transfer from, 138
  government corporations and, 189, 191
  government sponsored enterprises and, 212
  Roosevelt and, 118–119
  Truman and, 71
  twilight zone agencies and, 206
Department of Trade, 93
Department of Transportation, 24, 137, 179
  early attempts to establish, 174
  Eisenhower and, 72
  establishment of, 174
  Johnson and, 74
  Nixon and, 16–17, 82, 87
Department of Urban Affairs and Housing, 74
Department of Veterans Affairs, 55, 135, 174
Depression, 164–165
Derthick, Martha, 54, 103
Diefendorfer, William, III, 55
District of Columbia Reorganization Plan, 39–40, 74, 75
Division of Mental Health, 200
Dole, Robert, 28, 111
Domestic Council, 81–82
Domestic Policy Council, 103, 150
Domination, 79
Douglas Aircraft Company, 209
Drucker, Peter, 98, 110

Duberstein, Kenneth, 106
Duplication, 6–7, 11, 14, 15, 74

Eccles, Marriner S., 14
Economic Affairs Council, 102
Economic Impact Statement, 104
Economic Opportunity Council,
    142–143
Economic Policy Council, 103
Efficiency, cult of, 3–12
Ehrlichman, John, 57, 63, 80, 81, 82,
    86, 87
Eisenhower, Dwight D., 20, 23, 72–73,
    79, 83, 155
    executive departments and, 175
    Executive Office of the President
        and, 177
    regulatory and claims commissions
        and, 185, 186
Eisenhower, Milton, 72
Emmerich, Herbert, 24–25
Employment Retirement Income Secu-
    rity Act, 92
Employment Service, 138
Encroachment bills, 72–73
Enrichment Corporation, U.S., 196
Entrepreneurial management model,
    7
Environmental Protection Agency, 38–
    39, 97, 104, 179
Environmental Science Service, 124
Equal Employment Opportunity Com-
    mission, 92
Espy, Mike, 136
Evans, 80
Everglades National Park, 144
Executive branch, 51–77, 217–221
    congressional view of organization,
        27–50
    constitution on structure of, 161–162
    contest between bureaucracy and, 62–
        63, 67–68
    coordination and, 155–156
    government corporations and,
        193–194
    independent agencies and, 179

intergovernmental organizations and,
    204
lack of self-sufficiency in, 60–62
Office of Management and Budget
    and, 55–56
orthodox theory on, 5–6, 8–10
political implications of organization
    structure, 13
power in, 9, 41, 65–66, 218
primary task of, 219
regulatory and claims commissions
    and, 183–186
Smithsonian Institution and, 182
theory vs. practice in organization of,
    12–26
two-hatted arrangements and, 41–42
Executive departments
    list of, 165
    structure of, 172–176
Executive Office of the President, 143,
    176–178, 219
    Carter and, 92, 93
    Congress and, 43–44, 176, 177–178
    establishment of, 57
    list of offices in, 166
    Nixon and, 80, 177
    Office of Management and Budget
        and, 56
    structure of, 176–178
Executive Order No. 8248, 57
Executive Order No. 12044, 104
Executive Order No. 12291, 105
Executive Order No. 12498, 105, 106
Executive order No. 12838, 201
Executive Schedule Pay Rates, 171–172
Expenditure reduction, 11–12
Export-Import Bank, 194
Extension Service, 123, 135

Fair Deal, 84
Fannie Mae (Federal National Mort-
    gage Association), 76, 211, 212
Farm Bureau, 134, 135, 136
Farm Credit Act of 1953, 73
Farm Credit Act of 1956, 73
Farm Credit Administration, 14, 211

Farm Credit Board, 179
Farm credit system, 23
Farmer Mac (Federal Agriculture
    Credit Corporation), 211
Farmers Home Administration (FHA),
    14, 84
Farmer's Union, 134
Farm Security Administration, 14
Fayol, 4
Federal Acquisition Regulations, 210
Federal Advisory Committee Act of
    1972, 148, 200, 202
Federal Agricultural Mortgage Corpora-
    tion, 191
Federal Agriculture Credit Corporation
    (Farmer Mac), 211
Federal Aviation Administration, 87,
    114, 126, 127, 179
Federal Bureau of Investigation (FBI),
    33, 123, 171
Federal Communications Commission,
    71
Federal Crop Insurance Corporation,
    191
Federal Deposit Insurance Corpora-
    tion, 170, 192, 194, 196
Federal Elections Commission, 39, 44
Federal Emergency Management
    Agency, 92
Federal Energy Regulatory Commis-
    sion, 186
Federal government
  plans to reduce size of, 111–113
  Reagan and, 107–108
Federal Highway Administration, 119,
    127
Federal Home Loan Mortgage Corpora-
    tion (Freddie Mac), 191, 211, 212
Federal House Loan Banks, 114
Federal Housing Administration, 114,
    127, 193, 195
Federalist Paper No. 70, 197
Federal Loan Banks, 191
Federally Funded Research and
    Development Centers (FFRDCs),
    208–211

Federal National Mortgage Association
    (Fannie Mae), 76, 211, 212
Federal Power Act of 1920, 35
Federal Power Commission, 35, 183,
    186
Federal Reporting Services Act, 185
Federal Reserve Board, 114, 164
Federal Security Agency, 71, 174
Federal Trade Commission, 71, 130,
    183, 185
Federal Workforce Restructuring Act of
    1994, 112
Fenno, Richard F., Jr., 30
Financing Corporation, 211
First Secretary of Government, 72
Fisheries Committee, 31
Flemming, Arthur, 72
Florio, James J., 46
Food Administration, 164
Food and Agriculture Council, 103
Food and Drug Administration,
    150–151
Food and Nutrition Department, 93
Ford, Gerald, 56, 87, 104, 105
Ford Foundation, 208
Foreign Service, 124, 125
Forest Service, 119, 123, 126, 137
Foster, Vincent, 59
Foundations, 18, 166, 180–182
Four freedoms, 23
Freddie Mac (Federal Home Loan
    Mortgage Corporation), 191, 211,
    212
Freedom of Information Act, 181
French Canal Company, 188
Fulbright, J. William, 42

Gallaudet University, 195
Gardner, John, 52, 132, 136
General Accounting Office (GAO), 46,
    113, 129
  Federally Funded Research and Devel-
    opment Centers and, 210, 211
  government corporations and, 191
  Reagan and, 97, 99, 101
  Smithsonian Institution and, 182

"General Management of the Executive Branch" (report), 4
General Services Administration, 21, 41, 172, 179
Gilmour, Robert S., 7, 116
Gingrich, Newt, 28, 29, 31, 47, 110
Good, 177
Good Friday Earthquake, 150
Gore, Al, 3, 7, 27, 111–112
Government Corporation Control Act of 1945, 180, 188, 190, 191, 193, 195, 196, 208
Government corporations, 164–165, 167–168, 187–196
  mixed-ownership, 168, 191, 194, 196
  wholly owned. *See* Wholly owned government corporations
Government National Mortgage Association, 193
Government sponsored enterprises (GSEs), 191, 211–213
Governors' Conference, 48, 204
Grange, 134
Grants, 15, 107
Great Society programs, 84
Gulick, Luther, 4, 5, 6, 12, 70

Haldeman, H. R., 57, 81
Halperin, Morton H., 67–68
Hamilton, Alexander, 197
Harding, Warren, 83
Harlow, Bryce N., 25
Harriman, W. Averell, 147
Health and Hospitals Corporation, 98
Heclo, Hugh, 68, 140
Hepburn, William P., 28
Heritage Foundation, 6–7, 14
Hodges, Luther, 127
Holifield, Chet, 81
Hoover, Herbert, 5, 19, 34, 43, 71, 83, 138–139, 155
Hoover, J. Edgar, 119
Hoover Commission, 3, 4, 7, 9, 17, 21, 25, 43, 71, 202
  Eisenhower and, 72

Farmers Home Administration and, 14
  Nixon and, 78
Hoover Commission Task Force, 83
Horn, Steven, 55
House Appropriations Committee, 39–40, 198, 200
House Committee on Government Operations, 47, 81–82, 84–85, 176, 198, 200
House Committee on Government Reform and Oversight, 8, 16, 55–56, 113, 173, 196, 218–219
House Judiciary Committee, 33
House of Commons, British, 29
House of Representatives
  increase in number of subcommittees, 29
  Smithsonian Institution and, 180–182
House Public Works and Transportation Committee, 35
House Public Works and Transportation Subcommittee on Water Resources, 34
House Resources Committee, 31, 35
House Select Committee on Committees, 30–31, 37, 48
Housing and Home Finance Agency, 174, 175, 179, 193
Howard University, 195
Hughes, Emmet J., 89
Human Resources Council, 103
Humphrey, Hubert, 121, 164
Humphrey's Executor v United States, 184
Hydle, Lars H., 127

ICC Act, 184
Immigration and Naturalization Service, 33, 127
Independent agencies, 166, 178–180
Independent nonprofit corporations, 168
Independent wholly owned government corporations, 168
Inflation Impact Statement, 104

Informal (lateral) coordination, 145–146
Inspector General Act of 1978, 45
Inspector general offices, 129–130
Institute for Defense Analyses, 22, 208, 209
Institute for Peace, U.S, 207
Institutes, 167, 180–182
Institutions, 167, 180–182
Interagency committees, 20, 147–152, 197
   avoiding deficiencies associated with, 151–152
   reasons for failure of, 151
   types and purposes of, 148
Interest groups, 13, 28, 30, 137
Intergovernmental organizations, 168, 203–206
Internal Revenue Service (IRS), 111
International Communication Agency, 92
Interstate Commerce Commission (ICC), 71, 163, 169, 183, 185
Interstate Conference of Employment Security Agencies, 132

Jackson, Andrew, 51
Jackson Subcommittee, 149, 156
Johns Hopkins University, 209
Johnson, Lyndon B., 53, 74–77, 94
   Community Relations Service and, 127
   Great Society programs of, 84
   interagency committees and, 147–148
   White House staff and, 59, 65
Joint congressional-executive agencies, 202
Jones, David C., 122
Jones, James R., 50
Jones, Jesse, 61
Judiciary, 13, 221
Justice institutes, 167

Kappel, Frederick R., 187
Katzmann, Robert A., 130
Kaufman, Herbert, 37

Kennedy, Edward, 37
Kennedy, John F., 41, 72, 73–74, 126–127
   advisory bodies and, 200
   Community Relations Service and, 127
   interagency committees and, 147
   investigation of assassination of, 19–20
   National Security Council Planning Board and, 149
   regulatory and claims commissions and, 186
Kennedy, Robert, 20, 21, 123
Kerr, Clark, 139
Kettl, Donald F., 113
Kindness, Thomas N., 93
Kings River project, 36
Kissinger, Henry, 81, 86
Knights of Labor, 164
Koch, Edward, 98
Korean War, 22

Labor unions, 24, 127
Land grant colleges, 135
Landis, James, 41
Laski, Harold, 170
Lawrence, David, 178
Lawyers, 128–129, 187
Legal Policy Council, 103
Legal Services Corporation, 97, 196, 207
Legislative Reorganization Act of 1946, 29, 30
Level I agencies, 171
Level II agencies, 171
Level III agencies, 171
Level IV agencies, 172
Level V agencies, 172
Levitan, Sar, 153
Liern, Lawrence I., 138
Lilienthal, David, 108, 125, 126, 192
Lincoln Laboratory, 22
Lindsay, John, 98
Lindsey, Bruce, 59
Litton Industries, 80

Loan programs, 97–98, 118–119, 128
Local governments, 68
  coordination in, 146
  Reagan and, 107
Lockheed Martin Corp., 22
Logistics Management Institute, 209
Lovett, Robert, 147

McClellan, John, 41
McDonnell Douglas Corp., 22
McIntyre, James T., Jr., 92
McLarty, Thomas, 59
Management and Administration Council, 103
Mandate for Leadership II (Continuing the Conservative Revolution), 6–7
Manhattan Project, 125
Mansfield, Mike, 40
Marine Corps, 125
Maritime Administration, 24, 137
Marshall Plan, 17–18
Meese, Edwin, III, 103, 106
Merchant Marine Committee, 31
Migratory Bird Conservation Commission, 202
Mile's law, 17
Mixed-ownership government corporations, 168, 191, 194, 196
Moe, Ronald C., 7, 94–95, 116, 163–164, 207
Mondale, Walter F., 91, 93
Monroe, James, 162–163
Mooney, James D., 4, 145
Morgan, Arthur E., 193–194
Morton, Rogers C. B., 87
Mosher, Frederick C., 99, 133
Moss, Frank, 144
Mouzelis, Nicos P., 79
Moyers, Bill, 65
Multiheaded agencies, 46–47
Multiheaded government corporations, 167–168
Multiheaded independent agencies, 166

Multiheaded mixed-ownership government corporations, 168, 191, 194, 196

National Academy of Public Administration, 8, 27, 34, 86, 100–101, 129, 172
National Academy of Sciences, 15, 18, 198
National Aeronautics and Space Administration (NASA), 68, 120
National Archives, 21, 133, 182
National Association of County Officials, 204
National Association of Housing and Redevelopment Officers, 132
National Association of School Superintendents, 164
National Association of State Universities, 18
National Commission on Executive Organization, 55
National Conference on State Parks, 132
National Corporation for Community and Public Service, 196
National Council on Marine Resources and Engineering Development, 178
National Council on the Arts, 182
National Council on Vocational Education, 198
National Economic Council, 150
National Education Association, 21
National Endowment for Democracy, 207
National Endowment for the Arts, 182, 198
National Endowment for the Humanities, 182
National Foundation on the Arts and Humanities, 182, 197–198
National Highway Safety Agency, 33
National Historical Publications Commission, 198
National Housing Partnerships, 76

National Institute of Allergy and Infectious Diseases, 24
National Institute of Mental Health (NIMH), 200
National Institutes of Health (NIH), 170, 183, 198, 200
National Microbiological Institute, 24
National Military Establishment, 71
National Oceanic and Atmospheric Administration, 16
National Park Service, 87, 119, 144
National Performance Review, 3, 7, 56, 68, 99, 112, 115, 130
National Railroad Passenger Corporation (AMTRAK), 196, 207–208
National Resources Planning Board, 176
National Science Board, 18
National Science Foundation, 18–19, 23, 32, 38, 72, 131, 182
National Security Council, 19, 66, 72, 81, 150, 177
National Security Council Planning Board, 149
National Technical Information Service, 115
National Traffic Agency, 33
Natural Resources and Environment Council, 103
Naval Petroleum Reserves, 114, 126, 140
Navasky, Victor, 123
Navy Department, 173
Neighborhood Youth Corps, 153
Neustadt, Richard, 13, 73
New American Revolution, 78–89
New Deal, 21, 70, 84, 96, 136
New England-New York River Basin Committee, 203
Nixon, Richard M., 16–17, 42, 66, 90, 102, 104, 105, 134, 143
  domestic affairs and, 80–82
  executive departments and, 176
  Executive Office of the President and, 80, 177
  foreign policy and, 81

new American Revolution of, 78–89
  Office of Economic Opportunity and, 84, 154
  philosophy of government, 88
  Postal Service and, 180
  Reagan compared with, 106
  six great goals of, 82
  White House staff and, 57–58, 86, 87
Noll, Roger, 186
"Notes on the Theory of Organization" (Gulick), 5
Novak, 80

Oak Ridge National Laboratory, 22, 136
Off-budget borrowing, 113–114, 194
Office of Community Resources, 143
Office of Defense Mobilization, 20
Office of Economic Opportunity (OEO), 75, 84, 142, 150, 153–154, 178
Office of Executive Management, 72
Office of Federal Housing Enterprise, 213
Office of Federal Procurement Policy (OFPP), 43–44, 210
Office of Information and Regulatory Affairs, 105
Office of Management and Budget (OMB), 11, 15–16, 43–44, 55–56, 172
  advisory bodies and, 201
  Clinton and, 55, 115
  coordination in, 144–145
  executive departments and, 176
  Executive Office of the President and, 176
  Nixon and, 42, 81, 82, 85, 87, 89
  Postal Service and, 180
  Reagan and, 55, 104, 105–106, 109
  regulatory and claims commissions and, 185
Office of Science and Technology, 41, 74
Office of Scientific Research and Development (OSRD), 169–170, 209
Office of Technology Assessment, 208

Office of Territories, 126
Oleszek, Walter J., 30, 48
OMB 2000, 16
Operations Research Organization, 209
Orientation programs, 125
Orlans, Harold, 129
Orphan agencies, 15–16
Orthodox theory, 3–12, 17
  establishment of, 11
  Nixon and, 78–79
  primary concerns of, 5
Overlapping, 6–7, 11, 14, 15, 74

Pacific Northwest Electric Planning
  and Conservation Act, 205
Pacific Northwest Electric Power and
  Planning Council, 205
Packers and Stockyards Act of 1921,
  183
Panama Canal Commission, 38
Panama Canal Company, 192
Panama Railroad Company, 169, 188
Papers on the Science of Administra-
  tion, 10
Paperwork Reduction Act of 1980, 105
Patent and Trademark Office, 16, 33,
  114, 115, 195
Patterson, Samuel C., 30
Pension Benefit Guaranty Corporation,
  32
Performance-based organizations
  (PBOs), 114–115
Perkins, Frances, 48
Pettigrew, Richard A., 91
Pinchot, Gifford, 126
Pollock, 14
Pork barrel programs, 83, 84
  social, 98
Postal Service, U.S., 125, 179–180,
  187–188
Postal Service Act, 180
Postal Service Board of Governors, 44
Postmaster general, 119
Post Office Committee, 31
Power, 19
  distinction between authority and, 65

  in executive branch, 9, 41, 65–66,
    218
  Weber on, 79
Presidency. *See* Executive branch
Presidential appointments, 44–45, 102,
  112–113, 121, 122, 182, 212
Presidential records, 117
President's Commission on Postal Or-
  ganization, 187
President's Committee on Administra-
  tive Management, 17, 25, 57, 70,
  71, 79, 165, 178, 183
President's Committee on Government
  Organization, 72
President's men, 40–41
President's Reorganization Project,
  91–92, 94
President's Science Advisory Commit-
  tee, 20, 198
Privacy Act, 181
Private, government financed institu-
  tions, 168
Privatization, 3, 96–101, 107
Professionalization, 131–13
Professional Services Council, 210
Pryor, David, 97, 196
Public Health Service, 75, 194, 200
Public works, 129

Quality of Life Reviews, 104

Railroads, 23
Railway Association, U.S., 196
Rand, 97, 208, 209
Reagan, Ronald, 13, 66, 68, 96–109,
  121
  Appalachian Regional Commission
    and, 206
  main elements of strategy, 102
  Office of Management and Budget
    and, 55, 104, 105–106, 109
  orthodox theory and, 7
  privatization and, 3, 96–101, 107
Reconstruction Finance Corporation
  (RFC), 42–43, 178, 192, 193
Redford, Emmette S., 75

Reed, Thomas B., 28
Reedy, George, 59
Regan, Donald, 106
Regulations, control of, 102, 103–106
"Regulatory Agencies of Our Government" (presidential message), 186
Regulatory commissions, 128–129, 167, 183–187
Regulatory Council, 105
Rehnquist, William, 134
Reinvention, 3, 12, 27
Reorganization, 68–69
  Carter and ("bottom-up"), 90–95
  Johnson and, 74–75
  Kennedy and, 73–74
  Nixon and, 78–79
  orthodox theory on, 3–5, 11–12
  overemphasis on, 69
  Truman and, 71
Reorganization Act of 1949, 11, 71, 73–74, 101
Reorganization Plan No. 1, 47
Reorganization Plan No. 2, 55, 81, 82, 127
Reorganization Plan No. 9, 177
Reorganization Statute, 185
Report-and-wait provisions, 46
Republicans, 79
  abolition of executive departments and, 110–111
  Department of Commerce and, 33
  Marshall Plan and, 17–18
  National Security Council and, 19
Research Analysis Corporation, 209
Research centers, 168–169
Research grants, 15
Resolution Funding Corporation, 191, 211–212
Resolution Trust Corporation (RTC), 113–114, 194, 196
Resource Management Offices, 55
Ribicoff, Abraham, 52
Roback, Herbert, 82
Rockefeller, Nelson, 72, 147
Roe, Robert A., 34

Roosevelt, Franklin D., 12, 48, 59, 69–70, 76, 96, 137, 165, 193–194
  loan program and, 118–119
  Nixon compared with, 78
  White House staff and, 56–57
Roosevelt, Theodore, 11
Roth, William V., Jr., 31–32
Rowe, James H., Jr., 14, 46, 56–57
Rural Development Act of 1972, 85
Rural Electrical Administration (REA), 123, 137
Rural Resettlement Administration, 14

St. Lawrence Seaway Development Corporation, 115, 137, 186, 193
Salamon, Lester M., 96–97, 100, 128
Sallie Mae (Student Loan Marketing Association), 191, 211
Savings and loan institutions, 14, 113–114
Schick, Allen, 102
Schwartz, Herman, 212
Science Applications International Corporation, 211
Scientists, 131
Secretary of agriculture, 42, 119, 121
Secretary of commerce, 119, 121
Secretary of defense, 119
Secretary of education, 119
Secretary of energy, 119, 186
Secretary of health and human services, 119
Secretary of health and welfare, 42
Secretary of housing and urban development, 42, 119, 121
Secretary of labor, 120, 121
Secretary of state, 119
Secretary of the interior, 119–120, 121
Secretary of the treasury, 42, 119, 121
Secretary of transportation, 120
Secretary of veterans' affairs, 120
Securities and Exchange Commission, 113, 212
Securities Investor Protection Corporation, 196, 207
Selznick, Philip, 135

Senate
  Executive Office of the President
    and, 177
  increase in number of subcommit-
    tees, 29
  Smithsonian Institution and, 180–182
Senate Commerce, Science and Trans-
  portation Committee, 32
Senate Committee on Governmental
  Affairs, 14, 25–26, 48, 185–186
Senate Committee on Government Op-
  erations, 86
Senate Energy and Natural Resources
  Committee, 35
Senate Environment and Public Works
  Committee, 35
Senate Foreign Relations Committee,
  186
Senate Labor and Human Resources
  Committee, 32
Senate Select Committee on Presiden-
  tial Campaign Activities, 58, 86,
  89
Senate Select Committees on Commit-
  tees, 48
Shipping Board, 164
Shultz, George P., 85, 86
Simon, 196
Single-headed independent agencies,
  166
Single-headed wholly owned govern-
  ment corporations, 167
Small Business Administration, 41, 75,
  84, 135, 154, 179
Smith, Bruce L. R., 98
Smith, Frank, 36–37
Smithsonian Institution, 163, 180–182,
  202
Social pork barrel, 98
Social Security Administration, 47,
  172, 179
Social Security Advisory Board, 45
Society of American Archivists, 132
Society of American Foresters, 132
Soil Conservation Service, 35, 84, 123,
  125

Sorensen, Theodore, 73
Soviet Union, 20
Special Action Office for Drug Abuse,
  79, 178
Special pleaders, 28–29, 62, 64
Sputnik, 20
Staff
  congressional, 30–31, 37–38
  White House. *See* White House staff
Standing Panel on Executive Organiza-
  tion and Management, 8
Stanton, Thomas H., 211, 212
State governments, 68
  coordination in, 146
  Reagan and, 107
State institutes, 167
State of the Union Message
  1967, 75–76
  1971, 82
  1979, 90
Stone, Harlan F., 119
Strangeland, Arlan, 93
Strauss, Lewis, 41–42
Student Loan Marketing Association
  (Sallie Mae), 191, 211
Study Commission for the Southeast
  River Basins, U.S., 203
Sullivan, Harold J., 207
Sundquist, James L., 31
Supercabinet officers, 154–155, 156
Superdepartments, 156
Supreme Court, U.S.
  on AMTRAK, 207
  on executive branch power, 41
  on government corporations, 193
  on grant conditions, 107
  on legislative veto, 45–46, 104
  on presidential appointments, 44–45
  on regulatory and claims commis-
    sions, 184, 185
Surgeon general, 183
Sutherland, George, 184
Synthetic Fuels Corporation, 97, 195
System Development Corporation,
  209
Szanton, Peter S., 93

Taft Commission on Economy and Efficiency, 25
Tenneco, Inc., 22
Tennessee Valley Authority (TVA), 36, 44, 125, 126, 135, 191, 192, 194, 203
Tenure of Office Act of 1867, 44, 174, 184
Thatcher, Margaret, 114
Trade Representative, U.S., 39
Travel and Tourism Administration, 39
Travelgate, 64
Truman, David, 199
Truman, Harry, 18, 61, 66, 71–72, 80, 134, 194–195
Tugwell, Rexford G., 70
TVA and the Grass Roots (Selznick), 135
Twilight of the Presidency, The (Reedy), 59
Twilight zone agencies, 76, 168, 206–208
Two-hatted arrangements, 41–42

Udall, Morris K., 60
Union Pacific Railroad, 212
University-affiliated research centers, 168
Urban Affairs Council, 143
Urban Institute, 76, 209
Urwick, 4

Veterans Administration, 199
Veto, 45–46, 72–73, 104
Vice president, 155, 180–181

Waldo, Dwight, 10
Wallace, 136
War Department, 173
War Finance Corporation, 164
War Trade Board, 164
Washington, George, 78, 162

Washington Metropolitan Airports Authorities, 45
Washington Post, 87
Watergate, 25, 59, 65–66, 86, 177
Waterman, Alan T., 131
Water pollution control, 75
Water resource programs, 34–37
Water Resources Planning Act of 1961, 204
Webb, James E., 68, 120
Weber, Max, 58–59, 79, 86
Wellford, Harrison, 92
Westinghouse Electric Corp., 22
West Point, 35
White House Office of Consumer Counsel, 200
White House staff, 56–60, 64–66
    accessibility to Congress and, 41
    Executive Office of the President and, 178
    Nixon and, 56–57, 86, 87
    testimony before congressional committees and, 41
Wholly owned government corporations, 191, 194, 195
    improperly classified as mixed-ownership, 196
    independent, multiheaded, 167–168
    single-headed, 167
Why Not the Best? (Carter), 91
Wiener v United States, 184
Wildavsky, Aaron, 88–89
Wilson, James Q., 7, 123
Wilson, Woodrow, 117
Witcover, Jules, 91
Wolcott, 170
World War I, 164, 169
World War II, 22, 170, 209
Wydler, John W., 93